Dear Meag
Given to you with
            love

Together Forever
Being a Hero to Your Family

16/05/2017

Arie & Rivka Ringelstein

Copyright © 2015 Steven Ringelstein LLC.

Cover and interior design by Jamie Dickerson.

All rights reserved. No part of this publication may be reproduced, distributed, or transmitted in any form or by any means, including photocopying, recording, or other electronic or mechanical methods, without the prior written permission of the publisher, except in the case of brief quotations embodied in critical reviews and certain other noncommercial uses permitted by copyright law. For permission requests, write to the publisher, addressed "Attention: Permissions Coordinator," at the address below.

Steven Ringelstein LLC.

www.arierivka.com

sr@stevenringelstein.com

ISBN-10: 1517483301

ISBN-13: 978-1517483302

Dedication

I wrote this book in order for my precious family—

My children: Steven Ringelstein, Liat Ringelstein-Alus and Anat Ringelstein-Markizano

My sons-in-law: Shlomo Alus and Moti Markizano

My grandchildren: Itay, Dikla, Karin, Ram Alus

Leeran, Matan, and Maytal Markizano

To learn about our family roots, and how I created my life with my husband Arie Ringelstein—with whom I shared more than 50 years. The road we walked had its ups and downs, but the remarkable power of love kept us bound close together from the day we met until the day he passed away. And, magically, our togetherness continues to be a powerful force in my life even today.

A great portion of this book was written by Arie in his own words before passing away, and is integrated with my writings.

I hope to live to share the story of our family with my yet to be born great-grandchildren. I also hope to inspire you the reader through our family story to discover the gift of togetherness that makes the whole much greater than the sum of its parts.

Rita-Rivka Konig-Ringelstein

Table of Contents

About This Book • 1

Preface • 3

Map: Arie and Rivka's Journey (1934 – 2015) • 7

In the Beginning • 8

Chapter 1 The First Meeting (In Rivka's Own Words) • 10

Chapter 2 Moldova, Bessarabia, and the Pogroms • 12

Chapter 3 Arie's Parents—Jacob and Esther Ringelstein • 13

Chapter 4 Rivka's Parents and Memories from Childhood (In Rivka's Own Words) • 19

Chapter 5 Arie's Memories from Childhood (In Arie's Own Words) • 26

Chapter 6 Apocalypse Now • 27

Chapter 7 The Second World War (In Arie's Own Words) • 29

Chapter 8 Pogroms, and the Iași Death Trains • 35

Chapter 9 Rivka's Life During the War • 37

Chapter 10 Zionism and the Jewish State • 41

Chapter 11 After the War (In Arie's Own Words) • 44

Chapter 12 The Great Escape! • 52

Chapter 13 Welcome to the Children's Village! (In Arie's Own Words) • 56

Chapter 14 The Ship SS Negba • 63

Chapter 15 Living in the Promised Land • 66

Chapter 16 Kibbutz Gvat (In Arie's Own Words) • 68

Chapter 17 Kibbutz Gvat Year 2 (In Arie's Own Words) • 77

Chapter 18 The Journey to Israel (In Rivka's Own Words) • 86

Chapter 19 "Fresh Meat"—Becoming a New Military Recruit • 93

Chapter 20 The Military Life (In Arie's Own Words) • 97

Chapter 21 The First Meeting with My Future Wife (In Arie's Own Words) • 120

Chapter 22 The Wedding • 123

Chapter 23 The Honeymoon Is Over and Life Has Begun (In Rivka's Own Words) • 126

Chapter 24 Building a Family Together • 130

Chapter 25 The Blessings of Children (In Rivka's Own Words) • 136

Chapter 26 A Glass Half Full • 142

Chapter 27 My Working Life (In Rivka's Own Words) • 145

Chapter 28 Finding Balance • 153

Chapter 29 Bar and Bat Mitzvah Traditions (In Rivka's Own Words) • 155

Chapter 30 1987: A Year of Turning Points (In Rivka's Own Words) • 158

Chapter 31 Farewell to My Mom (In Rivka's Own Words) • 161

Chapter 32 Our Children (In Rivka's Own Words) • 163

Chapter 33 Starting a New Life in Canada (In Rivka's Own Words) • 169

Chapter 34 The Grandparents' Club (In Rivka's Own Words) • 173

Arie and Rivka's Family Tree (1800s to Present) • 175

Chapter 35 Honoring My Father (In Rivka's Own Words) • 176

Chapter 36 Emergency! (In Rivka's Own Words) • 178

Chapter 37 Arie's 70th Birthday (In Rivka's Own Words) • 180

Chapter 38 Arie's Health Takes a Surprising Turn for the Worse (In Rivka's Own Words) • 182

Chapter 39 A 50th Wedding Anniversary (In Rivka's Own Words) • 187

Chapter 40 Letters of Love • 192

Chapter 41 The Surgery (In Rivka's Own Words) • 205

Chapter 42 The Final Two Days (In Rivka's Own Words) • 212

Chapter 43 Arie's Voice from the Other Side • 218

Chapter 44 Eulogies • 220

Chapter 45 Memorial, Burial, Unveiling (In Rivka's Own Words) • 230

Chapter 46 Sitting Shiva (In Rivka's Own Words) • 232

Chapter 47 Arie's 75th Birthday • 235

Chapter 48 Rivka's 70th Birthday (In Rivka's Own Words) • 238

Chapter 49 A Greeting from Arie Channeled through Steven (In Rivka's Own Words) • 240

Chapter 50 My New Life (In Rivka's Own Words) • 243

Chapter 51 My Surprise 75th Birthday Party (In Rivka's Own Words) • 246

Chapter 52 Retirement (In Rivka's Own Words) • 250

Chapter 53 Rivka's Life Today • 252

Chapter 54 Together Forever (In Rivka's Own Words) • 255

Appendix I Arie's Meditation Transcripts • 260

About the Authors • 281

About the Book Cover • 282

Reference • 283

About This Book

Together Forever is a book about the journey of two people—Arie and Rivka Ringelstein—and what happened when they created a life and family together. The book follows these parallel lives and demonstrates how love pulled Arie and Rivka together over time and great distances. And love binds them together even today.

The word *together* can be used in a variety of different contexts, including…

To be in contact *together*

To go for a walk *together*

To be united *together*

To put your heads *together*

To consult with each other to find a solution *together*

To make plans *together*

To unite *together* as one person

We can see that this word can be used in many different ways, each of which reflects a different aspect of the power of togetherness. However, the power of togetherness is under constant threat by the strong fears that we feel in our relationships. These fears include:

The fear of abandonment

The fear of getting hurt

The fear of losing someone you love

Each of us needs to ask ourselves whether or not these fears are based in reality, and if all the happiness and other benefits of building a lifelong relationship and family outweigh the fear we feel. When a couple decides to be together forever, is it really eternal? For Arie and Rivka, the answer was clearly "Yes."

On October 15, 1934, Arie Ringelstein was born in Fălticeni, Moldova (now a part of Romania). Arie was given the name Leon, which is Hebrew for Lion, and he grew up on a farm where his grandparents raised chickens, cows, and wheat. There was a small community of Jews within this Romanian village who kept the Jewish tradition. Because they lived prosperous lives, they increasingly attracted the animosity of the other, non-Jewish people in the village.

On October 24, 1939, Rita Konig (Rita's name was changed to Rivka when she immigrated to Israel) was born in Iași, Moldova—also now a part of Romania—no more than 64 miles away from Fălticeni as the crow flies. The world into which Rita arrived was filled with news of war, inhumanity, fear, and terror. Nazi Germany, led by Adolph Hitler, was beginning its campaign remove the Jewish people from Europe, rounding up thousands of Jews in the occupied territories of Austria and Czechoslovakia and sending them to Poland. Against that scenery, many innocent lives were filled with torment and change as families were torn apart and hearts broken.

As the winds of war blew over Europe, Arie and Rita each followed separate paths as they grew and matured. But the overwhelming power of love gradually—and permanently—drew them together, until they were one.

At its heart, *Together Forever* is a story about the power of unconditional love and unconditional acceptance in the face of extreme hardship, and it offers a message of hope for people who feel lost in their relationships to themselves and others. This story—the story Arie and Rivka Ringelstein—clearly demonstrates that the old saying "love conquers all" really works.

PREFACE
BEING A HERO TO YOUR FAMILY

Purpose

The original purpose of this book was to share the untold stories of the lives of Arie and Rivka Ringelstein with their children, grandchildren, and future generations—to inspire, and to offer their wisdom and lessons learned. After the manuscript was completed and then read by a few close friends and family members, Rivka was invited to make the book public and to share with many other readers the accumulated wisdom learned about love, relationships, and overcoming unimaginable challenges.

How did this book come about?

Years ago, Arie Ringelstein started to write a book about his life. He had never written a book before, but he enjoyed reflecting on his life with the eye of a playwright. His writing was abruptly halted, however, when he passed in 2009. Arie's unfinished book captured Rivka's imagination, and it ignited within her a deep desire to complete it. However, Rivka had never written a book before, either. She started with a similar process of reflecting on her life, but filtered through the lens of grieving her husband and partner of 53 years. Her writing was healing, and it helped her transform the sadness, pain, and grief she felt into gratitude and love. Then the time came to bring the two books together, forging the single book you hold in your hands, and giving both Arie and Rivka their own voices to describe their lives from two uniquely different perspectives.

Who is this book for?

While this book can be enjoyed by anyone, it may be more appealing at first blush to people who are curious about how love and intimate relationships can turn ordinary lives into extraordinary experiences. Other readers will be drawn in by this book, particularly those who have an interest in history (particularly WWII, and the years preceding it), the establishment of the state of Israel from the perspective of the first generation of immigrants, and being a hero to your family—practiced and perfected over the decades, all the way up to today.

Why would you want to read this book?

Maybe you would like to learn how to allow love in your partnership to thrive, or maybe you are interested in the stories of everyday heroes who are not famous, but who do what is best simply because they love. Maybe you will be able to discover how much of a hero you are in your own life—and in the lives of others—and you'll find good reason to celebrate that. Or maybe you will be inspired by the art of contentment, and practice more of that in your life.

Why this *book?*

There are countless books about heroes from the Holocaust, and there are even more books about love and relationships. This book is different. It is not a guidebook, and it does not promote one proposed truth, nor one best way to live your life. It is a story about ordinary people who lived ordinary lives, but who were able to find unconditional love, unconditional acceptance, joy, and contentment in conditions and circumstances that most would find hard to bear. This book demonstrates how two people—united and bound by love—can together alchemize terribly evil, dangerous, and unpleasant life experiences into simple gratitude.

Where is the information in this book from?

First and foremost, Arie and Rivka share the details of their lives from the perspective of their own experiences, memories, and stories that created the Ringelstein family. Additional research was conducted to describe some of the world events occurring in Arie and Rivka's youth, as their memories couldn't account for all that was happening at the time. Rivka also interviewed other family members who had information about her parents and grandparents that was not personally known to her.

How much time did it take?

This book was written over a period of six years—allowing the book to cook in its own juices, and to be complete and ready to be shared with the world.

What can you expect from this book?

You might shed a tear, break into uncontrollable laughter,

and feel a full spectrum of emotions as you become intimate with the life events and experiences that Arie and Rivka share with readers. You might be challenged to consider the alternative healing methods that Arie used to treat his cancer, revealed at the end of the book. You might feel inspired—finding the hero in yourself and in the members of your own family.

Limitations

These are the shared stories of two ordinary people who became heroes to their family. The main limitation would be if you focus on these stories as only their own, and not allow them to become yours as well. There are opinions, beliefs, and worldviews in this book you might not agree with, and others that will compliment your own. It is our hope that you will find this book a positive addition to your life tools, and especially to be inspired to be a hero to your family.

Thanks to the following contributors

Arie Ringelstein

Arie Ringelstein was born in Romania in 1934. An orphan and survivor of the Holocaust, he found his way to Israel as a boy. Arie served in the Israel Defense Forces for years, and he was a commander on the front lines in five wars—leading his troops to victory each time. Because he was an orphan, creating a family was of great importance to Arie, who was married to his wife Rivka Ringelstein for 50 years. In his later years, he moved his family to Toronto, Canada, to enjoy the remainder of his life in peace. He passed in 2009, at the age of 75. Arie was well known for his unique ability to conquer any obstacle in his way, and to alchemize it into love, playfulness, and contentment. Arie was a hero to his family.

Rivka Ringelstein

Rivka Ringelstein was born in Romania in 1939, only 64 miles from the birthplace of her future husband. Rivka was an only child who, at a very young age, escaped the atrocities of WWII Europe—eventually finding her way to Israel to start a new life in the newly formed Jewish state. Her dedication, commitment, and hard work persisted over the many obstacles life presented. Rivka's love for Arie, and her unshakable courage, made her a hero to her family. Rivka survived Arie, and is now in her mid-seventies—enjoying a life of contentment in Toronto, Canada.

First editor
>Mary Holden

Second editor
>Vicky Millicent Hay

Third editor and writer
>Peter Economy

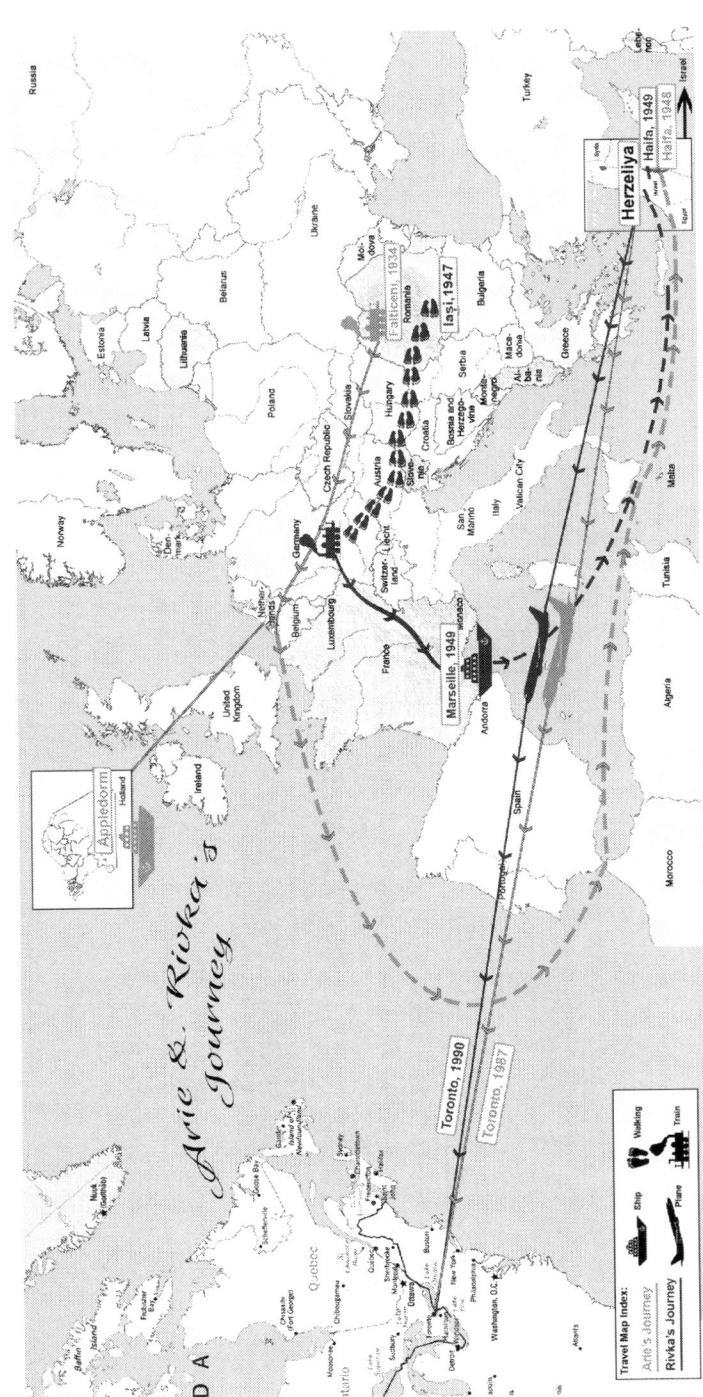

Arie and Rivka's Journey (1934 – 2015).

Graphic by Jamie Dickerson.

Please visit www.arierivka.com for detailed color map.

In the Beginning

Arie lay in his bed as a beam of warm light streamed through the window, high up on the wall. He could hear the comforting and rhythmic beeping of some electronic device, ticking away the seconds and tracing the final days of his physical life. In October 2009, after his cancerous stomach was removed from his already weakened body, Arie was in the hospital—in the Intensive Care Unit (ICU) at bed number 7.

Months earlier, before numerous rounds of chemotherapy, Arie had learned to meditate, and to relieve himself of the powerful emotional burdens and pain he was carrying in his back and stomach. As Arie watched the nurses' move quickly and efficiently around the room, he felt the warm touch of his life partner and loving wife Rivka holding his hand—and praying for her husband to get well. Arie was reflecting:

> *I can see myself when I was 6 or 7 years old. My Mom had passed away and I was wondering, "Will I die as well?"*
>
> *I realized that already, before understanding exactly what life is all about and what death means, I had strong desire to live. As I grew older, I started to understand the unavoidable journey of birth, life, and death.*
>
> *Regardless of how long I will live, eventually I will die. I imagine that I would feel I have not lived long enough. Today I do not want to die; I cannot bear the thought of leaving my wife, my children, and my grandchildren behind. Today my heart is filled with sadness to the possibility that my days of living are numbered.*
>
> *Once more I want to be touching the earth, smelling the flowers, and walking in nature. I want to feel once more the flow of water, jump into the ocean waves, and to be with my family and friends laughing together at how ridiculous life can be.*

After his deep reflection, Arie was embraced by a feeling of peace and well-being. He looked up and saw his bride Rivka gazing deeply into his eyes—and into his very soul. She pressed his hand.

When Arie thought about his relationship with Rivka—about the love that bound them together forever—he could see the statue of a passionate man kissing a woman. Their kiss connected them like a magnet and their separate bodies merged together at their hips and feet into one. Years before, Arie came across such a statue and bought it for his son Steven on one of their vacations to Sedona, Arizona, and they perfectly represented the togetherness he and Rivka felt for each other.

Arie smiled faintly at the thought, then held Rivka's hand a little tighter. And then his mind wandered back in time, to his childhood, and to the years before he was born.

Chapter 1
The First Meeting
(In Rivka's Own Words)

The way I met Arie was initiated through a sort of magical grapevine.

My cousin Sidi lived close to Arie's sister Bianca in Israel, and they were also close friends. Sidi told Bianca that she had a young cousin and maybe Arie would like to meet her. Arie decided to take a trip to Hadar Josef, a town in Israel not far from Tel Aviv, to meet with me.

At the time, Arie had completed his mandatory service in the Israeli army and he then continued his service as an IDF officer. When he arrived at the home of my parents, we talked a little bit, but there was no sign that this meeting was anything special. I had no premonition that Arie was my soul mate, my destiny, or anything more than someone I would meet once and probably never see again. I was young and did not give much thought to marriage at that time.

I do remember thinking that Arie was handsome, with beautiful green-brown eyes and medium brown hair. Although he was taller than me, he was not considered tall. His manners were very polite and that made him different than the other men I knew. I never dated any boys before as I was just used to going out with the girls in groups of boys and girls.

Later, Arie told me that he'd had an opposite reaction upon meeting me. He said to me that at that moment he knew: "That was it!"

Arie was my first boyfriend, and he continued to visit me on the weekends. After a few months of dating, however, I felt like I was falling in love with him. That progressed to realizing that we would like to have a family of our own. But we continued to date for almost two years.

My mom liked Arie very much. She treated him like a son. Arie even convinced my mom to go for a ride on his motorcycle, and he took me out on it, too. Although my mom liked Arie immediately, my dad wasn't excited about him and had his reservations. One of the reasons was that Arie didn't come from a wealthy family and he didn't have the savings necessary to start and maintain a family.

Another reason was that Arie had been brought up in a kibbutz, and this meant that he was not religious. Like many Jews who had survived the Holocaust, his Judaism became more cultural and ethical than religious; so he was considered secular. My parents kept kosher, were quite religious, and my dad would go to the synagogue every Saturday and of course on all the high holidays. It was important to my parents that my husband and I keep the Jewish traditions in our life after we were married.

Despite my parents' misgivings, we continued to date, and while doing so we went to see almost every opera that was in town, including *Carmen, The Barber of Seville, Pagliacci, La Traviata,* and the plays of Nabokov. We liked to go to the shows, and my mom would cook dinner for us. It wasn't popular to go to coffeehouses or restaurants, but occasionally we would treat ourselves to dinner at a Romanian restaurant to enjoy the dishes that reminded us of home.

It soon became plain to everyone that Arie wanted to get married and start a family—and he wanted me to be his wife. For Arie, family meant *everything*, especially since he grew up without parents and had a tough childhood. He had adopted my parents as his own.

Arie was so anxious to have a family that I would soon have to make a choice. Would I follow this man down the path that he laid before me, or would I turn in another direction altogether? I didn't yet know the answer to either of these questions.

Chapter 2
Moldova, Bessarabia, and the Pogroms

Historically, Moldova—together with parts of the Ukraine—is known as Bessarabia, and the Jewish people have lived in this area since the 1300s—first Sephardi, then Ashkenazi who arrived from Germany and Poland beginning in the 1500s. By the 1800s, it is believed that up to 230,000 Jews lived in Bessarabia, or about 12 percent of the total population. In rural areas, they were farmers, and in the cities they served as traders, peddlers, craftsmen, watchmakers, merchants, and cobblers.

Life was good for the Jewish residents of Moldova, but this was all about to change.

As a result of long-festering anti-Semitism, Russian political intrigue, and simple jealousy, the non-Jews of Moldova began the outright persecution of their Jewish neighbors. At the same time, Russian anti-Jewish laws were extended to Bessarabia, and decrees of expulsion were issued in 1869, 1879, 1886, and 1891 to Jews in a number of cities.

These actions—coupled with growing unrest among Moldova's populace—led to two violent pogroms in Kishinev—the former capital of Bessarabia, and the center of Jewish population and culture—in 1903 and 1905. The first resulted in the death of 49 Jews with more than 500 injured, and the second resulted in the death of 19 Jews with 56 injured. In addition, hundreds of Jewish-owned houses and shops were looted or destroyed, with millions of rubles in damages and thousands of families left homeless.

With the writing so clearly and unmistakably on the wall for all to see, Jews emigrated from Moldova and surrounding areas in droves—leaving behind their homes, their farms, their businesses, their personal belongings, and often their friends and families. But despite the extreme pressure for them to move, many Jews made the difficult decision to remain in the towns of their ancestors—hoping and praying for better times to soon arrive. Most of these men, women, and children lived to regret this choice. And, unfortunately, many paid for this decision with their lives.

Chapter 3
Arie's Parents—Jacob and Esther Ringelstein

Jacob Ringelstein was born in 1903 in a small village in Romania. He was the firstborn among the eight brothers and sisters who followed him. Jacob's family lived on a farm where they raised chickens and cows and grew wheat, and it is from this life that Jacob learned his love of nature. Only about five of the families in this particular Romanian village were Jewish and kept the Jewish traditions, putting them in a distinct minority versus the Christian majority.

Because the Ringelstein family lived a good and comfortable life, they started to be viewed as different from other villagers. They attracted a lot of jealousy and hatred from the other families in the village, most of whom were Christians. The Ringelstein family continued to grow, and the resources of the farm were not enough to keep sufficient food on the table. Jacob's parents established a restaurant to help fill the gap, and the eatery grew into a central part of life in the small village. People gathered there to not just to drink and eat, but also to dance and socialize.

Eventually, the family moved to Fălticeni, a village in a region of Romania called Moldova, where they bought a huge house and continued to raise chickens and vegetables to help have enough food. They also opened a small grocery store in front of the house to provide another source of income for the family.

At age 21 Jacob joined the Romanian army. At first, he was very proud to wear the Romanian uniform of his country, but it didn't take long for the ruling regime to become corrupt. And with this corruption came a blatant change in the regime's attitude toward Jews. The officers were from high-society families and very educated but they were anti-Semites.

When Jacob realized he would be humiliated—or worse—because of his Jewish faith, he talked to his parents about the situation. They came up with the idea of paying any price to try to bribe a senior officer into releasing Jacob from duty earlier than his two-year commitment. Bribing an army officer to win his freedom was abhorrent to Jacob, so he decided on a different pathway to the same result. During training, Jacob shot himself in the finger—his trigger finger. Jacob's wounded finger officially made him an invalid because he could no longer use it to fire a weapon. He was therefore released from the army.

With the help of his parents, Jacob entered the university and started to study bookkeeping. Again, because he was Jewish, he suffered many indignities ladled on by his classmates, teachers, and school administrators. To get outstanding grades, Jacob had to overcome all the prejudice and humiliation Jews were made to feel during that terrible time. High grades were not just handed out to Jews, they had to work doubly hard to pass.

But despite all the obstacles in his path, Jacob graduated from the university with honors and became the pride of the Ringelstein family, and of the other Jewish families in their small village. But anti-Semitism in those days was commonplace, and Jacob was unable to get a job. His only option was to start his own business, so he applied his business skills to become a talented bookkeeper. Demand for his services grew and he built strong business and social relationships throughout the community, and eventually the country.

When he was 26 years old, Jacob met the most beautiful girl he had ever seen. Her name was Esther, and she was born in Fălticeni in 1907 to a Jewish family named Kimel. Esther had three brothers and a sister. Jacob and Esther fell in love at first sight and were promptly married. After two years, the happy couple had their first child—Bianca, a beautiful, smiling, happy baby—and their son was born on October 15, 1934, when Jacob was 31 years old. They called their son Leon, which means *lion*, and the name served as a commitment the couple made to keep their son strong all his life.

The wedding of Esther Kimel and Jacob Ringelstein, Arie's parents, 1930

By then, Jacob traveled often to meet the demands of his clients, many of whom were located out of town. The economic situation had improved, and business was booming. In 1936 Jacob made one of his regular visits to Bucharest, the capital of Romania, where he had many clients.

**Standing: Jacob and Esther Ringelstein (Arie's parents);
Sitting: Samuel and Lea Ringelstein (Arie's grandparents)
Baby Middle: Leon (Arie) Ringelstein;**

Child Left: Bianca Ringelstein (Arie's sister); 1935

And then, out of the blue, it happened.

While he was on the train approaching Dolhaska, four men from an anti-Semitic organization called the Legionnaires attacked Jacob. Before he knew what was going on, the men had tossed Jacob out of the fast-moving train, where he hit the ground and rolled—right under wheels of a railcar. Jacob's legs were severed from his body, and blood spurted out of the exposed stumps in great torrents. Jacob was eventually taken to a hospital, but it was too late. Jacob died when he was just 33 years old—leaving behind his grieving wife and young children.

Esther understood immediately that she had to get over the terrible situation she and her children had been placed in. As a first step, Esther decided to learn a profession to be able to provide for her now fatherless family. She studied to become a dressmaker, a job that could help her make a living while working from home and caring for the children. In 1938, Esther made a momentous decision: to move to Bucharest, which offered much better opportunities for her to build a new life and make enough money to support her family. She rented a small apartment in a Jewish neighborhood, and quickly secured many new clients— along with their help.

The situation in the world was becoming worse with each passing day. The Nazis threatened the world with war, anti-Semitism spread, Romania made a pact with Nazi Germany, and war broke out in 1939 when Germany conquered Poland and started to kill Jews. Esther was lonely and desperate.

The hate that many Europeans felt toward their Jewish coworkers, neighbors, friends, and even family was reaching a boiling point as the 1930s came to a close. Already, Adolph Hitler had taken the reins of power as Chancellor of Germany—putting his country on a path that would ultimately lead to the Holocaust, and anti-Semitism was rampant throughout much of Europe. Consider this excerpt from historian William Manchester's book, *The Last Lion*:

...but in the 1930s it was quite an ordinary thing to see restaurants, hotels, clubs, beaches, and residential neighborhoods barred to people with what were delicately called "dietary requirements." ... Contempt for [Jews] was not considered bad form. They were widely regarded as unlovable, alien, loud-mouthed, "flashy" people who enriched themselves at the expense of Gentiles.[i]

As Manchester also noted, in 1930s Great Britain, Nazism had unbelievably become fashionable among the nation's upper crust. "Ladies wore bracelets with swastika charms; young men combed their hair slant across their foreheads."[ii]

But, in Eastern Europe, where there was a long history of anti-Semitism, events had taken a much more violent turn. Jewish personal property was destroyed, and homes confiscated or burned down. Jews throughout the region suffered a strong upsurge in persecution and violence directed against them, with many hauled off to jails or something new: concentration camps. It was a terrible time to be a Jew in Eastern Europe, and Arie and Rivka's families were caught in the middle of this social upheaval, with no obvious way out.

Esther met a good man who treated her well and with whom she thought to create a family and give her children a father. Esther became pregnant as their relationship blossomed, but the Legionnaires abducted her husband-to-be and he was likely murdered before they could get married. Whatever happened, he was never seen again. For Esther, the world had been destroyed yet again, but sadness turned to happiness when her daughter Dita was born.

Chapter 4
Rivka's Parents and Memories from Childhood
(In Rivka's Own Words)

When I was born in Iași, Moldova (now a part of Romania) on October 24, 1939, the world into which I arrived was filled with news of war, inhumanity, fear, and terror. Adolph Hitler, Germany's leader, had already been stoking the fires of World War II, building up to his master plan to remake Europe and eliminate millions of people, those he considered less than human, less than his concept of perfection, less than Aryan.

Against that backdrop of political unrest, many innocent lives were filled with torment and unexpected and unwanted change. Like many Jews, our world was about to shift then turn upside down.

My family had been subject to the winds of war for more than a generation. My parents were born in Bukovina, in the region of Chernovitz, which was under the Austrian regime ruled by Franz Joseph I of Austria at the time. It was home to many Jewish people. It is now the Ukraine. I remember that my parents used to say that even though they lived in one place, they lived in many different countries due to the fast-changing borders in Europe during the 1900s. Eventually, Chernovitz became a part of Romania (today it is part of the Ukraine).

My father, Jacob Konig, was the oldest in his family. He was born on November 29, 1906. He had a brother and two sisters. When his father, Zvi Ze'ev (born in 1885), went to fight in World War I for the Austrian cause and was captured by the Russian army as a POW. He was imprisoned in Siberia and he didn't return home until 1921. So at just 14 years of age, my dad Jacob became the provider for his family. This interfered with my dad's schooling because work by necessity became everything for him. After my grandfather went to war, his mom would bake the Romanian dish *malai* (cornmeal cheese cakes) and my dad sold them to make some money. In 1939, at the age of 54, Zvi Ze'ev died from lung cancer.

My grandma from my dad's side was Sara Scheter Konig, born in 1881. She died in Chernivtsi from gangrene during the month of February 1945 at the age of 64.

After the war, my uncle Herman—my father's brother—disappeared. To this day his whereabouts remain unknown. My two aunts, my dad's sisters Toni and Clara, were deported to Uzbekistan as were many other Jews from the area in 1941, and they returned to Chernovitz in 1945, then moved to Bucharest in 1946. In 1949, they made their way to Cyprus in anticipation of immigrating to Israel.

The memory of my father is still quite sharp in my mind. He was tall, with blue-green eyes. He was also handsome and physically very strong. At a young age he became bald. I know now that he loved me in his own fashion but could not really show it in ways I could understand. I surmise that his lack of warmth is partially due to the fact that his father was away for many years while Jacob was growing up, and he had to become the family provider from a young age. That is quite a burden for such young shoulders, a huge responsibility that must have made him a very serious person and old before his age due to a lost childhood.

Jacob Konig, Rivka's father, 1924

Work was very important to my father—he was all about work, and work was what kept him going.

My mother Peppi Reder was born on June 26, 1909, and she ultimately had fourteen brothers and sisters. Her father served in the Austrian army and was killed in World War I. He was buried in Vienna in the Jewish part of the cemetery for soldiers. Peppi's mother was a widow at a very young age and she had to challenge life and earn money for the family. She was very smart and she felt she had to prepare her kids for real life. Since she didn't have money to pay for their education, she sent every one of their kids to learn a profession in order to be able to make a living. She had a saying, "Even the king must learn a profession because there is no security that he will be king all his life."

Jacob Konig and Peppi Reder Konig, Rivka's parents, at their engagement, 1929-1930

Peppi was short with dark brown hair and green eyes. She was a very beautiful lady and quite the coquette. She liked to dress nicely, her nails were always manicured, and her hair was always beautifully arranged. She was also a very good cook. She always knew how to show me love and to pamper me. She was a very caring person, a good mother and later, a doting grandmother. My mother also shared a close relationship with her own mother, Feige Reder.

Jacob and Peppi Konig, Rivka's parents, at their wedding, 1930

My parents—who were married in 1930, about the same time that Chernovitz became a part of Romania—were financially well off and led a very socially active and good life. They dined out quite a lot, they went to shows, and my mother liked to sing—she had a beautiful voice. My parents eventually decided to move to Iași, which was the capitol of Moldova. They fluently spoke both German and Yiddish, which was the language spoken between the Jews.

Peppi Konig, Rivka's mother, 1933

In order to get a job, you needed to know the language, so my parents began to learn Romanian. In Romania, my mother's work ethic matched that of my father's. My mother worked as a hairdresser. I recall that my mom spent many hours on her feet cutting and styling hair and giving manicures. Since her clients were high society and rich people, they helped my mom find my dad a job as a hotel manager in the city. He kept this job for a long time and he earned money to improve the family's situation.

Baby Rita (Rivka) and her mother, 1940

Although my parents considered me to be a beautiful angel when I was born, my dad was disappointed that my mom didn't deliver a boy. Since we lived during the era of the World War II, it was very difficult to think about more kids. My mom did become pregnant again, but because the world was at war, she decided to have an abortion. The doctors were not well trained at the time and they botched the procedure. After that she could not have any more children. It was brought to my dad's attention after the abortion that it was a boy, and he was very sorry about that news—a disappointment he would feel for the rest of his life.

Rita (Rivka) Konig, 1941

My birth changed our family completely, and all the love my mom had within her she gave to me. My dad didn't know to express love, though inside he was very good hearted and I'm sure that he loved me although I was not born a boy. The same year I was born, my parents started to worry about our lives because of the widespread anti-Semitism and also because the German army started to march in to Romania and persecute Jews and transport them to the death camps. Because my dad was a manager in the hotel, he had built a network of connections with high-ranking people in the Romanian regime.

As the Nazi movement became more active, the hatred directed toward Jews became overt. While working at the hotel, someone reported my father for being a Jew. Being Jewish was enough in those days to put someone's life in danger. Nazi soldiers showed up to remove my father from the hotel and drag him in front of a firing squad. A minute before they were to shoot him with the other Jews they had lined up, the chief of the police who knew my father personally came and said, "Konig! What are you doing here?" The chief of police spoke rapidly in German to the men in charge and told them to get my dad out of the lineup immediately.

At the last moment, my dad's life was spared, and he was sent back to the hotel as if it was business as usual. However, the situation became more dangerous with each passing day. We had to hide in the cellar of our home and my parents watched me very carefully. During one of the bombardments, my dad was in bed and when the alarms went on my mom kept telling him that we had to run to the basement. Finally, he listened to her and as soon as we got into the basement a bomb landed in the middle of the bed where he had been lying. We spent a lot of time in the basement when I was just one year old.

But even in this terrible time, we found simple joys in our lives—eating, singing, dancing, and talking with our friends late into the night. We took time to savor the beauty of a flower on the side of the road, or the warmth of a winter fire in the hearth. These good times were deeply engraved into our memories, and they carried us through many difficult times ahead.

Chapter 5
Arie's Memories from Childhood
(In Arie's Own Words)

I was born in Fălticeni, Moldova (now, like Iași, a part of Romania) on October 15, 1934. My mom moved to Bucharest in 1938, which means I was about four years old, and I lived there until I was about six-and-a-half years old. Of course I don't remember a lot at that age, only the special events. Here are a few that stand out.

I remember sitting in a room with mom who was at a sewing machine surrounded by a lot of clothes, and she was laughing at my sister Bianca and me while we played. I was a very mischievous child. While chasing my sister I pulled her too hard and she fell, breaking a bottle that shattered into pieces and cut her face—right near her mouth. Of course this was a huge scare for my mom who ran to take her to the hospital where they stitched up her wound. I was with the neighbors and thinking to myself that from that day onward, Bianca would have to eat and drink with her mouth stitched closed.

I remember a day that I met a girl whom I adored in the neighborhood where we lived. We played together all the time. After a while all of the neighbors knew that I had proposed to her and promised to marry her after we grew up. We had all kinds of funny games. One of these games was to "play doctor" and touch our genitals. Everyone would laugh at us and thought we were behaving strangely.

Another thing I remember is that soon after we moved to Bucharest there was an earthquake. My mother woke me up in the middle of the night, and we ran under the stairs to hide. I found myself in the street with other people who had started to run from the earthquake. I was running and holding the hand of a woman who I thought was my mom—but it turned out to be a stranger! My fear and crying was overwhelming until I found my mom and she hugged me in her arms very tightly. This was a very scary moment that stayed in my mind for many years.

Chapter 6
Apocalypse Now

While the rise of Adolph Hitler and his Nazi thugs—along with their single-minded pursuit of genocide on a scale never before seen on this planet—is well known and documented, what is not so well known is the flood of anti-Semitism unleashed in Romania as Hitler's influence grew. This flood almost caught Arie and Rivka and their families in its deadly currents. One day, for example, Arie had left his family's hiding place in Suceava to look for food when he chanced upon a small detachment of German soldiers. He and several other Jews were stopped by the soldiers and led toward the train that would take them to the death camps. Arie, however, was able to take advantage of the ensuing chaos and he escaped this terrible fate. Only late in the evening, after it was dark, was Arie able to get home.

His grandma was so worried she hugged and kissed Arie and asked where he had been. Arie chose not to tell her the truth because he didn't want her to worry. He told her that he had gotten lost. After that day, Arie was so shaken and scared that he didn't ever want to leave his hiding place. Each time he saw a German soldier, he felt his body start to tremble. Arie realized later on that he extremely lucky. He was very close to being captured and put on a train to the concentration camps, where he would have certainly been killed. He was grateful to get the news that the rest of his family was also alive.

A few days later, Arie's family received a message that one of his dad's brothers, Mishu, was living in Iași with family, and that they were very anxious to meet their other relatives. In the evening Arie's family arrived in Bucharest, and his Aunt Matilda—a beautiful woman with blue eyes—welcomed them with love, and a beautiful blonde, blue-eyed boy who was about two years old named Tony was hugged by his dad. Arie's grandma was hugged by Aunt Matilda and she started to prepare a huge meal. Uncle Faivish was a very tall man with black eyes and a golden heart. He was always happy.

Later on that week, Uncle Faivish made all the arrangements for Arie's grandma to have surgery. She recuperated fast and after three months in Bucharest she decided to return to Fălticeni. It was really difficult for Arie to say goodbye to his grandma because Uncle Faivish decided that Arie would stay with them and his family would raise Arie. It appeared to Arie that this would the last time he would see his grandma, and indeed this turned out to be the case.

Years later, Arie heard from his cousin Samuel—the son of his aunt Shaina and uncle Meyer—that all of his childhood stories from Grandma were about Arie. Arie was very emotional about this, and his grandma always stayed in his heart.

Chapter 7
The Second World War
(In Arie's Own Words)

By 1941, we had moved back the city where I was born, Fălticeni, and I entered first grade. My father had already been gone a while. My mom rented a small apartment there, but after a while my mother got really sick, and we had to move in with her father, my grandfather from my mom's side, and my moms' sister who all lived there.

My mom's sister—my aunt, Nutzi—took care of my mom and Bianca and baby Dita and me. We were not allowed to enter the room where my mom and baby sister lay in bed, both suffering from the same illness—tuberculosis. We could only watch them through the door because the disease was very contagious, and very deadly.

The Romanian regime collaborated with the German army when the Second World War erupted. When I went to school I had to wear the Star of David on my clothes, a yellow sign, so that the Germans could spot us as being Jewish. But everyone knew that I was Jewish. Not only that, but I spoke a different dialect than the others—a dialect from Bucharest, while everyone else was from Moldova.

At home the situation was very bad. My mom's condition grew worse each day, and she died in 1942. A few months after that, my baby sister Dita died, too. Dita had been a beautiful little girl, only two years old, and she had barely been able to taste the goodness of life.

Right after my mom's death, my dad's family decided that my sister Bianca would stay with Nutzi at my grandparents' house from my mother's side—the Kimel family. But I was taken to my dad's family—to my grandparents, Lea and Samuel Ringelstein.

I was scared. I didn't know exactly what was going to happen to me. But after a while I adjusted to the situation. The house was big and on a central street. The name of the street was Doi-Granichei, which means "two watchers." In the front of the house they had a small grocery store. My grandma was the manager.

Our family was financially stable, and we were well-fed, happy, and loved. At the back of the house there were big rooms and a yard with all kinds of fruit trees, chickens, and ducks. In the house lived my uncle Eli, my uncle Joseph, my Aunt Shaina—who later on got married to a man name Meyer who also lived with us—as well as two other aunts Maria and Paulina. All of them were the brothers and sisters of my father.

Everyone helped with the business, buying and selling goods for the farmers. My grandma Lea was the one in charge of all the business dealings and who took care of everything. My grandma was the one who also had some time to pamper me, to hug and kiss me never mind how busy she was. She always found the time to take care of me and I loved spending time with her.

One of my uncles, Eli, tried to teach me a lot of practical things for life. He was the only one who was divorced, and he helped a lot with the business. My grandma also was the one who was responsible for giving me a bath and cooking for me. To give a bath meant that she had to go to the yard and pump the water from the well into a large pot, and then put it on the stove to boil so that we would have warm water to bathe in. There was no electricity, only oil lamps.

I didn't feel very close to my grandfather. He hardly talked to me. I didn't understand fully what his duties at home were, but everyone honored him like he was a king.

Because of the war, I had to stop my studies at school, so my grandparents enrolled me in a small yeshiva where a very serious rabbi taught me. I didn't know exactly what I was doing there, and I was very mischievous. I was punished severely for acting up; the rabbi would hit me with a ruler on my hand and with a belt on my tushy. It was horrible, I was suffering, and that is why I ran away from the place. No one could get me to go back there. I don't know how, but one day I found myself wearing a uniform and playing in the orchestra of the fire department of the municipality of the city. I was the focus of the concert because I was an orphan.

My uncle Joseph who lived with us in the house got married and moved to the city of Suceava. I started to travel with my uncle Eli to the villages in the neighborhood to buy and sell goods. He had two horses and a carriage. I was under strict orders when I was traveling with him to these villages not to say that I was Jewish and to remember that I had a different name—an original Romanian name. During those travels I experienced a lot of things. I enjoyed the scenery of the summer and the snow in the winter. I was very scared during one of those nights when the horses got wild and didn't want to move. My uncle noticed that a bunch of wolves had approached us. My uncle started a fire with the wood he had in the carriage and this saved us from the wolves. The wolves didn't go away though, so we had to stay awake till morning when they finally left and we were able to travel again.

My uncle made sure we always could reach the nearest village during the day where one of the villagers had prepared a room for us with straw so that we could sleep. When we got home I think we slept for two days in a row until I felt whole again. My grandma was very upset and she didn't allow my uncle Eli to take me with him on those trips anymore.

The city we lived in was a small. It had only one major street. I used to go with some kids to the edge of the city, and we would be wild and scream because we like to hear our echoing voices. Some of the kids said that the echo was the devil calling, but I didn't understand what this meant. I used to get myself frozen in the snow.

My grandma always welcomed me with love, hugs, and kisses and she would heat up my frozen hands with her own. One day some Romanian kids wanted to hurt me so I threw some stones at them and one of the stones hit a boy in the head. The father of the kid came to my home and started to yell at my grandfather and said that he would catch me and kill me. When I got home my grandfather was very upset, and he was chasing me around to hit me. Of course I was very quick and shouted at him, "You are an old dog!" This caused only more problems between me and Grandpa. He was very scary with a large white mustache. He was totally bald and never wore a smile on his face.

Fortunately for me, grandmother knew how to hide me from Grandpa when he was upset. She always told him to forgive me. Even though economically the situation was very difficult, we always had food to eat at home. I would help grandma with the fruit trees and the kitchen.

My grandma would have 100 ml of cognac and a cigarette every day. She used to give me a sip of cognac just to taste it, and she taught me to drink in the backyard. The toilet was just a hole in the ground in the backyard, so we had to be careful where we walked. I felt lucky that I didn't have to go to the toilet at night.

One morning I saw that my grandmother was very upset. An animal had come into the yard and killed all of the chickens, which meant that there were no eggs or meat to prepare for the family. The normal menu was soup with chicken meat and potatoes, and some beans that grew in the backyard. There was no bread, so we would instead eat *mămăligă*, which was a traditional porridge made of cornmeal (given the name "Turkish wheat" in Eastern Europe) and water. It is similar to what the Italians call *polenta*, but any Romanian will tell you that our version is much better.

There was a popular Yiddish song devoted to the joys of living in Romania, composed by Aaron Lebedeff in the 1920s. The song—"Roumania, Roumania"—included these heartfelt lyrics:

Dort tsu voynen iz a fargenign
vos dos harts glust dir vost kentsu krign
a mameligele, a pastramele, a karnatseleun
a gleyzele vayn, aha!

To live there is a pleasure
What your heart desires you can get
A mămăligă, a pastrami, a karnatzl (sausage),
and a glass of wine, aha![iii]

My grandma would work in the store and always explained to me that I needed to work with the cash and learn to be independent and develop my sense of business. I also learned from her to drink wine, which was normally stored in a big bottle called a *dabijan*. One of those days I went to take a sip from the dabijan, and I started to throw up because someone had put oil for the lanterns in the bottle instead of wine. My grandma nursed me back to health.

A few houses down the street, there was another grocery and the owner's name was Yanku Ringelstein. Apparently he was a cousin of my dad's. He was a very unfriendly person, and I could not understand how he had such a beautiful wife! They never had children. Every opportunity I had when I passed their store I asked for a lollipop. He would turn me away and never give me one.

The war got worse, and the Russians started to advance toward our area. The Germans were in Fălticeni, and the front was getting close to where we lived. It was a strategic place because it was near the mountains. The situation of the Jews got worse every day. Every man had been taken and recruited to the front for different types of work, and some of them had been killed. My uncle Eli succeeded in starting work in the army kitchen, and this way he was able to bring food to the family from time to time.

The battles were intense, and the Russians succeeded in pushing away the German and Romanian armies. One day the Russian army gave an order to spill all the wine and alcohol into the streets because they were afraid that the soldiers would get drunk.

I saw a big difference between the German soldiers—who were organized and clean, and who would wash their bodies even though it was cold and snowy outside—and the Russians. The Russian soldiers were wild, came with none of their own ammunition, and threatened everyone. Their women and children were stealing from everyone anything they could find. Later on I understood that it was the Russians who saved us from the evil German soldiers.

Food was getting scarce—just some old potatoes and cornmeal. The potatoes were frozen and tasted terrible—you could hardly swallow them, and they would make you sick if you did.

One day after the Russians had entered the city, I was walking in the street to look for food when I was surprised by a

Russian officer who touched my shoulder. I was afraid that he would kill me for stealing food, but he let me know that he was also Jewish. He knew that I was Jewish because of the star I was wearing. He gave me a full sack of food that I brought home to my family, and it lasted an entire week.

The battles were very hard and the city was always changing because people moved from one place to another. We hid in the basement to avoid being caught up in the strife. There was a separate entrance that we would cover with a rug and table and chairs so that no one would know we were there.

During this time, my grandma told me stories about my father—what happened to him, how he was killed, and the successes he had during his short life. I was not in touch with my sister Bianca during the war.

When the war ended in 1945, everyone was looking for their relatives, and trying to determine the consequences of the war, and what had happened to the Jewish community in Romania and the rest of Europe. We were informed that my uncle Faivish had been living in Bucharest during the war. He was married to a woman named Matilda, and they had one son, Tony, who was later known as Aaron.

Before that, my grandpa was very sick. He suffered from an enlarged prostate and couldn't urinate. A Jewish doctor by the name of Segal would come to the house to change the catheter. But one day my grandpa contracted an infection and died. My uncle Faivish accompanied me and my grandma on the train back to Bucharest, where Grandma was supposed to get an operation that would either save her life or end it. Strong woman that she was, after her surgery my grandma recuperated quickly, and after three months in Bucharest, she decided to return to Fălticeni.

CHAPTER 8
POGROMS, AND THE IAȘI DEATH TRAINS

As the Second World War raged across Europe, the Legionnaires, the Iron Guard, and other organized Romanian nationalist (and anti-Semitic) groups—with the tacit support of the Romanian government and police forces—embarked on a systematic program of murder and violence against the Jewish people. The pogroms that had raged across Moldova and Bessarabia in the early 1900s flared up once again, leading to the deaths of thousands of Jews.

These pogroms included:

- Dorohoi (July 1, 1940)
- Bucharest (January 21-23, 1941)
- Iași (June 29-July 6, 1941)
- Cernovitz (July 5-6, 1941)
- Edinets (July 6, 1941)
- Beltz (July 11, 1941)
- Kishinev (August 1, 1941)

And then there were the Iași death trains.

On June 30, 1941, the day after the Iași pogrom began, 5,000 Jews were rounded up by German SS troops, local police, and Romanian soldiers. The Jews were crowded into the courtyard of Iași's police headquarters where at least half were either beaten or shot to death. The survivors of this massacre were then herded onto two separate trains.

The destination of the first train was Calarasi, while the destination of the other was Podul Iloaiei. But these were no normal trains. These were freight cars specifically modified to become rolling death machines. According to one source:

> *Their captors then nailed shut the narrow ventilation slats in the cars. The train was decorated on the outside with slogans identifying the cargo as "Communist Jews" or "Killers of German and Romanian soldiers." The train, under the command of Sergeant Ion Leucea and a detachment of Romanian police, finally departed from Iasi in the early morning hours of June 30.*

For the next 17 hours the death train traveled a circuitous route to Tirgu Frumos, Pascani, Lespezi, back to Pascani, then on to Roman, and finally, back to Tirgu Frumos, where it halted temporarily. By this time hundreds had died. Three or four of the railcars were opened to remove the dead. The approximately 200 survivors found in the opened cars were escorted by Police Commissar Ion Botez and his guards to a nearby synagogue.

Those who tried to quench their thirst by drinking from puddles on the road were shot by Botez, while villagers were threatened with the death penalty if they offered aid to the Jews. Once they reached the synagogue the captives were subjected to further beatings and theft of their remaining personal possessions.[iv]

Hundreds of Iași Jews died in this first train. The second Iași death train—with its human cargo of 1,902 Jews squeezed into 18 railcars, along with 80 corpses—left soon after the first. After an eight-hour journey in the overcrowded, unventilated freight cars, only 708 Jews survived.

Arie and Rivka's families were caught up in these terrible pogroms and death trains, which gave them that many more reasons to find a new home—one where the Jewish people would be welcome and honored, instead of persecuted and murdered because of their faith and traditions.

With the birth of the modern state of Israel in 1948, the promise of this new home became more than just a dream. It became real.

CHAPTER 9
RIVKA'S LIFE DURING THE WAR

When Germany started regularly bombing the city, Rivka's family spent hours and days hiding in the cellar of their home. Rivka was only a baby, and yet she can still recall today the cold and damp of that cave-like hiding place. And while most children remember little of their early years, Rivka still has several very clear memories of her first seven years in Romania. She was an only child and she was treated like a princess. Rivka had a nanny, and she was rarely required to do any chores around the house.

Rita (Rivka) and her mother, 1945

The house was on a street named Stefan Chel-Mare, and during the winter, there was often a blanket of snow outside. Rivka has a photograph where she was standing outside with her mother and a friend. Rivka was wearing a special outfit for cold weather, and the women are wearing furs. Though the Konig family was not rich, their life was quite comfortable.

Romanian foods, culture, and music were part of the family's acculturation, and both German and Romanian were spoken at home. Rivka's parents spoke mostly German between themselves and other family members. It may be because of this early exposure to other languages that she grew up with a talent for languages: German, Yiddish, Romanian, Hebrew, English, French, and much later, Spanish.

The most popular food in the Konig household was mashed potatoes, although potatoes in any form were popular, including potato dumplings made from scratch. Rivka did not have a pet during her childhood in Romania, nor did she have much in the way of books or toys of her own, but she always loved music from an early age and there was constant music in the house.

While living in Iași, Rivka attended first grade at Notre Dame, a Catholic school run by nuns, and she still has a photo of her getting a report card when she was seven. That was the last year of formal schooling that Rivka would have for many years.

Rita (Rivka) Konig, age 7, graduating first grade with award, 1946

Both Jacob and Peppi (Rivka's parents) had to wear the Star of David on their clothing. This symbol was a sign to others that their family was Jewish. But to those forced to wear these Stars of David, it felt more like a condemnation for being Jewish. As the political situation went from bad to worse for the Jews, it became increasingly clear to Jacob and Peppi that it was time to leave their country, friends, and neighbors behind. The situation wasn't good for Jews, and it was getting worse with each passing day.

Looking back at that period of her life, the strongest sensation Rivka remembers is one of deprivation. Not of material things, but of the sense that she did not have any freedom, any personal power. Rivka believes that when a child is born into a family it should be a time of joy and celebration. Children are meant to experience joy and happiness with their parents and be surrounded by a sense of love and safety.

Despite the challenges faced by her parents, they showered Rivka with their love, and her mother did the best she could to keep Rivka sheltered and treat her like a princess. But the winds of war did not allow that to continue for much longer.

Being born right when WWII broke out meant that Rivka would not enjoy a normal childhood. The impact of World War II on Jews and non-Jews alike touched everything from attachment to possessions to camaraderie to shoe leather. Deep in her heart, Rivka knew that life was not quite right, but she did not understand why. She just knew she had to follow orders and that there was no room to be even slightly rebellious. In other words, Rivka never had the freedom to act like a child, lighthearted and free from worry.

Rita (Rivka) with her parents, 1945

During wartime you can't do what you want and that's that. By robbing Rivka of that childhood sense of freedom, the war robbed her also of the natural feeling that children are supposed to have that they can do anything they set their minds to, that the world is a place of infinite possibilities. It took her a long time to realize that she could change anything in her life, that there might indeed be choices to be made, and new paths to follow.

CHAPTER 10
ZIONISM AND THE JEWISH STATE

For centuries, the Jewish people have yearned to return to the homeland of their ancestors: *Eretz Yisrael*—the Land of Israel. While the boundaries of the land promised by God to his people vary somewhat depending on which biblical passage is read and who is interpreting it, the city of Jerusalem (known at different times in its history as the City of Peace, the Fortress of Zion, and the City of David, among other names) has asserted a strong pull on the Jewish people for thousands of years. The words *"l'shanah haba'ah birushalayim,"* or "Next year in Jerusalem," recited at the end of the Passover Seder, reflect this profound and heartfelt desire.

The long history of the Jewish people is punctuated by numerous diaspora, where men, women, and children were forced from their homeland, and spread across the face of the earth. The Ashkenazi migrated to Central and Eastern Europe, the Sephardi to Iberia (Spain and Portugal) and North Africa, and the Mizrahi to Babylon. Often left with little more than the clothes on their back, a strong work ethic, and a deeply rooted cultural identity that united them wherever they went, these people were left to their own resources to rebuild their lives, families, and communities.

And that they did.

Jewish settlers in these new lands quickly prospered, building successful farms, businesses, and communities. As Moshe Maor points out in his history of Zionism,

> ...the nineteenth century was "the best century Jews have ever experienced, collectively and individually, since the destruction of the Temple." Following the French Revolution, a new approach toward the Jews began to prevail with the spread of the ideas of the Enlightenment. Ghettos were opened, equal individual rights were granted and the occupational range was gradually widened with Jews acquiring a strong position in the professions of wholesale and retail trade. Jewish life began shifting from the periphery to the main metropolises of Europe and a

> visible Jewish presence was recorded in universities as well as in science and culture. This new and more humane approach toward the Jews led to a process of social and cultural assimilation in European countries."

By 1900, the global Jewish population numbered about 11.3 million people, with 80 percent of that total located within Europe.[v] But while they gained more rights and became pillars within their adopted lands, for the most part they remained outsiders—most obviously because their religion was different from the Christians who dominated most of these areas, but also because their great success often attracted the jealousy of their neighbors. In many cases, this jealousy turned into dislike, and outright hatred. Moshe Maor continues, "The Jewish population was routinely persecuted, massacred, expelled, forcibly converted, excluded from public service positions and threatened with physical, spiritual and cultural annihilation." Increasingly, Jews faced newly enacted anti-Semitic laws and official policies, passed to put the Jewish people at a legal disadvantage.

The combination of rising anti-Semitism among their neighbors, and the passage of laws targeting the Jewish population, increased the desire of many Jews to find a path back to their homeland—*Eretz Yisrael*. The Jewish national movement, which promoted the idea of the immigration of Jews to Palestine, was sparked in the 1870s, and the World Zionist Organization was founded in 1897, during the First Zionist Congress in Basel, Switzerland.

On November 2, 1917, Great Britain (which took possession of Palestine from the Ottoman Empire after the end of World War I) issued the Balfour Declaration, which stated:

> His Majesty's government view with favour the establishment in Palestine of a national home for the Jewish people, and will use their best endeavours to facilitate the achievement of this object, it being clearly understood that nothing shall be done which may prejudice the civil and religious rights of existing non-Jewish communities in Palestine, or the rights and political status enjoyed by Jews in any other country

During the course of the next several decades, more than

100,000 Jews attempted to immigrate to Palestine. Some were allowed by the British to stay (under the British *Aliyah A* program of limited legal Jewish immigration) but most were forcibly returned to Europe.

After the end of World War II, when the world was shocked by the atrocities visited on the Jewish people by the Nazis and the Holocaust, there was a consensus among world leaders that a Jewish homeland—a Jewish state—should be established in the Middle East. By September 1947, members of the United Nations Special Committee on Palestine (UNSCOP) recommended that Palestine be divided into two separate states: an Arab state, and a new Jewish state. The UN General Assembly ratified the UNSCOP recommendation on November 29, 1947, and on May 14, 1948, the modern state of Israel officially came into being, when David Ben-Gurion announced its founding.

Finally, after 2,000 years, the Jewish people had a home again, and in the late 1940s, the mass migration of Jews to Israel began.

Chapter 11
After the War
(In Arie's Own Words)

The economic situation of my uncle Faivish was excellent after the war. He became a contractor for huge buildings that needed glass for windows and doors, and he earned a lot of money. I remember him coming home with huge packages of cash.

My uncle hired a teacher who came to our home; he was a vice captain in the Romanian army, and he started to teach me mathematics, reading, writing, and some other basics which due to the war I had missed out on in school. In the mornings I used to walk with my aunt and my cousin Tony to Cişmigiu, where they lived in a very nice neighborhood. Their address was Covalchsku #16.

I used to meet a girl from the neighborhood who was about 16 or 17 and I was around 10-and-a-half years old. She started to kiss and hug me; pretty soon we were having sex regularly—even though I didn't even have any sperm yet. But I felt like I was in the heavens and went to see her at every opportunity.

At home everything was fine. I got to know the rest of the family, and I played with Cousin Tony. At night however, I really missed my grandma's hugs. I thought about her a lot and would not be able to fall asleep for a long time. Then one night I heard some noises, got up and saw my aunt and uncle; I think they were having sex and it woke me up! In the morning I was caught in the washroom, masturbating. My uncle started to laugh and he said he was proud of me.

A few months later another two uncles, Joseph and Mishu from Iaşi and Suceava respectively, came to visit. They were all happy to meet me and hugged me. The next morning, I stayed at home with my uncles while my aunt and cousin went to the park. A lady who was a dressmaker came to our home to do some repairs and sew some clothes for my aunt. The men started to talk to the dressmaker, coming on to her, so they wanted me to go away—they gave me money to buy cigarettes and ice cream. I got the point that they wanted to be alone with the dressmaker.

Uncle Faivish explained to me that he wanted me to go to a special school to learn a profession. He took me to a school in Bucharest called Chokanu, which means *hammer*. The manager of the school was an engineer whose name was Ringelstein, and he was a cousin of my uncle. I don't know what happened, or why that cousin of my uncle didn't want to accept me into the school, but almost a year passed without me attending any school.

In Romania a new regime had taken over, and one day there was a huge devaluation of the currency. My uncle lost a lot of money, and many people committed suicide because they were financially ruined.

One day Uncle Faivish explained to me that the Jews had organized themselves to take orphan kids to Palestine—now the state of Israel. He told me my sister Bianca was already at the orphanage, in the Hungarian part of Romania called Transylvania, in a small city by the name of Dobrovan. He made the arrangements and bought me a train ticket, and I traveled to the orphanage.

My uncle then gave me a small suitcase with a few clothes as well as some personal guidance on how to act. It was explained to me that I had to behave a certain way since the Romanians hated the Jews. I had to remember that my name was now "Yon," and to play the game that I was a Romanian traveling to Dobrovan to visit my aunt who was a nurse at the local hospital. I got a little bit of money and some sandwiches and I said goodbye to my uncle and got on the train.

The train was overcrowded with people—there were even people sitting on the roof! I sat between some Romanian men, and they started asking me all kinds of questions, and I told them the story that I was supposed to tell. They started to mess with me, and they said they would take me to their village so that I could help them with their farm. For them it was a joke, but for me inside I felt scared to death that one of them was going to take me away. My fright was so overwhelming that, when they announced the station of Dobrovan, I was hardly able to go in the direction of the door. The men kept joking that I was going to go with them. Just a few seconds before the train continued on the way, they threw me out of the window with my small suitcase.

I took a carriage to the orphanage and there I met my sister Bianca. A few months later I heard that my uncle Faivish had gone shopping at the market and was bitten by lice. He came down with typhus fever and died three days later. My aunt Matilda was pregnant and my cousin Tony became an orphan. I was very sad since I really loved my uncle.

After the long train ride and hours of traveling, I arrived at the orphanage in Dobrovan where all of the orphans in Romania had been gathered up by the Jewish Joint Organization (JJO) with the goal of transferring all of us to the new Jewish state.

The trainer-teachers were all very young and had received special Zionist training. We were put into groups by the different political organizations that were in Romania, and the kids were divided by age groups. All of us were trained in different subjects.

The orphanage was a huge building with small rooms. All of the beds were bunk beds to save space. Around the building there was a huge backyard. As soon as I got to the orphanage, I had to undergo many different medical checkups and fill out all sorts of forms. My hair was cut so short I was almost bald; this was to prevent the kids from getting lice. I got a few blankets and was told the rules of the house. The food came in very small portions, and at night it was terribly cold—so cold that I would tremble. I used to imagine Grandma Lea hugging me and keeping my hands warm.

After two weeks, I got a skin disease that most of the children in the orphanage contracted. I found myself isolated. They made us slather on an ointment that smelled so terrible it would make you throw up. It took about two weeks for me to get rid of that disease. I was very tired and weak, and I kept scratching myself.

A few months later I got a serious infection in my gums that caused me not to be able to drink or eat anything. The doctors decided they would have to cut my infected gums. I suffered terrible pain. Even with medication it took me nearly two months to get well. I was given special instructions on how to brush my teeth—up until then I didn't have the faintest idea that brushing teeth even existed. I started to brush all the time.

My sister Bianca and I would meet in between lessons, and she updated me about the family because she maintained correspondence with them.

One of those evenings when it was very cold, all of the kids huddled together around the stove in the middle of the room. Some of the kids started to misbehave and pushed each other close to the stove. I was already close to the stove when the kids pushed me and my left knee touched the burning metal. All of the skin on my knee was instantly burned, and I started to scream. They had to take me to the nearest medical center, and I was left with a scar that remained with me for the rest of my life.

There was not much food, and many of us had been undernourished during the war. So every day we got one spoonful of fish oil—it was horrible! We had to plug our noses and stop breathing in order to swallow. But it was mandatory, as were other new and incomprehensible rules that were foisted upon us.

After a long day of schooling in the subject of Judaism and Zionism we would play all kinds of games and tell each other horror stories about what had happened to each of us during the war. This is how we learned what happened to the Jews and how they perished in the Nazi concentration camps. We also learned about Israel, a country that we very much looked forward to arriving in—a country that would end the persecution of Jews for all time.

Soon one year had passed in the orphanage. We were told that the Jewish Joint Organization had joined with the Jews from America after the war to help the orphans first make their way to Holland and then on to Israel. This meant we had yet another new place to get used to.

We said goodbye to the orphanage after a year to find ourselves boarding the train at the same station I was at when I arrived—but with a small difference: this time there was only us on the train which mean that the JJO had hired the entire train to haul the orphans to Holland, where we would get more information and training before arriving in Israel.

Our orphanage was the first to board the train. Our trainers joined the trainers of the JJO who spoke English, and they joined all kinds of volunteers from America who were responsible for the food, clothes, candies, and blankets. At first we were running from one empty compartment to the other on the train, but as we traveled, kids from other countries boarded at every station, and we traveled day and night through Europe.

I was astonished to see the kids who were survivors from the Holocaust camps. They looked so thin, like skeletons. The trainers served food, chocolate milk, and all kinds of other delicacies, but what they were not aware of was that these kids had not seen food for a long time. As soon as they started to eat they became very swollen, and a few of the kids even died because they were not used to having any food. I was in shock, and this image followed me for years.

As we continued to travel, I reflected on the different phases of my life so far.

The first phase was in Fălticeni, before we went to Bucharest. I don't remember much of that.

The second phase was when I was in Bucharest with my mom and sister, during which I had just started to get to know the area. I was left with only vague memories of some of the events, like the earthquake, my mom working all day bent over her sewing machine, games with my sister, talk about the war. In a nutshell: a chaos of memories in my mind. I felt very lonely during that part of my life, as if nothing would ever make me happy.

The third phase took place in Fălticeni after we returned from Bucharest. The war was still on and Romania had allied with Nazi Germany. During that time, I was watching my sick mom from afar, without any possibility of getting close to her to hug her. Her death added a lot of sadness into my life, and I became very closed off. It was a big hit for me, even though I didn't fully understand the real consequences and my mind was foggy.

The fourth phase of my life was the time that I spent at my grandparents' home, where I was enveloped with love by my grandma. I opened up, and I felt that I was important to them. Grandma and Grandpa lived there, along with Uncle Eli, Joseph, Aunt Shaina, Maria, and Paulina, who was the youngest. I have been told that there was another uncle from my dad's side, Mishu, and his wife in Iași, and of course my uncle Faivish with his wife in Bucharest.

My uncle Eli was the one who dedicated a lot of his time to me and taught me about life. He taught me how to walk correctly, not to open my legs when walking because they used to bend in and were becoming crooked. I was told this was because I was undernourished and lacking vitamins and calcium. My undernourishment didn't change much and my legs stayed crooked, like a football player's.

Uncle Eli tried to teach me to be polite and to keep myself on the straight and narrow and not to be involved with bad kids. I was naturally so mischievous and liked to try everything at least once. I would listen to him sincerely, but whenever I was alone I couldn't help being mischievous. There was a saying that he kept repeating to me, "The sword cannot cut the head when the head is bending" which means we must know when to compromise—or give up—in order to stay alive.

My uncle Joseph was a tall man with blue eyes and a wonderful heart. He would tell me a lot about my dad and share all kinds of funny stories. He later on got married to a girl from Suceava and left the house, but he and his wife could not have kids, so they never had any children. I met him later on when the family left Fălticeni and we went to Suceava.

My aunt Shaina was the oldest of the girls. She was very serious. They made her a match with a man by the name of Meyer who didn't have any family; he was an orphan. He was a wonderful man with a golden heart. They got married and lived in a separate room at my grandparents' house. My uncle Eli helped them and they bought Meyer a horse and carriage; they started to work together driving through the villages and doing business with the farmers.

Aunt Shaina was very connected to my father and she kept telling me a lot of stories about him. She worshiped my father—just loved him very much. My dad would take her to parties and taught her to dance and introduced her to some of his friends. Aunt Shaina dedicated a lot of her time to me—it was like I was her own son. I could feel her love that strongly.

My aunt Maria was a beautiful girl with black eyes, full of energy and liveliness. All of the boys were chasing her—their desire for her was so great. She was the one who always gave me a bath. She would play with me, and it felt good to be with her. Later on a match was made for her, and she got married. But, after that, she was never the same—all of her energy and liveliness disappeared. Later on, I was told that the guy she married was impotent, but she couldn't get a divorce because that would be too shameful for the family. Because of this, she spent the rest of her life without knowing happiness. If she just mentioned to her husband that she would like to divorce him, he would threaten to commit suicide.

My aunt Paulina, the youngest of the girls, was very pampered. She used to take care of herself, and she was always afraid of getting sick. She would sleep with a hat on her head to prevent illness, and she never helped with any of the chores at home. My relationship with her was just polite, nothing special. She married quite late in life, after she made it to Israel, and she had one child—a son.

My grandpa was a very closed and serious person, and I didn't feel anything toward him. However, my grandma was everything for me.

From Grandma I received all of the love and happiness and liveliness and real life wisdom that I needed in my life. She was a superb role model on how to keep a family together. In my mind she always was the one who organized everything. She was good with the business, successful in every negotiation, and was able to deal with any issue—no matter how great or how small. She also was a very good cook.

Grandma worked as an agriculturist. She knew how to knit and sew clothes, and she had time for everything—especially when it came to showing love to everyone. The kids worshiped and honored her since she was the one who kept the family together.

While I was thinking about everything I had been through in my short life, I fell asleep, and in my dreams I saw myself being hugged by my grandma. I woke up and remembered that I was actually in the train traveling through a Europe that had been devastated by the war. Czechoslovakia, Hungary, Austria, Germany—everywhere you could see the destruction. Everywhere there were wandering people, like ghosts. People who once had homes—people who once had families.

I was especially left in awe as we traveled through Germany. The heavy bombing and battles left heavy destruction in their wake. The so-called German "heroes" were shadows of their former selves. They were wandering the countryside in torn clothes and starving—at one stop they begged for a slice of bread. Regardless of all of the terrible things the Germans had done to the Jews, we couldn't refuse to give the orphans on the streets some of our biscuits or chocolate. I was overwhelmed with pity for them, and I was thinking to myself that those kids were not to blame for the deeds of their parents. They were victims of the war, just as we were. I wished for a day when our generation would learn its lesson and bring peace to the world.

From time to time, my sister Bianca—who most of the time rode in the part of the train where the older kids were—came to see how I was doing. I told her about the thoughts that crossed my mind about the different phases of my life, and about my family. I also told her about the short time we had been together with Mom before she died. I told her about Grandpa, who was very tall and thin and didn't talk a lot, especially with me.

Bianca told me things that she remembered, and then she went back to her friends. After many days and nights traveling on the train through Europe, we finally arrived in Holland. It was a place like none other I had ever seen.

A new phase of my life was about to begin. I had no idea what to expect, but I forged on nonetheless.

Chapter 12
The Great Escape!

A year after the war ended, Russians invaded Romania, turning it into a communist country sympathetic with Russia. There was great chaos in the country and at home. Rivka and her parents lived in the same neighborhood as the sisters of her mom who had survived the Holocaust, as well as her grandmother from her mother's side who had lost six of her fourteen children. Some of the children were killed in the Holocaust, and some died from disease, because there was no medication available at the time to treat them.

The members of Rivka's extended family were happy to meet one another despite the challenging economic situation that made money scarce. Rivka's parents helped them financially as best they could. Rivka's family heard that the Jewish Joint Organization was helping Jews from Europe immigrate into Palestine, which would soon become the state of Israel. After hearing that news, Rivka's parents decided to leave behind their house and everything in it to try to escape to Israel.

In 1947, Rivka's family escaped. Leaving Romania happened so quickly that they did not even have time to pack. They were forced to leave everything in the house behind, from furniture to liquor bottles, clothing and silverware, furniture and linens—taking nothing from the house itself, only a few personal possessions each. Rivka's mother wore several dresses, one on top of the other. Shaike—her mother's brother—had a soap factory, and he hid the jewelry inside bars of soap that they took with them. That was it—no money, no food, and nothing to drink on the journey.

Rivka's dad Jacob Konig had a big stick to protect himself from the different animals they encountered, since they would be walking through the fields at night to cross the border. The group consisted of a few families including her mom's sister Erna, her husband Natan, and their daughter Herta. One time they had to run into a farmer's cornfield and hide there during the day. Rivka's mom covered Rivka's mouth so that she would not make the mistake of coughing, talking, or crying and reveal themselves to their enemies. Rivka remembers feeling like she was almost choked and never knowing when their ordeal was going to end.

But a successful escape would depend on one particularly important clothing item—a sturdy pair of shoes, because getting out of Romania required traveling on foot. Rivka's family reached the border into Hungary late one night. But just after they approached the Hungarian frontier, the Hungarian border patrol stopped the group of Jews. The Hungarians took everyone into custody, telling the families that they would be in jail for only one or two nights.

The children soon set up a wail of protest, loudly crying and making so much noise that they were soon released from the jail. At first Rivka thought that they were released because of the ruckus that she and the other children made, but she later realized that the reason they were released so quickly was because the border patrol had been bribed by Rivka's parents and the other families in the group.

After the experience in the Hungarian border jail, the families hid for a brief time on the farm of a non-Jew. This farmer hid them in his cornfields, deep among the tall stalks where no one would think to look. They were admonished by the farmer not to make noise or move around to keep suspicion at bay. The cornfields were but a brief reprieve.

Soon they began walking again, by night, and eventually crossed into Austria, where the group of refugees ended up at a camp in Linz. While in Austria, Rivka had the opportunity to meet her mother's sister-in-law Rosa, who was married to her mother's youngest brother, Herman Reder. Herman had been taken and killed during the war. Rosa remarried (her new last name was Zimmerman) and moved to Milwaukee, Wisconsin. For Rivka, it was nice to have an extended family in the different places they went. She had no idea then how emptied of Jews places like Hungary and Austria would be after the war. The Nazis were all too good at their job.

After a short time in Linz, the Konig family moved on to a refugee camp in Bad Windsheim, Germany, which was run by American soldiers after the end of the war. They lived there for two years. The camp was full of immigrants who had left homes throughout Europe at the end of the war. Jacob Konig knew how to speak German, and that made life a bit easier for his family. Some of the Jewish people in the camp did business with American soldiers—the soldiers bought cigarettes and other sundries from the refugees.

In May 1948, the state of Israel was established. It was a historic moment in Jewish history and it pulled European Jews to its new borders like a powerful magnet. It was a melting pot—and it was hard. Everyone was a newcomer in a new land. The people in the first wave of immigrants were largely from Russia and Poland, and they stuck together—no one spoke Hebrew.

In the second wave, Jews from Romania, Hungary, Czechoslovakia, Bulgaria, and Greece came and they kept together for the most part. These groups represented a larger group known as the Ashkenazi Jews, coming largely from Eastern Europe.

Then the third wave of immigrants came with a totally different culture. These were the Sephardic Jews from the Middle East—and in that group were the Ashkenazis who had previously relocated to the Middle East and had adopted the Sephardic ways. These Jews were dark skinned and had different foods, culture, and traditions than the Ashkenazi Jews.

Jews adopted the traditions of the countries they lived in and brought them to Israel with them. There was a small group of people already living in Palestine before part of it became the state of Israel (mostly Russian, Romanian, and Polish) who spoke Hebrew. Some of the ancient Sephardic Jews spoke a language known as Ladino that was a mixture of Spanish and Hebrew.

At the end of 1948, the Konig family left the refugee camp in Bad Windsheim to stay in the port city of Marseilles, France, for two or three weeks. There they lived in an encampment with other Jews who were in the process of moving to Canada, the United States, and Israel. The ones who wanted to move to the new state of Israel stayed in the same camp and slept in barracks. The living conditions were very basic. While Rivka's family was in Marseilles, her mother's sister, Mitzi Champanier, came to visit them. The Nazis had killed Mitzi's husband. In the Konig's extended family, there were many people whose immediate families did not survive the war intact, if they survived at all.

And such it was that Rivka spent nearly two years of her life wandering from country to country and never knowing what to expect from one day to the next. Because of this instability, she was unable to go to school or develop friendships. It was a constant struggle to get through each day.

One meaning of the word "courage" is voluntarily heading into the unknown even when deep inside the feeling of fear is stronger than anything else. Rivka's parents, Jacob and Peppi Konig, were very courageous to leave behind everything they knew and all they owned to go into the unknown—especially considering that they were already in their forties. But they really had no choice. Their lives were in mortal and immediate danger, so they had to make extreme decisions in order to stay alive. But they did, and they did so courageously. And for the many who did not and stayed behind to die, we all must forever mourn for them, and honor their memories.

Chapter 13
Welcome to the Children's Village!
(In Arie's Own Words)

We finally arrived at a small city in Holland named Apeldoorn. We were taken from the train station by bus to a huge forest, not far from the city. There in the beauty of nature there were small houses—like you would see at a resort. Given the name Ilaniah, the buildings and grounds had formerly been used as a mental asylum.

The people in Holland were mostly blond and white. They welcomed us brought fruits and candies. The entire place was decorated with flowers and welcoming banners written in different languages, "WELCOME TO THE CHILDREN'S VILLAGE!" We were supposed to be in Holland for four years and to go to school there.

A total of 500 Jewish children lived at Ilaniah. After the welcoming ceremonies ended, we were divided into groups according to our age and political party to be taught about our future life in Israel. Every group had a guide according to the country they came from.

The teacher and guides came from Israel, and the first goal was to teach us Hebrew, because everyone was speaking a different language—the village sounded like the Babylon from the bible. Bianca and I were in the group that was called Dror Habonim, a political party in Romania connected to the labor party in Israel, and then we were divided again according to our age.

In our rooms there were beds, blankets, towels, bedding, clothes, and soap to wash our things. The place looked like heaven—especially after spending a year in the orphanage.

After organizing ourselves, we went for a walk in the village. The village was in the middle of the forest, and roads and byways connected the different buildings. There were sports rooms and clubs for special events, and playgrounds. I was really impressed by the people of Holland who worked in the village; they all made us feel loved, and they looked like angels with their blond hair, white skin, and wooden clogs.

I was also impressed by the large quantity of bicycles everywhere. Everyone in Holland was taught from an early age how to ride a bicycle, and each person was given two bicycles—one for weekdays, and one more expensive bike for Sundays and holidays.

The first night at Ilaniah I slept in a bed with white sheets, and after riding the train for so many days, I slept like an angel. After breakfast the next morning, we were again divided into classes and given a daily schedule. We were taught Hebrew with teachers from Israel, and then we had hours to spend in sports—inside and outside—and all sorts of games. In the evenings we would sit around the fire singing songs from Israel.

Every program had an assistant for the trainers whose job it was to translate for every child to their own language, because everyone spoke a different language. This went on for two or three months until there was a miracle! After only a few months, suddenly everyone was able to talk to one another in Hebrew! Our studies were very concentrated, and we had to repeat the grammar like monkeys, and we turned it into a game to learn and remember the grammar.

We also studied math, history, the bible, geography, and what the Nazis had done to six million Jews—and how that led to the establishment of the state of Israel. They told us. "We are going to have our own nation where we will build our country and have our own manufacturing facilities and our own army." We were also taught the political way of socialism.

I excelled in sports, and I enjoyed talking to different kids and learning in class. But for some reason I can't explain, I felt lonely and sad, closed off, and angry. My forehead always had deep wrinkles, and kids were frightened by my look, and I would quickly knock down anyone who tried to hit me, even for fun.

One day one of those kids started to play boxing with me. He was less able than I was, but he surprised me when he hit me hard and I fell to the floor. I was so dizzy. All of the kids started to cheer for him and say that he was a leader and hero. I was so ashamed.

Afterward, that kid became my best friend, and he was the one to convince me to go and learn to be a boxer. In boxing classes, I met a child whose father was a professor at the school; this kid was very isolated and didn't have any friends. But he was a very good student since his dad taught him a lot, and he was knowledgeable. During one of those matches with this boy, I was hit very hard in my face and I fell down to the floor. I felt like my brain was leaving my head.

That was the end of my boxing career, because I never wanted to deal with that kind of pain again. This child who knocked me out also became my friend. I always dreamed about learning languages like him, but I never did.

While we were in Holland, and before we learned to speak Hebrew, I met two girls from Germany—one very tall and one very short. The tall one was blond with a body like an athlete. The other girl knew how to speak a little Hebrew. The tall one was not very smart—it was said to me that height diminishes the brain. I knew that I was a handsome guy because even though my feet were crooked, girls got attached to me. The smaller girl translated from German to Hebrew that her friend wanted to be my friend. She looked into my eyes and agreed. I wasn't thinking very clearly and said instinctively, "Tell your friend that she is too tall for me. The girls translated it and gave me an answer right away: "Tell him that he will grow taller with me!" We all started to laugh.

My sister Bianca also had a lot of admirers, and I heard all kinds of stories about her. Even though I was younger than she, I felt like I had to protect her because I was her brother. But who could face those big guys? They could hit me, and I would be crushed like a fly! One day two guys both wanted to date my sister Bianca, so they decided to fight; the winner would be the one to date her. They were hitting each other like hell, and I could not understand why people were able to hit each other so hard and still stay alive!

This battle over my sister perfectly reflected the history of mankind in my mind: People will fight in order to win. My opinion was that every solution to a problem should be reached through communication and not by force, because even when you use force, eventually the solution will still need to be reached through negotiation. I thought, why bother with the fighting in the first place?

In the evening, we would sit around the fire and sing songs in Hebrew. One of the American trainers had a voice like a bird when she sang—even the birds were listening to her. After sitting by the fire, I went for a walk with one of the girls, and we would kiss and hug. The other guys started to come to get my advice, and suddenly I became the most popular guy regarding advice about how to get girls.

The kids in my class saw me as a smart guy, and they wanted to be my friend. One of the most obvious gifts that everyone could see I had was patience, and the ability to listen to others. Only to listen without talking—this is what made them honor me and want to be my close friend.

For fun I used to go into the huge hall where the dining room was. Close to the ceiling there were all kinds of pipes that were probably used to heat the room during the winter. I liked to climb the pipes, and I would go from one side of the room to other, and even hold on to the pipes with only one hand. I showed my sister Bianca the muscles I had in my arms from all this climbing around.

For some reason we started to be very picky about the food we were being served. We would normally eat a lot of cheeses, veggies, and mashed potatoes, but the older kids organized a strike because they didn't want to eat only veggies and cheese—they wanted meat. I personally couldn't care less because I wasn't eating a lot anyway. The strike was successful, and the menu was changed.

Our activities also included different walks and traveling into the city of Apeldoorn and its surroundings. One week we went to the small city of Zandvoort, a seaside resort that we enjoyed very much. We rode in a car that was made of colored tin and had an open roof; it didn't have a real engine, but it had pedals like a bicycle. I liked the idea of that kind of car so much that I was thinking this could be the kind of car used in Israel because it was like riding a bicycle and provided strenuous exercise. You didn't need gas and there was no exhaust. Of course, the bureaucracy of the regime wouldn't let this happen.

We started to learn to ride bikes, too. I fell a few times like everyone else, and then I learned to keep my balance. When I felt more secure in my ability to ride, I went on longer trips along the byways in the forest that connected all the buildings. During one of the Saturdays that we had off from school, I took a trip with my bicycle while I sang to myself and enjoyed nature and felt happy. Without paying attention, I passed the buildings where all the religious kids were living. They started to shout at me in a chorus of Hebrew, "Shabbat goy! "I got scared and I fell off the bike and those religious kids started to laugh. They were screaming that it was a punishment from heaven because you're not allowed to ride a bike on Saturday. I picked up my bike and got out of there before I was attacked by those kids, and I never visited that area again.

One of the most enjoyable games we played was chess. I learned just by watching other children and the trainers playing. I liked the unlimited possibilities you have in a game like that, and the strategy of learning how to win over your opponent. It was a challenge for the brain. Chess became one of my hobbies, and I learned many of the basics and possible tricks. I also followed international chess competitions and tried to analyze the different strategies of the smart players, and how they used each strategy to their advantage.

In May 1948, David Ben-Gurion announced the establishment of the state of Israel, and he became the first prime minister of the new Jewish state. This announcement was made after the United Nations had voted in favor of the establishment of Israel. Immediately after the establishment of the Jewish state, the Arabs decided to attack the small country.

The more grown-up kids were required to undergo military training with the trainers from Israel, yet none of the training included actual weapons. After a short while, those older kids were sent to Israel to join the fight against the Arabs. In October 1948, Israel acquired a ship by the name of the SS *Negba*. It was decided that we kids should go on that ship to Israel after only a year in Holland—a much earlier departure than the four years we had planned to. This was fine with all of us—we were very excited to go to Israel and to be a part of the new country.

One day in October 1948, we said goodbye to our

children's village in Holland. All of the 500 of us—carrying small suitcases, some books, and souvenirs from Holland—boarded the buses to Amsterdam. Soon we were ready to board the ship. The SS *Negba* was on its way there. They didn't want to bring her empty to Israel, so they decided to cut short our stay and take us to the new Jewish state.

The boarding of the ship was accomplished in a very organized manner, and I remember being impressed by how big the ship was. It was interesting to be on a ship in the ocean. Guides from Israel divided us into rooms and gave us a hot meal. We were told it would take about 12 days to sail from Amsterdam to Haifa, Israel.

At the beginning of the trip, the weather was fair, but later—as soon as we were in the middle of sea—we were briefed on how to behave during an emergency if we needed to use the small lifeboats. We weren't thinking about that possibility too much, because we were playing on the ship and enjoying watching the waves. October 15, 1948 was my birthday, and the trainers decided to celebrate. The other kids whose birthdays also fell during the same month decided to have a bar mitzvah. I had not had one at the age of 13. I thought I was only 12 years old but I recalculated and realized that I was already 14!

My sister wrote a few words of congratulations and so did the trainers. We all got a little bit of attention, and that made me happy.

A few days before arriving in Israel the weather started to become windy. The waves were huge. The ship was a like a toy in the sea and listed from side to side. We were really scared, and most of the kids started to puke. I was keeping myself healthy and quiet; I knew that everything would be fine and went to check on my sister Bianca. I saw her sitting on the stairs, as pale and white as a wall—totally out of it and puking her guts out. I hugged and embraced her and promised her the storm would soon be over. She got up to hug me, but instead she threw up on me! I wanted desperately to escape, but I slipped and I fell with my hand in the vomit—and at that moment I threw up myself. I ran to my room and washed up. Later on the storm quieted and everything went back to normal.

On October 18, 1948 we started to approach the coast of Israel. We were astonished by the height of the incline of the beautiful city of Haifa, which was covered with houses. Everything was green, from the beach up to Mount Carmel.

We were given instructions to gather our personal stuff together for the arrival into Haifa. After the ship docked at the port, we got organized. People from the Joint Jewish Organization met us and issued each of us an immigration card with a small photograph. Upon my arrival in Israel, my given name was changed from Leon to a Hebrew name, Ariel—shortened to Arie—which in Hebrew means *lion*.

Once we left the port, we were divided into groups and sent to different *kibbutzim*, which are communal living and working spaces like farms. I was most impressed by the bright light and the hot sun on that day; I saw the tents in the fields dotted with the Jewish soldiers wearing helmets. Those were the soldiers who were protecting our country during the War of Independence.

I was surprised when the older kids who had left Holland before we did came to greet us when we arrived in Israel. They looked so tanned and dark! My first question was, "Will I also become so tan and dark from the strong sun in Israel?" I saw a lot of different Jewish religious people wearing black capes and hats as well as a few Christian pastors who had come to visit the Holy Land.

We were finally in Israel. I was home at last.

CHAPTER 14
THE SHIP SS NEGBA

If you were a Jew in 1948—particularly, a European Jew who had witnessed firsthand the atrocities of the pogroms and the persecutions and the ghettos and the death camps and the shootings and the mass burials—then it's likely that you were drawn to the newborn state of Israel like a moth to a flame. The moment Israel was re-created in its traditional homeland, the spirit of *aliyah*—literally, "ascent," or "going up," signifying an individual's return to the land of Israel from whatever country the diaspora had taken them—became stronger than ever, and Jews from all around the world made plans to immigrate.

Initially, the Israeli government had made plans for 100,000 new arrivals in each of the first three years of statehood. But Prime Minister Ben-Gurion realized that this number was far too low, and he revised the number to 150,000 immigrants a year for the first four years of statehood, for a planned total influx of 600,000 new arrivals. In reality, almost 700,000 new immigrants arrived between 1948 and 1951, doubling the country's population in just three-and-a-half years.[vi]

But how to get there? You couldn't just buy an airplane ticket and fly to Israel at that time, or drive your car there (assuming you had one). In 1948, there was a very small amount of immigration to Israel overland, however, the primary mode of transportation to Israel was by steamship.

For decades before the birth of Israel, ships had brought thousands of "illegal" Jewish immigrants to British-administered Palestine under the clandestine *Aliyah Bet* program. According to the terms of the British White Paper of 1939, only 10,000 Jewish immigrants were legally allowed to enter Palestine each year. This restriction was increasingly ignored, however, by the rising tide of Jews who were desperate to leave behind the anti-Semitism and persecution of their European homes. During the period, more than 142 voyages were made by 120 different ships—carrying their precious human cargo to *Eretz Yisrael*. More than half were stopped by the British Royal Navy, which had set up a blockade around Palestine.

However, when the state of Israel was officially created on May 14, 1948, this all changed. The Royal Navy withdrew its blockade and ships could freely bring immigrants into the country. Once the gates to Israel were opened, the ships—and the people—arrived. One such ship was the SS *Negba*, purchased by Israel from the Dutch government for the sum of $1 million in 1948. Together with the *Galila* and the *Kedman*, the *Negba* would carry many thousands of Jewish immigrants to Israel[vii]—including Arie and Rivka, though they traveled to Israel on separate voyages several months apart from each other.

The SS *Negba* preparing to depart from Marseilles, 1949

Passengers crowd the passageways of the SS *Negba* on its journey to Israel, 1949

The SS *Negba* arrives in port at Haifa, 1949.

Chapter 15
Living in the Promised Land

After arriving in Israel, Arie went to live in a kibbutz, Gvat, in the Jordan Valley, near Afula. The kibbutz was agricultural, and founded on the standard Zionist-Socialist principles, which meant that everything was shared in common by all the residents. Arie liked the kibbutz very much—it was an opportunity for him to attend school, raise chickens, and do farm work, which he enjoyed and during which he developed a love for agriculture and horticulture. He liked that on the kibbutz everyone had to do his or her share of the work. Arie arrived at Gvat when he was 14 years old, and he lived there until he joined the Israeli army (it was mandatory) at the age of 18.

On October 14, 1948—a beautiful, sunny day, Arie said goodbye to his sister Bianca, and he boarded a bus to Kibbutz Gvat. Since Bianca was older, she boarded a bus to a different destination, Kibbutz Givat HaShlosha, located in central Israel. The brother and sister agreed to keep in touch. It took about an hour for Arie and his fellow passengers to get to their destination. As they drove through Haifa and other cities, the driver told them stories about each of the locations they were passing through. Everything looked like painting from a saga.

They were very excited to be making the trip, and Arie and the rest especially enjoyed the warm welcome they received when they arrived at Kibbutz Gvat. They were told, "People, welcome to the homeland, and to Kibbutz Gvat, which is going to be your permanent home! You will no longer need to wander!"

The group was then assigned to rooms in a building with two floors. On one side of the building were the girls, and on the second floor were the boys. In every room there were four beds, so there were four children assigned to each room. After room assignments were made, everyone gathered in the kibbutz's dining room to be introduced to their new community.

Into the group that arrived from Romania, which included Arie, were added children from other Eastern European countries such as Russia, Hungary, and Bulgaria. Everyone spoke their own native language even though most knew at least a little bit of Hebrew. The guide asked everyone to be quiet and to listen to what he had to say.

He introduced the new arrivals to the teachers and other guides who were going to be their teachers each day at school. The guide explained that the children would be responsible for organizing themselves in their rooms, getting their bedding and school supplies, and checking the bulletin board for their daily schedule and whatever announcements might need to be made to the community. These announcements would explain such things as where everyone belongs, to which class they were supposed to go—and when they were supposed to go—what time they would have lunch, where the meetings were, and even what time everyone was supposed to go to bed and then wake up the next morning. They were told to meet again at 4:00 P.M. the next day, when they would be given a short walking tour of the kibbutz to learn more about their new home.

Everyone was feeling an intoxicating mix of excitement and anxiety. What would this new land bring to these refugees from across Europe? Had they truly found their permanent home? Would they really no longer have to wander the ends of the earth?

The new arrivals to Kibbutz Gvat would soon find out.

Chapter 16
Kibbutz Gvat
(In Arie's Own Words)

After the short briefing by the guide, we went to our rooms to organize ourselves. At exactly 4:00 P.M., we started our walk. The guide, who was a more mature person, introduced himself as Joseph, but he told us to call him Yoske. He had lived in the kibbutz since it had been established.

"I know every corner of the place," Yoske told us, "and I will be more than happy to walk with you and introduce you to it, and show you that my home is also your home. Let's start with the building where you are going to be living. It was built about a year ago, and it is called the 'Home of the New Youth Newcomers.'"

On the building were written the words, Beit Alyat Hanoar, which was the motto of the Gordonia movement—a pioneering Zionist youth group named after Aaron David Gordon. The main tenets of this movement were the salvation of Eretz Yisrael and the Jewish people through the revival of the Hebrew language and manual labor. The purpose of the building was to help the youth who managed to survive the horrors of World War II to come to Israel to build their new lives here.

Our guide explained that the kibbutz itself was divided into three different areas. The living area was comprised of a grouping of small houses with red clay roofs that could be seen from both sides of the byway. All of those small houses were beautiful, with flowers in the backyards, and the byways were made of concrete. To my young eyes, with its green grass and flowers blooming, the place looked like the Garden of Eden.

The second area had public buildings that include the dining room, kitchen, movie theater, and another room called a *beit tarbut* or cultural hall. There was also a sport hall and kindergarten, living facilities for the younger kids, and also rooms for where the babies were kept. Children didn't sleep with their parents. There were public showers, a home for the elderly—the parents of the other members—a synagogue for those who chose to maintain the religious tradition (few members of the kibbutz were very religious), and a first aid facility, because the kibbutz didn't have a hospital on site. We were, however, connected with the hospital in the city of Afula.

The third area was the industrial and agricultural part of the kibbutz, where the cows, horses, stables, chicken coops, and the garage for tractors and trucks were kept. There were also workshops, a manufacturing facility to create equipment for irrigation systems, and two pools—one for drinking water and another smaller one for other uses. The kibbutz was based on agriculture, so there were lots of fruit trees, wheat fields, and so on.

We were given explanations about everything we would need to know, and about the people who were living there. We were very excited to learn all of this and to know that, as of today, this would be our home.

After the briefing, we all made our way to the dining room to have dinner. We were very tired but happy and went to bed early—ready to start a new life.

During the course of the first two days, we learned about the structure of the kibbutz—how it was managed and the duties of the different members. We also learned the difference between a kibbutz and other settlements that were called *moshav* or *moshava*. Moshav were, like kibbutzim, Zionist cooperative agricultural communities, but with an emphasis on community labor.

The first main idea behind the kibbutz was to establish a large agricultural community that was managed by elected members. The second main idea was that every member was expected to contribute as much work as he or she could, and to receive according to his or her needs. All of the property in the kibbutz belonged to everyone, as long as they remained members of the kibbutz, and there was no money (nor any reason to have any).

Members were assigned to work in different areas of the kibbutz, according to work schedules that were prepared ahead of time. The cultural life of the kibbutz was managed by a group of people who were in charge and decided what lecturers to bring in and which movies would be shown in the theater. Four meals were served in the dining room each day: breakfast, lunch, a 4 o'clock snack, and dinner. Parents spent time with their kids each weekday before they went to bed and on weekends. The lecturer explained everything, including who was in charge of the different jobs—from who was responsible for purchasing supplies, to who was assigned to take care of the older residents.

I walked out of this lecture and I was thinking to myself that this is a real advanced way of living—it was a level of equality that only people with high intelligence or ideals are able to live. The philosophy "that everyone gives according to their capabilities and receives according to their needs" says it all. It is exactly like the sentence in the bible, "You should love your friends as you love yourself." I didn't think that even the communist regime in Russia would be able to attain this high level of life.

We were told that our daily schedule would be divided into two parts. We would learn half of the day and then work the other half of the day. And every few months we would be assigned to work in a different part of the kibbutz. After we learned about all the different kinds of work available, we would be able to decide for ourselves what we would like to do for a longer period of time.

During the evenings and weekends, we would have free time to spend with friends, play sports, attend shows, and participate in a variety of different fun classes.

In the building where we were living, there was a schedule to show everyone who was in charge of cleaning the rooms and showers because everything was to be shared—even the gardens and backyard of the building. We were allowed to use every facility in the kibbutz after the working day—including those that were designed for the older people. We started a routine and contented life with school, work, cultural life, and connections with the girls.

In school we studied math, geography, physics, music, and literature. We also learned a little bit about politics and socialism, but not religious things. We had been taught about the religious holidays in Israel and the agricultural life according to the seasons. So we actually celebrated all of the Jewish holidays according to the Bible. During one if the Bible lessons that I didn't like very much, I started writing a story while daydreaming. The teacher caught me and took my story away and then sent me out of the class. That teacher later became a well-known professor who wrote many books explaining the translations of the Bible. Other topics discussed in class were focused on Zionism and the establishment of the state of Israel, the Holocaust, and also different political views on how to lead the country.

When we studied Israel, we were taught to love our country, and that we would one day visit all of the places that we learned about. This would include Masada and the Negev, which were the locations of important battles for the ancient Jews, and places where many tourists went to visit. We would also visit the monument at the border outpost Tel Hai in the northern part of the country, built to honor the Zionist pioneer Joseph Trumpeldor and seven other Jews killed in an attack by the Arabs in 1920. Although they died, the group bravely fought a much larger force, and they inspired Jews throughout Palestine to fight for their homeland. His famous last words were, "It's good to die for our country."

We were also taught about sex, and this was done separately for boys and girls. The men taught the boys and women taught the girls. During those lessons, everyone was very aware and alert and curious. Even though some of us had already had sex, a lot of the students still didn't know anything about it. During one of those lessons about the human body, I was called to explain about the different parts of the human body on a skeleton. Still confused from the sex lessons, I pointed to the throat and explained what the purpose of a period was instead of what the purpose of the esophagus was. Of course the whole class started to laugh and get wild, and that was the end of the lesson for the day. The teacher was not able to stop the laughing.

During one of my discussions with a girl I used to have sex with, I learned that she was concerned that she had not yet started her period that month. I was unaware of the details of how babies were born, so I did not put two and two together. We had been told what a period was, but we had not been told that if you don't get your period that it might mean you are pregnant.

So I asked her, "Why do you even want that dirty stuff?"

Luckily she got her period and was not pregnant. With other girls, I learned my lesson and I was more careful to pull out because at the time we didn't know about condoms yet.

I really liked music classes and I wanted to play an instrument and attend the chorus. Our music teacher was a composer. His name was Daos, and he was a Jew from Germany. He worked as a teacher but was not a member of the kibbutz. His wife taught us how to draw and paint and she was very nice. However, Daos was a very troubled, angry, and crazy person, and he was unable to conduct an entire class. He used to write on the blackboard, "If you are going to talk, I will not talk" So we would continue to talk and get wild and he wouldn't talk.

I took part in the chorus and also in the music group playing the flute. I asked him to teach me to play the piano, but after a short test he said that I don't have a musical ear and that I would never be able to play. Anyway, I continued to play the flute in the group and he would always spot me and stop me from playing saying, "Ringelstein you are faking!" It was very embarrassing.

One time I didn't even play, I just moved my fingers without actually playing. And even then he kept screaming, "Ringelstein you are off!" This time I couldn't keep quiet and with chutzpah I yelled at him, "How can I be off when I'm not even playing? If I am off, then you are not a real composer!" Of course he got mad and he threw me out of the class and that is when my music lessons and music career both ended.

Fortunately, I did much better in my history, literature, geography, and theater classes. My voice changed when I was almost 15, and I was very active in marionette shows. There was a member of the kibbutz who loved it very much, and that is how he decided to open the marionette theater. He taught me how to create the heads of the dolls and how to use them technically, how to move the body, how to move the strings, and how to read a story as if the doll was talking.

I then joined a group in the kibbutz to put on a play in the theater, "The Kings New Clothes," and I landed the role of the prime minister. I received a lot of praise for the way I performed. I started to read a lot of material about the theater and how it was developed. I became very anxious, thinking to myself that this would be my career in life. I looked with different eyes at the various shows and saw each one individually. I started to imagine that I was identifying with each of those different roles and I really got the feeling that one day I would become a theater actor.

I was also very interested in philosophy and different philosophers, and I attended different debates and discussions and expressed my views about humankind. We had been going to school the first half of the day, and after lunch we would get dressed in grey and blue overalls and high boots to go to work. We also wore a *kova tembel*—a "hat for a dummy"—to protect the head from the burning sun.

Our working hours were from 1:00 to 5:00 in the afternoon. My first job was to work in the vegetable garden, where we would gather potatoes and take care of the tomato vines. We were taught not to walk over the cucumber plants, otherwise, they would grow to be very bitter. We received explanations about each of the vegetables and how to take care of them to get the best results. I enjoyed this job very much, but after only a few days of work I ended up with a lot of back pain and I wasn't very excited about it anymore. So I looked for an opportunity to change to a different job.

I started to work with the fruit trees where we learned how they were developed, and we picked apples by climbing on a ladder where we were able to see the world from above. I also worked with the chickens, which reminded me of my grandma. I learned how to feed them, how to collect their eggs, and how turning on a light in the coop at night keeps the chicken awake for longer hours to produce more eggs. Later on I went to work with the cows in the barn and I milked them using an electrical wire and rubber that we put onto the cow's teats. We pumped the milk into special equipment that would then pasteurize it.

In the stable I met the horses, and I fell in love with them at first sight. I also worked hard collecting their waste, distributing their food, and washing and brushing them. Some of the horses were kept for riding while others were reserved for fieldwork, but later the tractors replaced them. The horses reminded me of my Uncle Eli with whom I would ride to the villages. I also learned to ride the horses, at first without the saddle and, then with the saddle. I liked to brush and pet them very much. I would look into their eyes and talk to them without any voice and just feel the heat of their body.

In time I started to ride the horses and I developed very strong connections with them. We would become like one body and both of us were happy to ride fast and enjoy the breeze and the beautiful fields. One day my friend Yossi Ashkenazi and I grabbed two horses after our work was done, of course without permission, and we started to gallop across the fields in the direction to Nahalal. On our way back to Gvat, it started to get dark, and all of sudden Yossi disappeared. I stopped my horse and looked for him. I called his name, "Yossi! Where are you?"

And then I heard a very weak voice nearby, battling pain. I saw Yossi on the side of a ditch, and next to him was laying the horse. Yossi was in terrible pain, and he told me that the horse hit something and he didn't see the ditch. He also thought he had broken his leg. I helped him get up first, and then I helped the horse get up. The horse appeared to have hurt his leg, too, because he started to limp. Little by little we made our way back to the stables. We finally arrived in the middle of the night and quietly entered the stables. We gave the horses water to drink, and I took Yossi to his room. In the morning, I went to school and Yossi stayed in his room. Later on he crawled to get first aid because of his swollen knee.

The next day the guys at the stable discovered that the horse was limping, and that Yossi's knee was hurting and he was not able to work. Yossi didn't say anything about me, so I was saved. I never dared to take a horse without permission again, but I continued to enjoy riding them during my time with them in the stable—with permission only.

During one of those days when I was working in the stable, I witnessed one of the horses having terrible pain after an accident when a carriage turned over and caused him to break his leg. They couldn't save the horse, so the man in charge of the stable decided to put him down. As he was aiming his revolver, I can't forget the look in the horse's eyes—how he understood that they were going to put him down even though he had never before seen a revolver. He was trembling and begging to be able to continue to live. The man shot him and this put an end to the horse's suffering. I couldn't fall asleep at all that night because I was so sad.

After that, I went to work with the lambs and I learned how to cut their wool coats. I enjoyed taking them to the fields to pasture them and to be in nature. I also worked in the garden and I learned about all of the flowers and I was very proud to work for the kibbutz and to know that my work in the garden was helping the flowers bloom and making everything look very nice. I liked to work with the tractor. Of course I was only an assistant at first, because I was not allowed to drive the tractor at my age. But I was able to convince one of the members to allow me to be his assistant and to drive the tractor. I worked with the tractor until I changed jobs again and was assigned to work in the kitchen and dining room.

One of the members of the kibbutz was in charge of the dining room, one was the cook, and all the others took care of the many other dining tasks. The food was normally served from carts, with different dishes on every shelf. There were dishes of meat, vegetables, and potatoes. The dining room workers had by then already placed bread and other appetizers and side dishes on the table. Of course, after the meal, everything had to be cleaned and the table needed to be organized for the next meal.

All of those jobs had to be done by the members of the kibbutz, per their schedule in the kitchen. I remember how one of the members, Haim Givati, who was the minister of agriculture in the Israeli government, would serve other members food when it was his turn to work in the kitchen. Everything looked so natural—it didn't seem out of the ordinary to us for a minister in the Israeli government to work in the kitchen of our kibbutz.

After finishing my work, I went to the shower with all of the other members of the kibbutz, and this was a real experience because everyone would tell jokes and stories, and sing like in the opera. I enjoyed being able to sing without being worried that someone would say I was tone deaf, and also because I wasn't the only one to do it! In the evening hours we would hang out at the club and play Ping-Pong, chess, and checkers, while some of the people would read or listen to music. I personally enjoyed folk dancing and also dancing in pairs, which I would win because I would always be the last one on the dance floor.

Before I knew it, a year had passed since we arrived at Kibbutz Gvat. During my first year, I visited my sister Bianca at Kibbutz Givat HaShlosha. Later that year she left the kibbutz and went to live with Uncle Itzhak, my mom's brother who had lived in Israel since before WWII. I had heard a lot of stories about him—that he slept so lightly that even the sheets didn't get wrinkled!

Uncle Itzhak was a construction contractor—he was independent and worked very hard. He was married and had one daughter, Pia, who was the same age as my sister Bianca. My uncle was a very tall man who didn't talk very much, but you could sense that he had a good heart. He told me a lot of stories about the difficult times he endured living under the English regime in Israel, and how he had been slapped by an English policeman for standing in the bus because, according to the law, you were only allowed to board the city bus if there were seats available.

The romantic idea that my sister Bianca had about living in my uncle's house was cut short because there were constant feuds between Bianca and Pia. This mostly came about because Pia would envy my sister whenever they went out together to parties. My sister was more beautiful than Pia, and more successful with the guys, and this caused friction. Pia was quite ugly, but my aunt of course sided with her daughter, so Bianca's life in the house became a living hell.

During one of those parties, Bianca met a guy by the name of Simon. Not surprisingly, Simon fell in love with her at first sight. So at the age of 17 she got married, and by age 18 she gave birth to her first son whom she named after my father, Jacob. And I became an uncle at the age of 16. They lived in downtown Haifa with Simon's parents since he was an only child.

In the kibbutz, we had a beautiful party to celebrate the one-year anniversary of our arrival. There were shows to dramatize the first steps of our arrival, and songs and a chorus. I read a beautiful poem and also gave a speech and thanked the members of the kibbutz for the opportunity to have a new life in Israel. Everyone was really touched, especially when I said this was our last stop in our wandering and that we would stay in Israel forever, and build a beautiful country. This led to much applause, and everyone spoke highly of me and the nice things that I had said.

CHAPTER 17
KIBBUTZ GVAT YEAR 2
(IN ARIE'S OWN WORDS)

During my second year in the kibbutz, I started to feel more and more connected to the place. This was my home, the members were my family, and the children had turned into my only friends.

We continued our routine of a half-day of school and the other half work. We kept changing from one job to another according to what the schedule said, and according to the needs of the different seasons. If fruit needed to be picked, then we picked fruit. If seeds needed to be planted, then we planted seeds. Working like this in the different areas of the kibbutz for such a long time enabled us to specialize and reach a more professional level of expertise. For example, when I worked in the garden, I went to attend a weeklong seminar in Haifa to study the different types of the flowers, the different seasons in which they could be planted, and how to best take care of each type of flower.

I liked my job, and I researched the history of every flower to know the origin, its name, and from which countries in the world the flowers had been brought to Israel. From the moment they started to bloom and decorate the garden, I would care for them with love, water them, and make sure the earth around them was clean. I talked to them as if they were my babies, and I couldn't stop wondering about the beauty of the creation of them. You plant a seed, and it develops into a plant and then a beautiful flower, each one unique, each with its own spirit.

All flowers are friends—they don't envy each other, and they become one big colorful chorus. I am the maestro, the one who conducts the beautiful music, and it is my privilege to listen to it. This is their way to thank me for my devotion to them. A few months later, I was transferred to work in a different place but the connection that had been established between flowers and me was so strong that every time I would pass, they would sway in the wind and release their wonderful smell to greet me.

In the evening, after our homework was done, we would gather in the club and stay busy with different games and dancing. Some of the kids brought ballroom dancing records to play, which wasn't normally played in the Kibbutz. This music was instead normally played in the capitalistic society in the city. We would dance late at night, after the trainer went home. There were very gifted kids with good taste, and they knew how to dance very nicely. One of the girls decided she would teach me how to dance the tango in two steps—one step, two step, one. She had big tits, so I would get close to her and my imagination started to work overtime. As I felt the heat of her body, my body started to shake and I was very excited. That night we finished the tango behind a tree by the light of the moon, hugging and kissing and having sex. We stayed friends for a few months, and she succeeded in teaching me how to dance.

On some nights we would sit around the fire, and there would be a few groups of couples who would walk behind the chicken coops to kiss. The member of the kibbutz stationed there to watch the coop would feel uncomfortable with all the kissing and move to another place. When he moved, another group of kids went into the coop and stole some chickens, a third group came with a big pot of potatoes, and a fourth group came with the chicken to cook it! We ate the chicken, which still had some feathers on it.

Someone would play his harmonica, and in short order we were very happy to be out there spending our time there—enjoying one another's company until the wee hours of the morning.

That same year we also went for a trip to Galilee, and I was impressed by the beautiful scenery and high mountains. We received many lectures from our trainers about every date in history, which meant that the stories in the class started to become a reality. I imagined all of the kings and the stories of the Bible, and it seemed like a dream. Then we ended our trip in Tel Hai, taking pictures next to the lion statue, which was a memorial for Joseph Trumpeldor and the other brave Jews who fought the Arabs and were killed with their guns in their hands. I agreed with a young man from Russia who said that we have to build our country and be ready to die to protect it. Because of Trumpeldor, we were able to take trips in the mountains of Galilee, and with his death he gave us life. I was ready to give my life to my country and to my people if it became necessary. I wouldn't think twice about it.

In the coming months, I was transferred to work in the vegetable garden. The work was very hard, and I had to bend over all day, which made my back hurt—especially spending all of those hours in the heat of the sun. I remember one time when I returned from work and got into one of the carriages that were backed into a tractor to rest for a minute. I was sitting very tired there on the potato sacks when the tractor started to climb a little bit and hit a big stone. The hinge that kept the carriage connected to the tractor broke and the carriage started rolling down the hill, faster and faster. I don't know how, but I managed to jump from the carriage at the very last minute, and this saved my life. I got a few scratches, but I was fine. The carriage turned over just after I jumped and all the sacks of potatoes scattered everywhere.

After this incident, I told that guy who was responsible for preparing the work schedule that I had to change my job. So I temporarily joined the truck driver who would bring milk to the kibbutz every morning from the Tnuva dairy cooperative in Haifa. I enjoyed traveling in the cart to watch the scenery of the city and get to know new and different people. During one of those trips, I was sitting in the back of the truck because in the front cabin there was a lady—a member of the kibbutz—who needed to make a trip to Haifa. I was sitting on the milk crates enjoying the breeze when, as we arrived at Tnuva, the driver (who probably came on to that lady and wasn't paying attention that the road was about to end) stopped the truck suddenly and I was thrown on top of the cab. I bounced off the cab and landed on a wire fence where I remained hanging. They had to call for first aid—all of my clothes were completely torn and I was bleeding from every side. They took me to the first aid station where I received medical treatment. I wasn't able to work or study for a whole week. This was how I finished my work with the truck driver.

In school, everything became quite routine and we had to study a lot. Our social life was really full. We drove to the nearest city, Afula, a few times during the week just to have fun and get an impression of life outside of the Kibbutz. I used to play football for many hours, different positions every time—sometimes as a goalie and sometimes on defense. During one of our games, I bumped into one of the guys from the opposing team. We both flew into the air and the other guy fell on his hand, breaking his wrist. They called the doctor in the kibbutz and took the injured player to the hospital in Afula. The doctor fooled with his wrist and fixed it right away. I couldn't believe how fast he could do it!

After the football games I would go to the dining room and drink a lot of water—I wasn't hungry at all. I also played volleyball and tetherball. One thing I never enjoyed, however, was swimming, I'm sure it was because I had never been taught how to swim. One night, however, I dreamed that I was swimming in the water with the other kids, and I was swimming wonderfully. So the next morning I woke up, put on my swimming suit, and walked over to the big pool. I felt very secure of myself and I ran into the pool to play with the other kids. But the pool was really deep and I slipped on the green algae at the bottom, and of course I did not swim like I had in the dream. I started to swallow water and I thought I was drowning. I heard the kids screaming.

I saw a guy by the name of David running toward me to help. Everyone called him Tarzan because he was an accomplished athlete, had muscles, and was an excellent swimmer. He came running very fast and in a flash I was yanked out of the pool and tossed onto the concrete. I didn't want to see water ever again, even though I had really wanted to learn to swim.

After about a month I began to put my bad swimming experience behind me, and David became a very close friend of mine. He convinced me to come to the small pool where taught me how to swim. I really owed my life to David who saved me and who also taught me how to swim. He originally came from Hungary; he was very strong and courageous. He worked in construction, which was very difficult work, and was also a boxer.

During one of my trips with the other kids from the kibbutz, we visited the beach in Nahariya. There were all kinds of games, picnics around the fire, singing, and other fun activities. Of course, every one of us came to swim, and I liked to play in the waves. A whole group of kids decided to swim in the ocean towards a small island of rocks, which looked quite close. I started to swim there with them, but because I was still a weak swimmer, I decided to not go on. When I turned around to head back to shore, I swam and swam, but I could not get to the beach. I saw the kids playing but I was too embarrassed to scream for help because I knew the girls would laugh at me. With all of the strength I had, which was really nothing, I succeeded to get to the beach, very tired and pale. I decided that I wouldn't try to swim so far ever again, or play with the strength of the ocean.

The kids who had managed to get to the island were thrown by the waves into a huge cliff and were injured. Some of them severely cut open their bellies and were not able to return to the beach. The coast guards of Nahariya were brought in on small boats to save the kids. We were lucky that this trip did not end in a disaster or tragedy.

During the trip, the guides tried to integrate all of the kids who had come from different countries, which at the time included Romania, Poland, Hungary, and Bulgaria. Each of us had a different story of survival from the war. The kids of the kibbutz who were born in Israel were very proud of their country. They didn't know the tragedies that we knew, and they didn't have horrible dreams that we had. They were real *tzabar*—a nickname given to kids born in Israel because they are like the cactus plant. Even though on the outside they seemed to have prickly thorns, on the inside they were really sweet once you got to know them.

I remember asking myself, "Where is the equality that we are always being taught?" The kibbutz kids learned all day long and only during the summer break did they have to work. And we had half a day of learning and half a day of work—we were actually supposed to learn more than they did in order to be able to cope with all the learning we lost during the war when we couldn't go to school at all. The answer to that I never did understand. Anyway, we were not able to get close to those kids of the kibbutz—at least not during the one trip. A real integration would have happened only if we were to be together at school as well, and then we would be equal and it would truly make us feel like we belonged to the kibbutz.

A few months later I started to work again in the fields, this time for a longer period. I liked to hear the quiet nature and the birds. You could also hear the noise of the tractor, which dragged a plow. They would drag for kilometers, and I had time to think about the whole world. I was thinking about the material they taught us in school, about general history, and specifically the history of the people of Israel.

I followed the Jewish and other holidays without any religious connection. I enjoyed learning about different types of lifestyles in the world, and the different regimes during the course of human history. I studied democracy in all its different forms, along with kingdoms, communism, dictators, and the perfect life in the kibbutz. I thought about my purpose in life and the goals I should try to attain.

I became interested in the military, which I would have to join at the age of 18. I used to go up to the fence and look into the air force base in Ramat David, which was on the border of the kibbutz. I got really attached to the airplanes I saw there, and I thought about the possibility of joining the air force and becoming a pilot. Different thoughts crossed my mind. One day I thought about being an actor in the theater, and the next day I thought about becoming an air force pilot!

One of my friends at the kibbutz had a twin sister—they were Holocaust survivors from Poland. The two were beautiful, short and always good hearted with smiles on their faces. The girl's name was Pnina and the boy was named Itzhak. He had very strong muscles and liked sports. One of the things that made us all laugh was when he would walk on his hands in every direction, up and down the road and on the stairs.

Itzhak went to join the army, filling out the forms and lying about his age. He was only 16-and-a-half years old. He would come to the kibbutz in his uniform to tell us stories of life in the army. He impressed the other kids and was very proud of himself. A few months after he joined the army, he took a command car without permission and without a license and drove wildly down the road. The car flipped over and he was killed on the spot.

They brought Itzhak to be buried in the Kibbutz Gvat and we were all very sad and heartbroken to see the sad face of his sister Pnina, as if part of her was being buried with her twin brother. But life went on anyway. We took part in school, work, lectures, trips, sports, girlfriends, and life without any worries.

There was a story I remember from the kibbutz about a little girl who asked her mother, "How was humanity born?"

The little girl's mother grew up in a traditional religious

school and house, and she told her daughter that God created Adam and Eve and that they had kids and this went on from one generation to another.

A few days later, the little girl approached her father and asked him the same question: "Dad, how was humanity born?"

Her father had been a member of the kibbutz for many years, and he had studied evolution. So the little girl's father told his daughter that life started from very small creatures that had only one cell. These creatures eventually developed into animals, and then into monkeys. Then he announced to his daughter that the human's origin is from the monkey.

The girl became totally confused and went back to her mom and asked her to explain the story her dad had just told her. Her mom said simply, "Look my daughter, the story I told you was from *my* side of the family. Your dad told you the story from *his* side of the family."

I passed the audition for the kibbutz theater group, and another kibbutz member and I were chosen to be representatives for the Theater of the United Kibbutz. I was very excited and treated it very seriously. I was sent to Kibbutz Na'an for two months where they had an organized group, supervised by a kibbutz member by the name of Hugo, who was also the stage director and a movie producer. The name of the show was "Seven Episodes of Life in a Kibbutz," and I was given a few roles, such as being a young father who is putting his son to bed in the children's room, and a work organizer preparing the work schedule. The rehearsals began and were held every day, making it very hard to work, but I enjoyed them very much.

After the rehearsals, I would spend some time in the apartment of one of the girls, Zohar, who was about 20 years old. She helped me with the homework required to replace my schooling at that time. Zohar was very cute and always smiling, and she taught me a lot of things beyond what we learned in school. We became very close friends and I enjoyed being with her after working hours.

Two months later we started our show and performed all over the country, going from kibbutz to kibbutz each day. The show was a great success. They took our photographs and they published them in the newspapers. The reviews were very positive. After six months of being on the road with the show, I returned to Kibbutz Gvat and I went back to school and to work, and my life was soon back to normal. I got some assistance from the teachers in order to cope with the material that I had missed out on in school. I also had to pass the exams that I had missed.

The six months I spent in the theater group gave me a new perspective on life. I enjoyed being on stage very much and to live every day playing the roles in the show. Every evening I was excited to get into the role and begin, and even though you have this experience and the illusion that you are representing a different image, I reached the conclusion that every role you play you are actually presenting yourself, and what makes you so special. You know that every person deep inside has all of those different gifts in life that are being expressed very strongly. It is just like every cell in the body has the same concept as the others but each has its own unique role. The success of the show was measured by the way you were able to identify how each character was being represented. You have to be able to present that image so that others can feel the integration and also so the family or friends of that person agrees that you are playing the role exactly like him.

I learned to look at people from different angles, their way of talking and walking. I learned that I could actually learn much more about a person by listening, as opposed to most people who are trying not to pay attention to what the other person is saying, but rather just showing that they are better than you. I learned to listen without criticism, and to see life through the point of view of the other person. Like in a chess game, you learn by watching adults play without being active in the game itself or giving advice.

This was a really satisfying period of time in my life, to have the opportunity to learn about other people. In the kibbutz, life settled into a steady routine of studies, work, and parties. We learned about the different political parties, the democratic regime, and the differences of opinions and ideology of how to run the country and how to build a home for the Jews of the world. We also learned about using arms to protect the country from feuds with our neighbors, the Arabs. We started training before joining the army. Different ideological opinions spread through the United

Kibbutz, which split it into two different parties, including the lefty which was close to the Russian philosophy at the time it was the USSR.

About a year after I joined the army, the United Kibbutz and the Kibbutz Gvat went their separate ways. Half of the members of the Kibbutz Gvat established a new kibbutz not far from Gvat by the name of Yifat.

Time was passing so fast and so did our major exams toward the end of the school year. The Israeli government Office of Education had not yet created exams, so we just got a report that said we had graduated from high school. In that way, four years passed in the Kibbutz Gvat and before we knew it, we had reached the end of an era. We had a big party and I gave a nice speech where I expressed my excitement toward joining the army and I promised that Gvat would be our only home.

The principal and the secretary of the school also gave speeches. They had watched us grow from children into young adults. They congratulated us for joining the army and were very happy that we had all been formally nominated as official members of the Kibbutz Gvat. After the speeches, our theater group performed a show with humorous pieces about life in the kibbutz from the kids' perspective. Of course, part of it was making fun of the teachers and trying to imitate them. We enjoyed a wonderful meal and then danced together one last time. Everyone was very happy.

It was indeed the end of a particularly pleasant era of my life. But I was still young, and there were new adventures waiting for me just around the next corner. I couldn't wait to see what they would be!

CHAPTER 18
THE JOURNEY TO ISRAEL
(IN RIVKA'S OWN WORDS)

In January, 1949, my family left Marseilles for Israel on the SS *Negba*. It was the first time I had been on a boat and at sea. Only three months before, the *Negba* had also delivered the love of my life to Israel. But I did not know that yet.

Trying to describe my memory of being on that ship as it crossed the Mediterranean Sea for ten days is easy: It was awful! My mother and I were very seasick. It was cold and stormy and the ship hit an iceberg. The crew had to radio an S.O.S. for help and we honestly did not know if after all we had been through, we would survive our journey to Israel, or instead end up on the bottom of the sea. Fortunately, the ship was not badly damaged, and we were able to continue on our voyage. I hardly remember anything of the ship—no cabin or berth—only being very sick.

But on January 10, 1949, the ship did arrive on Israel's shore in Haifa, and I remember the overwhelming feeling of freedom. For the past two years, from age seven to nine, I had been on the move with my parents. I now had a home—Israel was my new homeland.

When we first arrived, we lived in a small, military-style tent in an immigration camp in Ra'anana. Today the city of Ra'anana is one of the most populous cities in Israel, and it has a significant population of wealthy people. But back then at the tent camp, my family was given only the basic necessities of life, which were provided by the United Jewish Appeal. I had a bed with an iron frame and a small mattress. I do not recall having three meals a day, but food was provided.

We could not keep food in our tent because there was no refrigeration, and a coyote-like animal called a *shakal* was always around. Once, a storm came up and blew our tent away. I had no sense of privacy, but we were no different than every other family there.

After six months living in a tent, we moved to a tin barracks in Kefar Salame. Although it was just a small step up, the barracks seemed luxurious compared to the tent. The terrain there was sandy, so there was not much vegetation or many trees except for the eucalyptus trees that had been brought in to dry out the former swampland. The barracks were shared by Jews from Russia from the first wave of immigrants, as well as from Poland, Romania, Bulgaria, Czechoslovakia, Yugoslavia, and Hungary.

Our accommodations in the barracks comprised just one room with a kitchen in one corner, a bathroom with a shower in another corner, and iron-framed beds that were more like cots. All the families lived this way. We knew it was temporary, so we didn't get too close to other people. I didn't make any friends there. Language was a barrier, and I was put into a school where every student—no matter what their age or native tongue—was taught together in one room. It was challenging because I did not speak, write, or even understand Hebrew yet.

While I spent my days at this school, my dad would get up early and walk in the dark fields to get to a bus station. He had to take a stick to protect himself from the *shakals*. Then he would board a bus and ride for two hours to work at a silo where food for chickens was processed on a large farm. Because he was fluent in the German language, he was lucky enough to get this job. Jewish newcomers from Germany owned the farm. Later on, the land on which the farm was built was turned into one of the most prestigious cities in Israel, K'far Shmaryaho, where only the rich could afford to buy a house. Commuting to and from work took up a lot of his time, and he used to get home pretty late at night. My mom commuted by bus to work at a hair salon in the city of Tel Aviv.

After two years in camps in Europe, and then six months in a tent and six months in the barracks in Israel, we were finally able to move into a *shikun,* which in Hebrew means to live in a building as opposed to a tent or barracks. The place we moved to was called Hadar Yosef, where we found a one-bedroom house with a kitchen, washroom, and a veranda. My dad closed up the veranda to turn it into a hair salon during the day for my mom to work in.

At night the veranda would serve as a bedroom for my grandma Feige Ziporah Reder. (*Feige* means bird in Yiddish; *Ziporah* means bird in Hebrew.) My grandma wanted to live with us because she liked being around my mom who was the youngest of her kids, and she felt comfortable with us.

I remember Grandma Feige as a very organized person and personally very clean lady. Before she went to bed each night, she removed the scarf from her head that she had worn all day long, and then she folded it neatly and organized it with the rest of her clothes. She used to say to my mom, "When the husband comes from work, first you feed him and make sure that he's okay. Then you can talk to him!"

I had a very good relationship with my grandma. She was quiet and a good person, despite the fact that she'd suffered so much in her life. Her husband died young during the First World War (he is buried in Vienna), making her a widow at 49 years of age. She encountered further loss when seven of her fourteen children died during the course of her life, some of diseases that could not be treated at that time, since no proper medication was available, and others during the Holocaust. Six of the seven who remained alive eventually moved to Israel, but one, my aunt Mitzi, stayed in France. I also recall that my grandma suffered from diabetes.

I really admired my grandma and her fortitude during the kind of life she'd had to live. Imagine her strength and her courage! She never remarried; she raised all fourteen of her children on her own; and she did all the household chores without any of the high-tech equipment that we have today. She even moved to a new country late in her life. She made sure that each and every one of her children had a profession so they would be able to make a living, no matter where they chose to spend their life. Grandma Feige used to say that even the king had to have a profession because he could not be sure that he'd be a king forever. So not only was she kind and good and loving, but she was also very practical and had solid commonsense.

One Friday night, my mother had worked late in the same room where my grandmother slept. My father got up early that Saturday morning, and I heard him walking into Grandmother's room. I heard him moving her bed, and I had a hunch that something was not right. I was so scared. Then he called out to my mom and said, "She doesn't look so good, your mom." My mom jumped out of bed. My mom was so upset and blamed herself when Grandma Feige died. My mother worried that because she had been so tired from working she hadn't heard her own mother's call.

My grandma passed away at the age of 88 very peacefully in her sleep. Friday night is the beginning of the Sabbath or *Shabbat* in Hebrew, and that meant she was a *Tzadika* in Hebrew, a holy person. Her funeral took place that Sunday. My grandma is buried in Israel.

The passing of Grandma Feige was the first time in my life that I had to come face to face with the meaning of a death in the family—especially someone so dear to me that I loved so much. I was 15 years old by that time, but it was very difficult for me. I had to learn to overcome and to be strong for myself and for my parents. The death of Grandma Feige Ziporah marked the end of an era and the beginning of a new time for me, my parents, and the rest of our family.

Since my formal schooling had been interrupted when I was seven, I was happy at age 10 to get back to a real school in Hadar Yosef. I was placed in third grade at David Yellin elementary school. I already knew a little bit of Hebrew, but everything was so difficult. There were no books, no dictionaries, no encyclopedias. I had to struggle to understand and remember everything.

The school's principal, a man named Baruch Yopel, was a good man who knew the difficulties we were going through. He looked funny and all the kids made fun of him, but his manner is why I have not forgotten his name. He kept things organized, made sure that the kids came to school, and confirmed that once we got there, everyone was taken care of. He was a very considerate person and always ready to help.

During those years, I was quite fortunate to make friends with a girl named Mazal Sevillia who had emigrated from Egypt with her family and three siblings. The Jews from Egypt were very educated. They spoke English, French, Arabic, and Italian. Before they learned Hebrew they mostly spoke French. Mazal's family had books, so I spent time studying at her house. This friendship was an important part of my daily life.

The Israeli economy was not good during those years, so

food had to be rationed. Rationing meant that we got meat and fish only when we had coupons for them, of which a certain amount was given by the government to each family according to the number of family members they had.

Because my parents went to work early in the morning, I was the only one left to take care of the house. Before going to school each morning, I was responsible for going to the store to purchase fish and meat with the coupons and to get ice for the icebox. In those days, there were no electric refrigerators like we have today; back then we had iceboxes to hold the ice and keep our food cold. This was called the Dov Yosef Era because that was the name of the man who was Minister of Rationing and Supply. After I completed my chores, I would go to school. After school I went to Mazal's house to do homework, then back home where I would clean house and cook dinner for my parents. They were not young when they arrived in Israel—they were in their 40s—and they would come home from work tired and exhausted.

While in grade six, I started to learn English. I read Pocket Books written in English. I was told that if I want to learn to speak English, the best way to practice was to talk, even if I made mistakes. I also used to read books in Hebrew. The reading in both languages helped me write letters and other correspondence in a professional manner later on during my career. I liked to read lots of books, play basketball, and meet some of my friends from school on the street to chat. Occasionally we would meet at the community center where music was played so that we kids could dance.

I did not get to spend quality time with my parents because they were always busy making a living. We never went on trips or weekends to a hotel or resort, and we never went abroad, as these diversions were too expensive—luxuries we could not afford.

After completing grade eight, I went for two years to Tihon Ironi Alef high school in Tel Aviv. I had to ride a bus or two to get to the school. I did not graduate from Tihon Ironi Alef, but I continued my education at a commercial school where I learned to type on a typewriter in both English and Hebrew, and where I also studied office management. I added different topics of interest and languages to my course load. Later, after I started working, I continued my education—over the years attending different courses on management, managerial decision making and strategy, and import-export customs and duty.

After graduating from school, I got a job at a travel agency as an errand girl, performing all the errands on foot. I was 17, and I soon learned firsthand how difficult it is to earn money. But I knew I had to stick to working, and to have discipline in order to succeed. As a child I was brought up with very strict rules by a father who behaved like a dictator. Everything had to be done his way or no way at all. During my school years, my dad always wanted me to be the best in the class. He was never satisfied with my grades even though I was considered a very good student, and he would always say, "You can do better."

But since I was so shy and insecure, I did not participate much in class or raise my hand to show what I knew; it was by virtue of my exams that I got the excellent grades. I sensed that he always thought that I was not good enough and would not be able to be the person he wanted me to be. By doubting all of my achievements, he was in essence saying that he was never happy with me the way I was, and this caused me to develop an inferiority complex.

When I started to work and would go out with friends, my father's strict rules continued. I had to be home not later than 11:00 P.M. no matter what the other kids my age would do. This caused me to develop even more insecurities, as well as limiting the opportunities I had to spend time with friends.

My mom was different. She was not so strict. She was more flexible and always encouraged me and appreciated me and was happy the way I was. But she had to honor my dad's rules. My mom and I used to discuss life, and she warned me about boys. She used to say that boys wanted only sex, and that I should take care of myself by not falling for them. Unfortunately, she never explained to me in so many words *how* to take care of myself. I had to use my own instincts and self-discipline to learn all that was needed.

That kind of attitude of parents toward children was well known in those years. Parents would educate their children the way they had been educated themselves, without knowing whether that was the best way or not; it was simply tradition that went on from one generation to the other. For example, in those days it was unheard of for boys to live with girls without getting married; it was considered a sin and quite scandalous. This way of thinking came from the history of the Jewish people in Europe—their mentality came from always living in small villages and knowing everything about everyone. They developed the habit of keeping secrets to avoid being the shame of the village, which meant that even couples that did not get along continued to live together and not get divorced to ensure shame did not fall upon the family.

The fact that I was brought up in such a strict environment caused me to make certain decisions in my life that were different than what I would have otherwise made. It took me a long time to come to terms with the fact that I was indeed good enough and that I was not an underachiever. Eventually, I succeeded in making myself understand that this was my *dad's* story and how he saw me. From that moment forward, I decided that I was not afraid of anything or anyone. I took a stand and decided that I could do whatever I put my mind to. I could succeed *more* than I ever thought I would be able to.

Over time I defeated my inferiority complex. I started to act courageously, to go forward into the unknown—even if inside me I was still full of fear. I did not let my fears overcome me. I developed a lot of confidence and I used this confidence to my advantage in the years to come.

Chapter 19
"Fresh Meat"—Becoming a New Military Recruit

Arie's dream of helping to defend his newly adopted nation against its enemies came to pass as he began his career in the army. During his mandatory military service, Arie moved through basic training and then officer school.

In November 1952, a long line of buses took Arie and the other recruits to the army offices in the city of Afula to register and fill out all of the forms. Then trucks took them to an army base in the center of the country, to decide where everyone would serve. On the way to the base, everyone was very excited and singing. They thought about the different units that they could possibly be assigned to—the air force, paratroopers, artillery, and more. Arie was particularly excited about the possibility of being assigned to the air force because he had been watching the military aircraft flying around the base close to Kibbutz Gvat. He would sit by the fence for hours watching the airplanes take off and land—dreaming that one day he would become a pilot and fly those planes.

The welcome to the base was very strange and unexpected. There were soldiers in uniform screaming at the recruits, "Fresh meat!" Later on, Arie and his fellow recruits understood that it meant they had just joined the army, and that those who were screaming at them had joined only a week earlier! In just a few day's time, Arie and his new friends would be the ones to scream these words at the next group of recruits to arrive on the base.

The recruits were organized and given a briefing and daily schedule as well as different uniforms for working, training, and casual activities. They were told to keep everything clean and to stay clean-shaven. The uniforms came in a few different sizes, but for those who were too thin, the uniform was too big. A few moments later, other soldiers of higher rank started to scream at Arie and his friends, and they became slaves.

The second part of the day they had to undergo all kinds of medical exams. They each were issued a soldier card and identification tags to wear around their neck. Beginning at that moment, they went from being civilians to being a number. The new soldiers were divided into groups and assigned to rooms where everyone slept in bunk beds. The new recruits were given sheets and instructions on how to use all of the equipment, when to wake up, and the routine they would have to follow in the morning. Recruits wake up in time to eat, work out, shave, and clean their rooms—all before the 8:00 A.M. checkup to see if everything had been done.

In the briefing they were told that they would be at that base for only a short while, and that a higher-ranked officer would interview them and place each person at a different base depending on the officer's opinion. Arie had requested to be placed with the air force, but there was no guarantee that he would be. That night, Arie couldn't sleep with so many thoughts racing through his head. He thought, "Is this the Israeli army I was so anxious to join? And is this how they treat people?"

Arie was totally confused.

In the morning the soldiers woke up Arie and his friends with screams and whistles, and they tore the blankets off their bodies and shouted, "Be ready in five minutes!"

The new recruits got in line and began their morning run and exercise. This woke them up quickly, and from that moment they were in a race against time to be able to do everything they needed to do, including shave, polish their shoes, and make their beds before the morning checkup. For breakfast, they stood in line with their tin trays to get what the cooks were serving, usually eggs, bread, cereal and tea. They taught the recruits how to stand when they were at attention and at ease. They taught them how to turn left and right, all while standing in a perfectly straight line.

The guy in charge was a sergeant, so his voice was always ringing in the recruits' heads while they walked like robots, sweating. Their shoes were tight and they dreamed of a recess that never arrived. The recruits wanted to become better at each of the exercises in order to become a better army.

During the course of the week, representatives of the Israel Defense Forces (IDF) came to interview the recruits, and Arie was happy to be told that he would be joining the air force. After a week and a half of torture as he waited to be sent to his new post, Arie found himself on the way to the air force base. There he met a brand-new group of people—a group that was on a different level than those at the other base. They were members of the kibbutzim and moshavim, and Arie found a common language with them. They all had one goal in common: to become fighter pilots.

They were treated much better, but there was still a very strong sense of discipline. To be a pilot took about a year, and there were different stages of training, including theoretical studies, airplane design, and of course flying lessons. They were told that every week they would be reassessed, and that only a few of the best recruits would be selected to continue their training.

To avoid being thrown out of the air force pilot training program, the recruits tried their very best to follow every order—to "swallow every frog"—because the high-ranking officers and trainers tried to crush them no matter what. Arie had the feeling that he was not good enough in physics and he was not strong enough to take on the required physical tasks. After a couple of months, Arie was called in to see the officer in charge of the course. He told Arie that he really appreciated the efforts Arie had made, but that he was sorry to tell him he was not fit for the course. He explained that it wasn't because Arie wasn't good enough, but it was because the air force dedicated a certain number of hours for each soldier to become an excellent pilot. The officer in charge went on to say that anyone can become a pilot, but to be a fighter pilot you need be a different type of person.

The officer suggested that Arie stay in the air force and that he should enroll in a course for airplane maintenance and become an airplane technician. This was a great profession at the time, and would serve as excellent experience—both for the air force and as a civilian. Arie thanked the officer for being so fair and open with him, and for his offer, but Arie explained that if he was going to stay in the air force, he would not be able to overcome the overwhelming desire to steal an airplane and fly.

So Arie asked to be transferred, and a week later he was sent to an army base in Beit Nabala.

Arie had to make his own decisions the best he knew how, without being able to consult or get advice from someone close to him. He had to shape his own life and personality with the tools he had. Remarkably, he succeeded in becoming the formidable man he was: a loving husband, a loving father, and later on, a loving grandfather. His gifts of giving and loving and cheering up other people by telling jokes—always with a smile on his face—were the always-so-visible qualities that explained why people loved him for who he was.

Arie's fulfilling, new life in the army was just beginning.

Chapter 20
The Military Life
(In Arie's Own Words)

A new chapter of my life started in army field Regiment 52, which was part of the Givati combat brigade—one of the first to be created when Israel was established. In comparison to a democracy where people are free to express their opinions and views, I learned that the army is a dictatorship, like a country of its own within a democratic country.

We were divided again into different classes, and there were different guys from different levels of society with different ideas about life. That is how we started training for six months. We received personal training, and also training as a class and as a battalion—all to enable us to act as one on a team. We received physical training, ammunition training, night training, and live-fire training. The trainers were sergeants and they would treat us like slaves, with strong discipline and punishment.

There was very strong discipline about water—we were told to only use it in case of emergency. As a result, we would get very dried up in the heat. The trainers would drink water all the time, and we were not allowed to have a sip! If one of the soldiers tried to get a sip of water, then a trainer would pour out his water bottle so that when we finally were allowed to drink, that soldier would not have any water.

During the live-fire exercises, they would shoot real bullets in front of our legs, and this was how a lot of accidents happened. One night the trainer kept screaming at us to walk in a straight line, but a very tall man named Drukman suddenly jumped in front of the line where the trainers were firing, and he was killed on the spot. We were all very depressed, especially since the discipline was so strong. The trainers took advantage of every opportunity to make our lives miserable.

The punishment given by our trainers was collective. If one of the soldiers had done something wrong, we were *all* punished. Sometimes after a long hard day of exercise, the trainers would wake us up in the middle of the night, tell us to get dressed, make our beds, put on our equipment, run 100 meters outside, and then return to our beds. We had to do this every fifteen minutes, and with every delay the punishment was made longer. At the end of our training, we had to walk 120 kilometers as a battalion, and this was how we celebrated the end of our recruit training. But we became a professional fighting team, ready for any mission.

When we finished our training, we were awarded the symbol of the infantry ground forces to wear on our uniforms, and then we were granted our first quarterly week of vacation. I spent most of my vacation at the Kibbutz Gvat, and for two days I went to visit my sister Bianca. After the vacation was over, we went into training and exercises again. During those years, many Arabs tried to infiltrate Israel, and the military had to constantly fight with them.

We were divided into smaller groups, and some of them were assigned to the Jordan Valley. Each group was led by an officer, all of whom later earned higher ranks. We went through different exercises to learn how to fight the enemy, and this was how I became a professional soldier and overcame fear. But I found myself fighting a battle over the man inside me who was a man of peace, and the man inside who was being ordered to fight for a good cause for the state of Israel—which would require you to kill or be killed

My group was stationed in Abu Gosh on the way to Jerusalem. We were assigned to different tents near Latrun, which was then under Jordanian rule. During those years, many Arabs tried to infiltrate Israel, and we had to fight them. It was kill or be killed. Every night when it became dark, we would spread out in an ambush formation until morning—ready to surprise any trespassers who might have plans to attack Israeli homes in the settlements.

One morning, after being in an ambush the entire night, I returned to my small tent and felt a sting in my toe that was horribly painful. The doctor gave me two injections in the toe and the pain disappeared. It was the sting of a yellow scorpion, so the guys turned on their flashlights and we shook out all of our blankets until we were able to find it. We took the scorpion, put gasoline on it, and with wood started a fire. The scorpion folded his tail, stabbed himself, and committed suicide. We learned that the entire area was full of scorpions, which were hiding under the rocks. We had to start checking our beds each day to be sure there were no scorpions hiding in our blankets.

Although we tried to be very careful, a few weeks later I was stung again. Since this was the second time, I knew what it was. I immediately ran to the doctor and got a shot so I didn't suffer so much. During our military activity we had to walk through all the villages and the Moshavim to show our presence and dedication to protecting them from the trespassers.

Eventually, I was assigned to another course—this time to become a corporal and head of a class. The soldiers loved me very much because of the humane attitude I showed them, and they were ready to perform any of my commands with love. During one of those exercises, I wanted to make sure the soldiers walked without a gap between them, so I pushed them closely together. A soldier told me, "If it was anyone else pushing me I would kill him, but since it is you, and I like you, I know that you are only doing it to help me." I gained a lot of satisfaction from my work.

It didn't take long for me to earn the rank of class sergeant. On one hand, the soldiers were sorry that I was moving on to a different course because I was so nice to them, but on the other hand they were happy for me earning a higher rank. As a sergeant, my work was easier and I had more time for myself. During one of my most interesting times as a class sergeant, we were sent to Mount Scopus (Har Ha Tsofim) in the eastern part of Jerusalem where a Hebrew university, hospital, and library were located. During the treaties between Israel and Jordan, it was agreed that Jordan would allow Israeli police forces to protect these facilities—transferred to the mountain on Jordanian armored buses under Jordanian supervision. These exchanges of men would occur every two weeks.

We were sent disguised as Israeli police. The feeling of being in a Jordanian armored bus without any windows or ammunition while a Jordanian armed soldier watched over us was very unpleasant. The Jordanians followed us into the Jordanian jurisdiction up the mountain, and they took back the people who had already been there for two weeks. As soon as those big gates closed behind us, we went for a walk to see all of the places on the mountain that we were there to protect.

We were given a briefing on all of the places to watch over the next two weeks. We were very excited to see the library and laboratory; everything looked like people went on vacation—it was all big and modern. In one of the glass jars in the laboratory there was a fetus. It looked alive, like it was about to be born. We then were assigned to different rooms and were given orders for what exactly we needed to do. We were working in a factory that created wire fences, and because of the treaties we were not allowed to have any ammunition or make any changes. Regardless, using the Jewish brain, we were able to smuggle in ammunition, and the Jordanians didn't suspect anything.

We had to watch the area day and night and make observations. After about a week, we had a few clashes with the Jordanians and a very serious situation arose. My people were told to clean the ammunition, which was kept in a special grease to prevent the equipment from rusting.

We were all in a small room working by candlelight and we cleaned the ammunition with gasoline and a special cloth. Two people started to fight and the gasoline turned over. Within a few seconds the fire was burning our mattresses and then the whole room. A few solders started running out and I yelled, "Where are you running to? Bring me a fire extinguisher and cover the fire with the mattresses that are not yet burning!" In this way we were able to put out the fire.

To tell you the truth, I couldn't run out of the room even if I had wanted to because everything was on fire! A few of the soldiers got burned, but one soldier was really badly hurt and he was transferred to the hospital in Jerusalem. This saved his life. There was a very serious investigation, and the two soldiers who started the fight were punished. At the end of the investigation, I was highly honored by an officer. Eventually, the situation became much quieter, and after a few months we went down the mountain and were granted a weeklong vacation.

Another experience I remember during my course as a class sergeant was when I was supposed to do some training with a new weapon that the army had acquired from France to be used against tanks—something called a *bazooka*. During the lecture I gave, a group of officers accompanied by a French general came to get an impression of how the new weapon was working out for the Israeli army. I was totally shaken up! I got over it, however, and during the lesson I pretended that the visitors didn't exist. I liked being a trainer and I proved to have really good knowledge in the use of this new weapon. After that lesson, I received high praise from the French general and the rest of the staff.

I returned to the battalion and participated in a reunion of the Givati brigade. I led the march along with those who were marching with flags. A photograph of us was published in the newspaper and that photo is kept in my album. I was very proud and I felt that I was fulfilling a very important mission.

Each soldier received vacations from time to time, but for me they were very difficult. At the beginning I used to go to the Kibbutz Gvat, however, all of my friends were serving in the army as well, and their vacations didn't match mine. So I stopped visiting the kibbutz. For some of my vacations, I would go visit my sister Bianca.

One day I was called to have a checkup to become an officer. After about a month, I became a trainee in the officers' course of the infantry, which lasted about six months. The attendees were trainees from all of the different divisions in the army. Some of those different divisions were professionals who had to undergo more courses according to their profession, such as communications, information, or artillery. It was just like for doctors who need to specialize in their profession—like an eye doctor or an ENT. We had to specialize in the army too.

There is another experience I had at the graduation for the recruit training (Tirunut), which was to culminate in a military march on Independence Day. This training was three months of very tiring, diverse exercises led by a sergeant. The privates and sergeant kept torturing us until we acted just like robots and were able to walk in unison. These exercises included all kinds of walking, to the left and right, linking arms, and looking this way and that. After a while, it was hard to understand even what they wanted. We heard an order and like a robot we would respond. Even at night we would dream about it. We were yearning to get to the parade to finally finish this nightmare.

We survived our ordeal, and on Independence Day, we attended the military march in Haifa. We gathered at Mount

Carmel, not far from a small city by the name of Tira, which was the starting point of the parade. The excitement was great, and we were issued new uniforms that had been nicely ironed. We wore berets and the sleeves of our shirts were emblazoned with the Givati Brigade emblem—the symbol of the well-known infantry unit. I felt very excited and happy when we organized ourselves to start the parade.

The army orchestra was marching in front, starting with different melodies. The Israeli flags were waving and people stood on either side of the route, welcoming us with loud applause. In spite of all the training and rehearsals, it still was painful to carry the personal weapon which weighed about 4¼ kilograms. Even though we kept changing shoulders, it still hurt. We would start with the gun on our shoulders but then we would have to carry it straight in front of our body. Despite the pain and my numb hands, I felt a huge pride at the entrance of the city of Haifa on our way to the center of the city, Hadar HaCarmel.

While I marched, many thoughts crossed my mind. In the not-so-distant past, the Jewish people were brought to slaughter by Nazi Germany, and here I was marching with the Israeli Army—the Jewish army that protected the people of Israel and vowed that never again would we be brought to slaughter. I felt a huge honor to be a part of the Israeli Defense Forces, and I knew how much bigger the responsibility to protect this state would be, especially since all of the people watching us had high hopes that they would be able to depend on us and trust us in a time of need.

I was selected to take the officer training course. The welcome at the officers' course was like the welcome for any of the other courses of the Israeli Defense Forces—you had to fill out all kinds of forms and check out your equipment, blankets, and clothing. To differentiate us from the other soldiers, we had to wear a white band on the sleeve of our shirts under the symbol of the infantry, as well as on our berets. This identified us as trainees. We were divided into classes and given rooms. We had to spend the rest of the afternoon hours cleaning our personal arms and organizing our beds and everything else.

In the evening, we were all brought to a big hall, and on the stage we were introduced to the trainers. Each of the trainers had much experience in the IDF, especially with battles, as well as experience in being trainers. The commander of the school came to train all of the trainees and would be there for the next six months. He pointed out to us the importance of the school to introduce a younger generation of officers who would be responsible to lead the IDF into victory over our enemies in defense of Israel. He explained that the survival of our country would be dependent upon our professionalism and the force of the leaders who would lead the IDF to victory.

We were told that the training sessions would be very difficult, and include learning war tactics, analyzing situations, and that there would be a very strong physical training component. We would also learn about humanity and keeping the purity of arms, that is, not to kill the enemy just for the act of killing—only if you are attacked. Only the trainees who were able to complete all of these missions would have the privilege to serve in the IDF as officers. Every class had a meeting with their commander, and we received a copy of the training program for the coming week.

I found myself assigned to a class where all of the guys were at least one head taller than me—they were all big guys and most of them had served in combat units. And many of them were from the famous parachute division with a lot of combat experience who had already participated in different operations in enemy territory. I started to feel a little bit inferior. On the other hand, it gave me a strong will to prove to myself that I could be as strong as they are. That gave me the strength to overcome all of the physical and theoretical obstacles.

Among my trainers was a guy from the parachute division—Moshe Vahetzi—whose nickname was "Moses and a Half" because he was so tall! In a few years, he became the chief of staff of IDF. He was a member of a kibbutz, very modest, and a good friend with a golden heart—he had a good head on his shoulders. During that course, I developed strong relationships with the other trainees and I received lots of help from them during the difficult training. In one exercise, I was chosen to play the role of the injured soldier because I was very slim and lightweight, and it was easier to carry me on the stretcher or over their shoulders. Not only that, but if the trainers had decided to have somebody else play the role of the injured soldier, I would have had to walk in the middle of the stretcher, and my shoulder didn't even reach the stretcher because the other guys were so much taller than me.

The exercises included personal training, ammunition training, obstacle courses, and many other types of training. One day I felt something very strange, like a small ball coming out of my colon. When I looked in the mirror I got so scared I ran to the first aid station and they told me I had hemorrhoids resulting from my exertions during the training. I was given some medication and suppositories, and I learned what hemorrhoids are. Most of the time I could be found in the different training areas in the field.

Every trainee had to perform all kinds of commanding calls, and then analyze in front of everyone how he had performed his duty according to the different criteria and situations, the transfer of the orders through the communication equipment, and more. I was very happy about the positive comments that I received after performing an exercise where I was the commander. I felt very secure due to all of the help I had received from all my friends who became my subordinates during the exercises. I treated my job very seriously and felt that everyone was really cooperating—not because they were such big and strong guys, but because of their camaraderie. We had to wear heavy ammunition, and I had much trouble with the helmet, which hurt my head—especially at the roots of my hair. I also had trouble with my boots, which caused me a lot of pain because of the prominent bone in my foot. Without the help of my friends, I wouldn't have been able to sustain my personal morale, and I would have failed.

Every field exercise started in the war room by presenting a problem on a sand table as if it were on enemy territory, with fences and mines around the base. The goal was to conquer the base, which required conducting an assessment of the best possible actions that needed to be taken to succeed in conquering the base with a minimum of casualties. In parallel with that, another group of trainees played the enemy, and they had a different assessment to make: to find the best solution to protect the base. During the exercise, the trainers would announce how many soldiers had been injured or killed. After the exercise, we had to organize the conclusions and comments in a written exercise, and the trainers made notes with each remark notated and turned into a grade. Those trainees who were not fulfilling the exercise completely were released from the course, which kept us under constant stress to excel.

During the exercises with the caterpillars and tanks, we had to learn about cooperation between the infantry and the corps. We engaged in different exercises where the tanks passed over different excavations, and we would get out and throw Molotov cocktails—the same as had happened during World War II. We also engaged in many exercises in cooperation with the artillery corps. We learned how we could get their assistance when we needed it. We were also taught how to get in touch with the air force and how to ask for their assistance. During a major part of our course, we were given lectures on the policy of the country regarding national problems, economics, psychology, handling of prisoners, and general education.

I felt very bad during our occasional vacations from the officers' training school. Everyone had a family, a home, and friends from school. I would visit my sister Bianca, and her family lived in a totally different world. I didn't have anyone to share my world and experiences with, to tell about my difficulties and challenges with the course. Each time I returned to the school from vacation, I was sad because everyone would talk about their families, brothers, sisters, and friends, and I would have to stay quiet. I didn't have anyone to tell about. I felt very lonely and sad. Sometimes I would go to Kibbutz Gvat, proud to wear my uniform, and proud to be a cadet in the officer school. But most of my friends in the kibbutz were also in the army, so I didn't get to meet them at Gvat. I couldn't find myself and I couldn't feel comfortable.

The training continued day after day, and we became physically stronger and stronger. We started to think differently and we solved a variety of different problems. We would take a problem, break it into small pieces, and try to solve it. That way we could expand our horizons regarding the political situation in the country and in the world, and the connection between both. In other words, we became men ready to lead soldiers through every task that was needed. We were taught that there are more important things than your own life. This, of course, is totally against the idea that as a human being your own life is most important.

After being followed and measured by the trainers 24 hours a day—with everything being noted—we received a grade for everything that allowed us to reach the big moment where we were able to become officers in the IDF.

Our graduation ceremony was scheduled to take place in Jerusalem, and we prepared for the ceremony and the parade. The great day arrived, and I stood in line with my ironed uniform and officer hat, waiting for the entourage of the prime minister of Israel, David Ben-Gurion, who at that time was also the minister of defense. The chief of staff of the IDF was Moshe Dayan. Other commanders of course were the trainers and participants.

The ceremony started when the entourage of the prime minister marched in front of the trainees, giving each one of us a lieutenant rank. Photographers were taking pictures the entire time. Then came Prime Minister Ben-Gurion and Chief of Staff Moshe Dayan. There was a Yemini guy—a very tall guy—who stood next to me. It was a dream come true to see the first officer in the IDF who was a Jewish man originally born in Yemini. Most of the newcomers came to Israel from Europe, so this was really a big deal. Since I was standing next to that man, a photograph with me, the Yemini man, the prime minister, and the chief of staff was published in all the newspapers. That picture is in my album as well.

Graduation ceremony for Arie's (Second from the right) Officer's Course of the IDF, 1953

The ceremony ended with a speech by Ben-Gurion, about the huge responsibility on our shoulders to strengthen Israel and to be brave against our Arab neighbors, whose one goal was to throw us into the ocean. Only a strong IDF would deter war and bring peace to the state of Israel and let it bloom into the entire area.

As soon as the speeches ended, we continued to march through the streets of Jerusalem while the people in the street applauded us from every angle. We marched with a huge amount of pride and excitement. A few years down the road, I realized that an entire column of soldiers marching with me in the parade was killed during IDF operations in war.

When we finished the march, all of the new officers got together with their families, friends, and brothers. They received hugs and kisses and presents, and were greeted with great happiness. Here again I found myself lonely in the world, outside of the happiness. No one came to meet me and show me how proud they were of my achievement to become an officer in the IDF. Only after visiting my sister Bianca did I receive a present from her and her husband—a golden ring with an engraved lion, which made me very happy.

We returned to the base and received our grades and our unit assignment, which we were to report to after a week's vacation. I spent my vacation with my sister Bianca in Haifa and I traveled between her home and the Kibbutz Gvat. I was very proud to go back to Gvat wearing my IDF officer's uniform. At the kibbutz, I met one of the girls and we had a very good time after a long period of time not being with any women. The interesting part about that was I didn't feel any connection to her other than the sex itself. After the vacation, I went to my new unit—the Golani brigade based near the city of Naharia. My first organizational duty was leading logistics. I learned my duties, and later on I was sent to a special officers' course for this profession where I was taught the importance of the job, and that every fighter receives administrative assistance from seven soldiers. This way I learned a new subject. I passed the course with excellence, and it was here where I found myself in the south of the country with the entire brigade in 1956 when the Sinai War against Egypt erupted.

In addition to my duties as a logistics officer, I was also an administrative assistant to the commander of the base. The commander was a redheaded captain named Ze'ev Gur-Arie. He was born in Germany and his original name was Wolfgang Lotz. He served in the British army before immigrating to Israel. He spoke fluent English, drank a lot, and would get very drunk. He also spoke German and Arabic, and was busy catching all of the riding horses that were taken from the Egyptian army.

The commander of the brigade had a very special personality. He was a lieutenant general by the name of Benjamin Gibli, and he was transferred from the job of head of Intelligence after a group of Israeli spies was caught in Egypt. This event was called Parashat Lavon, the name of the minister of defense at the time. During the 1956 Sinai War, I had the privilege to work closely with Lieutenant General Gibli and to see how a leader handles a battle—being totally cool, giving clear commands to commanders, asking assistance from the air force, and leading a brigade to victory. In this war, we received much assistance from the French army, and it was a complete victory for our side. We were settling down in Gaza where a military regime was put in place and the Military Governor was a commander on top of the civilian manager.

During the first stage of the war, a large group of Egyptian prisoners was surrounded by wire fences and watched by the military police. I was a witness of some very wild behavior by the IDF soldiers in the administration units who beat the prisoners without justice. Most of the soldiers in that particular event in the IDF were born and lived in the Middle Eastern countries. I assume that the hatred for those Arabs was so great because they lived with them and their customs and characters, and therefore they tried to get revenge.

In the line of my duty, I felt that I was contributing my part by being in charge of the logistics—making sure that our military got all of the necessary goods such as food, clothes, gasoline for the cars, and water. I took care of all of the administrative issues when we entered a city named Kahn Yunis in the Gaza Strip. While we were there, we were surrounded by kids and adults who tried to sell us cheap souvenirs, pens, and lighters. They were all carrying photos of the President of Egypt, Gamal Abdel Nasser.

During this period of time, the civilian and army authorities worked well together, and life became routine. Soldiers received vacations, and I would stay as an officer on duty. I liked my life—I was treated like a king. They made sure I got breakfast and coffee in my room, and they didn't bother me. For the weekend, I would spend my time with one of the female soldiers, and we would have a good time. After the war, she served in the marines as a switchboard operator. I kept in touch with her and visited her at the base on the weekends. I didn't have any feelings of love or connection, it was just to have a good time.

Later, international political pressure on Israel began—led by the Americans—so Ben-Gurion decided to retreat from all the areas that we had conquered, pending an Egyptian agreement to also retreat from the entire Sinai desert. United Nations forces would be placed in the Sinai to establish a buffer zone. While I was in Gaza, I found a motorcycle and a warm outfit for pilots to be used in bad weather and rain. I taught myself to ride the motorcycle and I brought it back with me to the base.

After the war, I was transferred to another unit to attend a course as a trainer and Captain Ze'ev Gur-Arie (the spy Lotz) was also transferred. After a few years I met him on the street in Tel Aviv. We sat down and had coffee together. He told me he had been released from the army and had different business abroad. He didn't elaborate much, and I didn't have any reason to be skeptical about his stories. The truth came out later that he was actually engaged with the Mossad. He earned the rank of major and was sent as a spy to Egypt. He was given a new identity as a German businessman since he knew the German language fluently. They had him marry a German girl and he was sent to Egypt to establish a riding school for horses. There he connected with different businesspeople, and especially army officers who wanted to ride in his school.

Because of his connections, he was able to get into high society events to gather intelligence information by listening to the officers discussing issues. They never imagined that he actually understood and fluently spoke Arabic! From time to time he would go to Germany for business trips, and then he would find a way to get into Israel to update the Mossad.

During the preparations for the Six Day War, Lotz was not satisfied with the information he had gathered, so he rode his horse to the border and mingled with the Egyptian army forces, took photographs, and then forwarded them to the Mossad in Israel. The Egyptian commanders asked him politely not to enter their military zone, even though they were friends. There is no doubt that the information he transferred into Israel had a very great impact on the victory over Egypt during the 1967 Six Day War. A short time before the war erupted he was caught, however, the Egyptians didn't know he was an Israeli spy. After the war, Israel succeeded in getting him released through the intervention of a third country and only after he made it to Israel did the Egyptians find out he was actually an Israeli spy.

After the 1956 war, Lieutenant General Benjamin Gibli was transferred to fulfill different roles in the IDF, however, Ben-Gurion insisted that he not be promoted to a higher rank. So even though he was awarded the role as the Chief of Staff, Central Command, and although he was a very dedicated and smart commander, he was not promoted. He was then released from the army and he went back to his hometown, Petah Tikva. After a short while, he landed a job as the general manager of a company by the name of Shemen, which was an oil manufacturing facility in Haifa. He was able to use his talents to do very well at this job.

After a few years, I met him one day in a supermarket standing in line at the cash registers. He was still very modest—a tall man like an American cowboy in the movies. He passed away at the age of 86 in great shape. He did not manage to write a book about the truth of the incident known as Parashat Lavon (Hasek Habish), where a group of spies was caught and executed in Egypt. All that was known was that he was the head of the intelligence division of the army. He had put together a group of Jewish Egyptian citizens living in Egypt who, without professional training, were recruited as spies. When they were caught by the Egyptians, the Ministry of Defense blamed Gibli, recruited the spies without approval from the minister of defense, Lavon.

Gibli claimed that he had received approval from Lavon orally, but the politicians—who included Ben-Gurion and Moshe Dayan—preferred to put the blame from the political people on to the shoulders of Gibli. And that is how he was deposed from his job. It was clearly an agreement between the political people and the military. Gibli would accept responsibility for the tragedy, but he would still be allowed to serve in the IDF.

Eventually I was assigned to an isolated base located on the top of a high mountain between other mountains. There was a central building and fields of tents. This was the central school for class commanders of the infantry where students learned about all the different arms of the IDF. It was a very basic and thorough school designed so that commanders would be able to fulfill their different duties in cooperation with the different armies of the IDF. After filling out all the forms, and getting our personal guns and so forth, we were assigned to different tents. The new officers were gathered in a huge hall where we were introduced to the team. The commander of the school was a lieutenant general, and under his command was a major, a few captains, and some lieutenants who served as the commanders in the different classes. We would, in turn, become the commanders of those classes when new trainees would arrive for that same course, the Commander Grade.

A few guys who were not officers had fulfilled their duties as administration of the school, including cooks, administrators, drivers, and logistics. The head leader was a sergeant major in the army. Those guys were responsible for the discipline within the military school and also for the training of the trainees through a variety of different exercises. The commander told us about the different subjects we were going to learn, and explained that our duty would be to build a strong structure of commanders that was very professional. We were divided into classes and started our very difficult training, which lasted about one month.

We studied the art of being a trainer—how to present a lesson within the assigned schedule, and how to build new leaders. We had exercised the different stages of a lesson many times, including how to present the subject, and how to finish the lesson. The focus was on the way we presented ourselves, the way we stood, how we used our voice (louder or lower) to avoid causing the trainees to fall asleep, and of course a full knowledge of the material. At the end, we had to pass exams and we had to be able to answer questions that were brought by the trainees. The month passed very quickly, and we were all very proud and ready to start our duties.

We got a one-week vacation before becoming the new trainers in the new course that would open when we returned to the base. The new class of trainees was assigned to me as a commander the day after I returned from vacation, and the course started with celebrations for the newcomers to the IDF School of class commanders. We trainers were on stage with the administrative people, and there were some speeches about the schools. We were really proud to be on stage and to be introduced as the trainers. It was very exciting. This was the moment when I became the commander to about 20 trainees. For the coming six months. I had to teach them combat and keep them together as a team. My job was to turn them into leaders and commanders who would take the IDF to victory whenever they faced a situation that would test their abilities. I was very confident in my important new duties, and I had a lot of energy. I worked hard and always served as a good example to my trainees.

I was very strict—I demanded that my trainees get the job done perfectly, but in the process I was very honest and fair. In addition to my duties as commander and trainer, I felt like I was the father to 20 soldiers. I would listen to the stories about their lives and family situations, their wishes and dreams, and what they were thinking about—even some very personal issues. I was only about two or three years older than those trainees, each of whom came from a different level of the society, with experience and knowledge from other forces. For example, there were trainees from the marines who had a huge amount of experience in combat. The same was true with the men from the parachute units—just brilliant guys. Also some very brilliant guys from intelligence, as well as helicopter pilots who had gone through a lot of training for takeoff and landing on the American aircraft carriers.

I constantly struggled with myself to keep the boundaries between being the commander who keeps some distance from his soldiers, and the good father who is worried about his kids. The most important thing was to honor each one of them as a person and to appreciate their talents.

I worked hard to prepare the lessons so that I would be professional about the issues I was teaching, and so that my students would feel that I wanted to teach them everything I knew. I reserved a lot of my free time for personal discussions with them or group discussion about different issues outside of the military, and they trusted me. At the end of the course, I acquired many new friends, who I encountered throughout my military career.

Many years after I was a trainer, I already had my own kids and I was about to take a trip to the United States. I received a phone call from one of the trainees from the school. He told me that they had organized a get together for the whole course class in Tel Aviv, including all of the other trainers and commanders of the school. I was invited, along with my family. I explained to them that on the same night at 1:00 A.M., I was already scheduled to fly to New York. They didn't let me give them any excuses, however, so I promised I would come.

My wife Rivka was busy making final preparations for the trip, but she pressured and convinced me to go the party without her. I took my oldest son Steven with me, who was 12 years old at the time. We got to the event in Tel Aviv and the banquet hall was fully organized and decorated. They had many photographs and a model of the school where I served as a trainer. It was very emotional to meet all of those young soldiers who were already bald with bellies! Some of them were wearing suits, while some were in their IDF uniforms with their officer ranks. We hugged and told stories from the old days. They showed a movie from our time at the school, and everyone tried to identify themselves as young men. They also had funny stuff where the trainees made fun of the trainers and told all kinds of stories about them.

The team of trainers was introduced on the stage. Sadly, quite a large number of the trainers were not present because they had been killed in various IDF activities over the years. The commander of the school, then-Lieutenant General Eli, was also not there. He was among those who had been killed. I liked him very much. He looked every part a teacher and educator, and I liked to talk with him for hours. He used to spend much of his time watching nature—especially animals—and he would use examples of the smart behaviors of different animals.

A group of guys surrounded me and told my son how strict I used to be—in their words, I really gave them a hard time. "I tore their asses." But nevertheless they respected me, loved me, and trusted me with their lives. My behavior toward them was similar, I respected them, and I helped them to be the people they became with my stories and jokes which gave them energy during their lives. I was very excited to listen to their warm words and to be one of them, however, I had to leave quite early in order to get to the airport.

During the time that I was the commander in the courses, there was great tension on the northern border of the country with Syria. According to the treaties, we were not allowed to keep any military forces on the border between Israel, Syria, and Lebanon. The name of this place is Givat Hahityshvut. A decision had been made to conquer this spot and evacuate the Syrians. The commander of this operation was the vice chief of staff, General Laskov, who later became the chief of staff of the IDF.

In the early evening, we boarded trucks with our different armaments, and we traveled to the gathering point, which was the police station in the north of the country called Tzemah. There we met other IDF forces from different armies, and after a few hours we received a briefing and intelligence information on the size of the Syrian regiments, where they were advancing, and where they were situated. I remember riding in the truck on our way to the north with our ammunition, helmets, and faces colored with camouflage. It was really quiet—everyone was still and thinking to himself.

For most of those soldiers, it was their first experience with combat. Although I had experienced combat, I started to think about the possible dangers of getting hurt or even killed. People were having a good time in Tel Aviv drinking and dancing, and here I was about to end my life without having the opportunity to enjoy everything that life had to offer. The minute we got to our assigned place, I felt a heavy responsibility on my shoulders to perform the mission.

A few hours before daybreak, we were given the command to attack.

It was a very dark night and very cold. We were shaking, and I'm not sure if it was because of the cold or if it was because we were afraid of the unknown. The attacks started with mortars and artillery guns. We cut the barbed-wire fences and broke into the trenches. There was chaos, explosions, hand grenades were thrown, and guns were fired. All of my fear and thoughts just disappeared, replaced by the commands we had learned and taught to the trainees.

The Syrians were totally surprised by our fast raid, and ran away, leaving behind many causalities and combat equipment that was of Russian origin. The only thing I took for myself was a Russian fur hat, which had special flaps to protect your ears. After conquering that position, there was a sudden rain of fire from mortars and artillery guns on the Syrian side. We started to dig ourselves deeper into the trenches, and the fire stopped only after the IDF artillery guns were directed toward Syria. We were all very proud that we had participated in that combat and we felt very secure and happy.

During the continuation of my army service, I went for a course of commanders of the Mefakdei Pluga-Company Commander, and then I was transferred to headquarters to perform my duties, where I had courses in general education, foreign affairs, and more. In my new duties, I was stationed in the north of the country—in Nazareth—in a base located at the police building. This was a building used since the English regime was in the Israel. The general commander was Itzhak Rabin who later on became the chief of staff of the IDF, and years later became the prime minister of Israel. He was assassinated in November 1995 by a Jewish radical religious guy after a political get together in Tel Aviv. The spot where he was assassinated has been given the name Rabin Square.

In my new duty as an assistant to the operation officer, I was promoted to the ranks of first lieutenant. I learned new things and the focus was put on how to work as a team at the headquarters, how to prepare programs and commands to the different units, and how to supervise their performance. The area was always in the news because we had endless clashes on the Syrian border. I was kept busy updating the maps in the war room, preparing materials for the meetings, and especially learning about the situation on the ground. I had the opportunity to get to know many top officers, including the commander of intelligence, the commander of artillery, the chief medical officer, the logistic commander, the military rabbinical rabbi, and their assistants, with whom I worked very closely to coordinate events.

I was really impressed with General Itzhak Rabin. When he

was in the war room, you could feel that he was a real leader, and everyone respected him. He knew how to assess different situations and you could feel that his level was much higher than any other officer in the room. He had an analytical brain—always straight to the point—and it was an honor just to be close to him.

One time we went out to the area where there was a clash on the Syrian border. The Syrians opened fire and we officers tried to hide behind every possible rock. The only guy who acted really cool—looking around to observe where the source of the fire was coming from—was Itzhak Rabin. With his strong, tranquil voice, he commanded the artillery to open fire in the direction of the source of the Syrian fire. That provided the cover we needed, and we were able to retreat. I worshiped Itzhak Rabin, and he served an example for me for many years to come. He was very modest, even shy, but a very handsome man with blue eyes. Every female soldier was in love with him, however, none of them had the courage even to get close to him.

At that time, the Arabs who lived in Israel were put under martial law. So it was my honor to be invited with the other senior officers to the different Arab villages, while being welcomed in the Arab tradition—they were known for their hospitality. The head of the village and other dignitaries welcomed us, and we walked among them and shook their hands. We gathered in a huge tent with lots of rugs and pillows covering the floor. There were a few speeches and then it was straight to the feast.

The women were in the kitchen preparing the food because they were not allowed to participate in events of this kind. The women would look from behind the curtains from time to time while the men were eating. The main course was roast lamb that had been specially prepared for that event, with pita, hummus, and tahini. We ate without cutlery, using only with our hands like in ancient times. At the end of the meal we were given black coffee with cardamom.

This is where I learned the Arabic tradition that it is a big honor for the host to hear the guests let out a burp after they finished the meal, showing that they enjoyed the meal. The purpose of those meetings was to build a good relationship with the local Arab leaders and to solve their day-to-day problems, since they were living under Israeli military jurisdiction. In that forum, they would present a list of different issues they wanted the military to take care of. We promised that every problem would be handled separately.

I used to attend a lot of those meetings, and each was an experience in itself. One time we were invited to a wedding in the village of Abu Gosh, on the way to Jerusalem. The wedding was held outside in an olive grove. All of the men, including the groom, had been separated from the women, including the bride. What made that evening so special was the belly dancer. The men would push their hands into her big bosom and leave huge amounts of money.

After the ceremony, the bride and groom walked up to the second floor of a house at the end of the olive grove, and sometime later the groom came out onto the veranda and showed the bed sheet stained with blood, which proved to the family and guests that the bride was a virgin. The women would scream happily and the celebration began in earnest. This was truly an unforgettable experience.

During my free time I would go out to the city of Nazareth to have lunch in the restaurant or to have black coffee with cardamom. There were a lot of female soldiers at the base, and I became friends with a few of them. We took a few trips together, but of course, we could do this only when the situation was not tense and we could get some vacation. Usually only the officers on duty would stay on base with a team of soldiers—guys and girls—and of course the people who were on duty to guard the base. I would go home every evening to see Bianca. I started to help her and her husband with the kids, especially at night when their kids Jacob and Esther were crying and my sister and her husband would argue over who would go down to take care of them.

I remember when my niece Esther was teething and she was suffering so much pain. I would hold her to help her relax and she would fall asleep in my arms. Simon was working as a police officer at the station in Haifa Port, and his salary was quite low. They lived on a mountain in Ein Dor, which at the time was called Havasa. They acquired a Swedish hut (a name used for the kind of barracks) and from the outside it looked like a nice house with a nice backyard. My sister Bianca took advantage of this location and she opened a daycare center for young kids. That way she could also make some money.

Because I signed up to work in the army as an officer after completing my mandatory service, I received a monthly salary. My salary was deposited directly from the army to my bank account. My necessities were very little—I would eat at the base, wearing only my uniforms as clothes. My sister Bianca and her husband were always complaining that they didn't have enough money, so I started to give them my salary each month to help.

Many times I traveled to Naharia to visit my uncle Eli and his wife Rachel. I always felt very good with them. I still had the motorcycle that I brought with me from Gaza. It was painted in a khaki color and it had a military license plate. I decided to drive my motorcycle every day, even though I didn't have a driver's license. I was very thin and I could barely hold the motorcycle. I failed my first military motorcycle test because I was so insecure. We had to stop on our way up a large hill, turn off the engine, and then restart it again by pushing the kick starter hard with my leg. This wasn't easy for me.

I continued to get lessons, took my civilian test, and I got my license. However, in order to drive a military motorcycle, I needed to get my military license. When my civilian license arrived at the military license office in Jaffa, the chief warrant officer on duty decided that trying to get a license in two places was a criminal offense, so he banned my civilian license. I sought advice from everyone to see if there was a solution. Help came from one of the officers in the Chief Engineering Officer Headquarters. He was a good friend of the chief warrant officer who had banned my license, and he arranged for me to get my military license based on the fact that I had received my civilian license. It was a miracle, and I learned my lesson that if you have a problem, you should share it with everyone because you never know where help will come from.

The officers on the base heard my story and organized a surprise party for me. One of the girl soldiers from intelligence who was very good at drawing prepared some nice sketches and caricatures. Mine had me riding a motorcycle with a headline that read, "Be careful, he got a license!" A lot of the girls were eager to catch a ride with me on my motorcycle. I liked those girls when they were sitting behind and hugging me. I would try from time to time to stop suddenly so that I could feel their tits on my back. What can I do, I was always mischievous. They never complained, so I assume they enjoyed it too.

I joined the army on November 26, 1952, and was released on August 28, 1963. I then continued in the reserves as a major until August 23, 1988. All told, I served two years and six months of mandatory service, eight years and four months as an active-duty officer, and 24 years and six months as a reserve officer. I was proud to serve my young country of Israel and to help protect it and our people from the many enemies that surrounded us, and whose main goal was to destroy our nation. Sometimes it was exciting, sometimes terrifying, sometimes boring, and sometimes a lot of fun. No matter what feelings I was experiencing at the time, however, it was always satisfying to me.

Chapter 21
The First Meeting with My Future Wife
(In Arie's Own Words)

During my visits with my sister Bianca, I met a couple of her friends, Sidi and Dorel. They had two small kids, and sometimes when I had a free evening they would ask me if I could babysit for them. While I was babysitting I also met Itzhak Goldenzweig from Jerusalem. He was 16 or 17 years old, and we became friends right away. We would play chess while watching the kids to pass the time.

One day Sidi told my sister Bianca about her cousin Rivka—an only child from a very good family originally from Romania. And so my sister and her friend convinced me to travel to Hadar Yosef to meet this girl who was still in high school. It seemed very strange to me, and I was very much in doubt about the long-term hopes for this match. It seemed too old fashioned to me. In my head I thought you could meet a girl when you went out with friends, and if you find that the two of you are serious, then you decide to get married and have a family—of course only when you fall in love.

Anyway, Bianca and Sidi were insistent, and I was eventually convinced to meet Rivka. I dressed in my lieutenant's IDF uniform, grabbed my motorcycle, and drove all the way to Tel Aviv.

In a small, cute house in Hadar Yosef, I met Rivka, my future wife.

Her parents invited me to eat lunch with them, and I remember the moment when our eyes met and I saw the mischievous warm smile light up her face, reflected toward me. She was so beautiful and naïve and innocent—so full of light. I knew right away that this girl was destined to be my wife. This was my first time in my life where I felt what love was all about.

Lieutenant Arie Ringelstein, IDF, when he met Rivka, 1958

The table was set in the traditional way of the Jewish people who came from Chernovitz—well known as the best hostesses and as the best cooks with their special dishes. The discussion flowed. I was very thin and a bad eater, but Rivka's mother Peppi prepared huge portions. When she set them on the table, I pushed them toward the center of the table because I thought all of us were supposed to share them. I quickly realized that this was actually only my portion, and it was only the appetizer. In truth, the food didn't interest me at all—I was staring only at Rivka.

Rivka Konig at the time she met Arie, 1958

Her parents started to interrogate me about my financial situation—how much I earned in the army—and of, course, my family history. It was during those discussions that we discovered my uncle Mishu—my father's brother, who was living in Beersheba—was also a good friend of Rivka's parents when they lived in Iași. Sometimes they would go have a drink and eat at the restaurant Mishu owned. Rivka's family was religious, and you had to wear a yarmulke while eating—they only served kosher food. They regularly went to synagogue, and they were not allowed to travel on the Sabbath.

These issues didn't bother me at all. At the end of the meal I had an opportunity to take Rivka out for a walk. We talked and talked, and I felt that I was in love. I liked her and she liked me, the spark of fire was there. We were discussing different issues, laughing and enjoying every minute and we didn't feel the time pass. We exchanged phone numbers and decided to keep in touch. We could hardly wait for the next opportunity to meet.

CHAPTER 22
THE WEDDING

When it became apparent that the couple would get married, Arie asked Rivka's father to give them his blessing. Rivka's mother said, "What? So fast!" But the couple decided that they were going to get married anyway. Privately, Rivka's father said that she was too young, and he made his point by loudly asking, "This is the first guy you dated, and now you want to marry him?"

But it was *bashert*. It was meant to be! What does "meant to be" mean? It is the feeling that something bigger than you is calling forth what is about to unfold. This feeling of a natural attraction that propels you to move with it as if you have no other choice at the moment.

Their winter meeting gave way to a summer wedding. The Tel Aviv Banquet Hall had just opened, and it was chosen as the venue for the July 8, 1959, evening wedding.

At that time, the bride traditionally rented a wedding dress instead of buying one. Rivka chose a big, beautiful one with many layers of skirts. A rabbi from the military rabbinate of the Israel Defense Forces performed the ceremony.

The wedding of Rivka Konig and Arie Ringelstein, 1959

There was quite a celebration after the wedding ceremony, with dinner and much celebrating. The newly wedded couple received gifts to furnish the apartment they planned to move into, including many knives and tablecloths, and bottles people used at the time to make their own soda. There were no gifts of money, but Rivka's parents helped the couple get an apartment in a three-story building that had two apartments on each floor.

Arie and Rivka took their honeymoon trip to the seaside city of Netanya, about a half hour's ride from Tel Aviv. Today, Netanya bills itself as the "Israeli Rivera," and it is a sparkling and lively city with beautiful beaches, long seaside promenades, and countless cafes and restaurants. They spent a week there immediately after the wedding, and enjoyed their days and nights filled with fun and relaxation—enjoying their special status as newlyweds.

But, of course, the honeymoon had to eventually end, and the reality of life together soon interceded. After the honeymoon, the couple settled into their apartment in the city of Ramat Gan, just east of Tel Aviv. The apartment had a living room, bedroom, bathroom, kitchen, dining room, and a small den. The building was in the middle of nowhere, and there was a lot of sand around it, as the area was not yet fully developed. Ramat Gan was established as a suburb of Tel Aviv in 1921, and the first residents built a moshava specializing in the farming of barley, wheat, and watermelons. By 1961, the small agricultural colony had grown into a business and industrial powerhouse with just under 91,000 residents, textile mills, furniture makers, canning plants, electrical manufacturers, and more.

To move to Ramat Gan, Arie requested and was granted a transfer by the army from Haifa to Tel Aviv.

Rivka's parents at Rivka's and Arie's wedding, 1959

Chapter 23
The Honeymoon Is Over and Life Has Begun
(In Rivka's Own Words)

About four months after the wedding, in November 1959, I took a job with El Al Israel Airlines. I had already earned a diploma for office management and typing, and I could type in both English and Hebrew. I went to the employment office to look for a job, and I found an opening for a typist at Lod Airport, Israel's largest international airport, and a one-hour commute from where we were living in Ramat Gan. The facility was later renamed the Ben Gurion Airport in honor of Israel's founding father and first prime minister. I wondered what Arie would say about the commuting time from home to work and back. He advised me to try it and said that if I didn't like it, I could stop.

At that time El Al's main office was in Tel Aviv, but the operation and maintenance hangar were at the airport in the city of Lod. I worked in shipping and receiving, typing the shipping orders, and ordering spare parts for the aircraft. It was my job to order parts from different suppliers who were outside of Israel. When an aircraft was grounded, it was labeled AOG, meaning Aircraft On Ground—not able to perform flights—which had a direct impact on the company financially.

It turned out that I was very good at the job, and I was transferred to the office of Ephraim Ben-Arzi, the president of the company. Born in Poland, Ben-Arzi joined Israel's early defense force—the Haganah—in 1929, and later became an officer in the British army and a general in the IDF. He was good at his job—very smart—however, he lacked relationship and communication skills with people. I noticed that the men who came from the army felt that they were from heaven and others were beneath them, and their behavior expressed that by continuing to give orders as if they were still serving in the army!

Although I was employed by the airline, I had never been a passenger on a jet. I got my first chance to fly through the company. The International Air Transport Association (I.A.T.A.) stipulates that as an airline employee you are entitled to get a no-cost, space-available ticket for yourself and for your partner and children whenever you wish to travel.

El Al had a policy that after you had worked for the company for two years, you and your spouse were eligible to apply for and receive these space available tickets for travel. So, in August 1961, Arie and I made our first overseas trip by airline together—flying from Israel to England, France, Switzerland, and Italy. At that time there were no Boeing airplanes in El Al's fleet. We flew on a British-built Bristol Britannia aircraft, nicknamed the "Whispering Giant," which carried approximately 139 passengers and had four powerful turboprop engines.

England was nice. I remember looking at the names signed on the guest register of the hotel we stayed at, and noticing that a lot of Arabs were staying there. I mentioned that to Arie and he was surprised. He asked me, "How do you know?" And I said, "I just reviewed the registration book and I noticed." Arie knew I had a photographic memory.

France was the next place we went. We visited my aunt Mitzi Champanier and her son George. Mitzi was my mom's sister who lived all her life in France. Tragically, during the Holocaust her husband had been reported to be Jewish and was taken away and killed by the Nazis. George was married, had two daughters, and was in the clothing business. He ran both a factory and a store where people would come to purchase clothes *prêt a porter* or "ready to wear" in French. He also exported clothing to Lebanon. He was a wealthy man who owned two homes, one in the city and one in the suburbs of Paris on the Riviera.

During our visit to Paris, we went to see a show at the well-known Lido nightclub. The show included dancers who performed the can-can. I was so young. There was a dress code, and when you came in you were obliged to order drinks. Arie ordered champagne. He did not drink, but that night we finished an entire bottle of champagne between the two of us! Arie couldn't stop laughing—we were laughing and laughing and hiccupping all the way back to the hotel. We also visited museums like the Louvre and walked up and down the Champs-Élysées.

Because I understood some French, and because I was shy, I would whisper to Arie what to ask when in a shop. When the answer would come Arie would not reply—he would just say

"Merci!" After I heard the clerk answer, I said to Arie, "Okay, let's go!" Once when we were browsing the shop windows in Paris, we saw the flip-flop sandals that were then very popular in Israel displayed in the window of a shoe store. When Arie went into the shop to buy a pair, he spoke in Hebrew to the clerk while she spoke French to him. I thought the scene was humorous because he grabbed her arm to take her to the window to show her what he wanted and they were both speaking different languages. The clerk kept saying in French, "Je ne comprends pas ce qu'il veut!"—"I don't understand what he wants!" Arie liked to joke with everyone and he was always happy.

After France, we visited Switzerland and then Rome. For the entire trip to Europe, we flew only when space was available on an aircraft. By the time we arrived in Rome, we were just about out of money, so it was time for us to go home. But to our surprise, there were no spaces available on any of the flights to Israel! So we stretched what little money we had and had some more fun and memorable times while waiting for space on a flight home.

The hotel where we stayed in Rome had two beds, which Arie found to be unacceptable. He called the front desk and asked to have the beds put together. We were used to double beds, but these beds were separated by a nightstand. Arie liked always to joke, and at one time he used his hands to make motions to ask the clerk if in Italy couples don't ever make love!

Nearly out of money, at one meal we ordered just pasta because it was cheap and filling. We stuffed ourselves with the pasta, grateful for what food we could get. When our empty pasta bowls were taken away, we were surprised then they were replaced by a second course that we did not expect—roast chicken.

Eventually, we used up the last of our funds and I was forced to go to the station manager of El Al and tell him that we were stuck in Rome and out of funds. I asked if he could loan us money until we got back to Israel and I could pay him back. He was a good guy, very understanding, and agreed to provide us with a small loan. After a week, we were able to get back home. But before we left, we visited the Trevi fountain and threw coins in with a heartfelt wish: We don't want to stay any longer! Let us go back home!

The first two years of our marriage were spent struggling to make a decent living in order to be able to start a family. The point was not just to have children, but to be able to provide them with the best life we could—considering the fact that we were children of war—and also to give them much love and appreciation. I am proud to say that we succeeded in achieving our goal beyond our expectations.

Chapter 24
Building a Family Together

After their trip to Europe, Rivka learned that she was pregnant. Conditions in the hangar office at El Al varied with the season—summer was very hot and winter was very cold, and Rivka had to commute for an hour to the airport office by bus. But throughout the pregnancy, her friend Ninette helped Rivka at work.

Ninette had come to Israel from Egypt, and she was fluent in several languages: Italian, French, English, and Arabic. At El Al, she worked on the IBM machines, and she and Rivka were office neighbors. They also commuted together each day on the El Al buses that were grouped by routes defined by where employees lived. To help pass the time during the daily commutes to work and back, Rivka taught Ninette Hebrew, and Ninette taught Rivka French.

On her office calendar, Rivka circled May 15 and said, "That is the day I will go to the hospital."

Sure enough, her water broke on May 15, and she was soon on the way to the hospital. Rivka had taken some Lamaze classes prior to giving birth and even toured a hospital to see women who'd just delivered their babies. She witnessed everything—including all the blood that remained after the birth process—and the whole scene looked quite scary to her. Although Rivka's water had broken, there were no contractions, so the doctor had to induce labor to make the contractions begin. She did not take medication for the pain and was at the hospital for hours and hours. Arie and Rivka's son Steven was born around 12:30 P.M. on May 16, 1962.

Delivering her first baby was quite an exciting experience for Rivka. To give life to a newborn baby and to experience motherhood—these were amazing feelings for her to experience. The birth of their son brought much happiness to both Arie and Rivka.

They named their son Zvi, after Rivka's grandfather from her father's side. *Zvi* is the Hebrew word for deer. Later on his name became Steven.

Rivka's father Jacob brought the *mohel* to perform the *bris*, the Jewish naming ceremony during which the baby boy is also circumcised and welcomed into the Jewish community. Steven's bris was held at the synagogue, and Arie was beyond excited to have a son to continue the Ringelstein name. When he came to the hospital to pick up his wife and son and bring them home, the staff was preparing for another baby to be picked up. Arie was so excited that he almost picked up the wrong baby!

Those first days as a young mother were very interesting and exciting for Rivka. She used her strong maternal instincts and quickly became very organized. She woke up early each day, and by 10:00 A.M., her house would shine. She used cloth diapers without a washing machine or dryer—carrying big pots of soapy water to the gas stove and boiling them to clean and sterilize the diapers. She then used cold water from the bathtub to rinse the diapers before hanging them outside on ropes to dry. There was plenty of sun to dry them.

But the baby was difficult. He had problems with feeding. He'd eat 50 grams and throw up 100 grams, and it was always a struggle to feed him. Because Steven was so difficult, Rivka could not go back to work after three months, the standard amount of time allotted for maternity leave. He was skinny and tiny—his parents fed him boiled cornflower and cocoa and made pudding in hopes of putting some meat on his bones.

One day it was Arie's job to feed baby Steven and he kept turning his head. Arie got so nervous that he spilled the whole bowl of pudding on Steven's face. Rivka got mad and said, 'This is what happens? The one time you had to feed him during the whole day?" She was extremely frustrated, but knew that this problem with Steven's feeding needed to be addressed. Arie and Rivka had heard that there was a skilled pediatrician in town, a Dr. Rahamimov. He was from Bulgaria and was disabled, but he was very good at what he did. He agreed to treat Steven.

Dr. Rahamimov's rules for feeding were to give food every day at the same time and in the same quantity then, if he refused to eat, only water to drink until the next meal. Steven's parents were strong and followed the rules, but it was not easy. No toys, no TV shows—no distractions during feeding. Rivka had to sit and feed the baby without interrupting the process until the next meal. She could not even put sugar in the water. Steven would cry at feeding time. Rivka would cry at feeding time. Eventually, however, he began to eat normally. Because of the difficulty in caring for the baby, Rivka was not able to return to her job at El Al until seven months had passed.

During those seven months, Rivka raised Steven without help. She took him outdoors on walks and laid him in the sun to get tanned. When Steven was just one or two months old, Arie and Rivka took him with them and with their friends to the beach and on picnics. There was no two-day weekend at that time—people only had Saturday off from work.

When Rivka went back to work, she hired a neighbor from another apartment building to take care of Steven. The woman agreed to take care of him in her home, so Rivka used to drop him off at her apartment, then was at the bus stop by 6:30 A.M. for her hour-long commute to the office. When she returned home each day, she would pick up Steven, go home, and start to cook dinner. It was hard for her to leave Steven, to know that a strange woman was taking care of him. After two months of Rivka's being back to work, Steven contracted pneumonia. Arie and Rivka were afraid that the disease could turn deadly, so Rivka asked if she could go to work later in the day.

Eventually, the couple decided that they were not going to put Steven at risk anymore, and so they looked to hire a nanny who would come to their home and take care of him there. Fortunately, Steven soon recovered from the pneumonia and life returned to some semblance of normalcy in the Ringelstein household.

Despite his difficulty feeding, Steven was precocious. He started everything early. He stood on his own at seven months and walked well before his first birthday. And on his first year birthday, in May 1963, his parents threw a big party in their house, recording the proceedings with their Grundig tape recorder. The birthday party took place on a large porch, and Steven was dressed like a little man. Everyone asked him questions and Arie and Rivka recorded his answers with that tape recorder, consisting mainly of baby gurgles and mumblings.

In 1963, Arie was offered a new job in the army. He was still engaged with them on a salary basis, and they offered him a promotion to major. Unfortunately, that involved moving from Tel Aviv to Beersheba, the largest city in the Negev desert, which is in the southern part of Israel.

After Israel declared its independence in 1948, and Beersheba was won from Egypt by the IDF, a flood of Sephardic and Mizrahi Jews moved to the city from the surrounding Arab countries and as far away as India. Later, in the 1990s, Beersheba became a popular destination for Ashkenazi Jews from the former Soviet Union, and today it has more chess grandmasters per capita than anywhere else in the world.

However, in 1963, Rivka did not want to leave behind her home and her job at El Al. So she told Arie that she was not willing to live her life as dictated by the army. It was well known at the time that the army could transfer soldiers to any location at any time. Arie's promotion meant that Rivka would be forced to quit her job and move the family.

Rivka told Arie that an army career would mean that he would be controlled by the army and could be transferred to a different city or base anytime they chose. They would always be on the move, and Rivka was not ready for that type of life for their family. Since family meant so much to him, Arie made the decision to leave the army and look for a job in a civilian place of employment. This was not easy for him. He was an officer—the one used to giving the orders to his subordinates. All of a sudden, he had to take orders from others. Arie was always a person ready to compromise, so he did what was necessary to keep the family together.

Arie soon found a job at a construction company—Naveh, founded in 1963—and he earned three times as much as he was being paid in the army, which was a boon for his small family. It was his job to purchase materials for both residential and commercial construction.

Naveh's owner could hire and fire employees at will, and although he paid workers three times as much as other companies, he treated his employees like dirt. The engineers who worked for him put up with him because of the pay, but Arie, with his pride and ego, found the owner a very difficult person for whom to work. When the owner raised his voice during an argument, Arie threatened to quit. The owner said, "I will raise your salary, just don't quit." The owner begged Arie not to leave, but Arie's ego and work ethics were more important to him than a higher salary, so he left that job after less than a year.

Arie was such a people person that he quickly found another job working for a manufacturer of linens, Kitan Demona. Their factory was in the south, and Arie worked as an assistant to the chief buyer. Part of his job was to research the best prices. It was a lower salary than the position he had at Naveh, but he didn't care.

After some time, Arie moved into a position in the purchasing department for El Al, working in the Tel Aviv office. He did purchasing for everything the company needed to operate its fleet of aircraft. He knew many wholesalers, and it was easy for him to work there. The spare parts and interior items were imported from abroad.

Arie knew well the ins and outs of purchasing, and it was common in that kind of business to be bribed—companies would offer incentives to the buyers to send them orders for the materials and equipment they sold. Arie, however, followed what he called the Golden Rule: he refused bribes. As he would tell Rivka, "For me it is important not to take a bribe. My integrity is very important. I don't want anyone to point to me and say to my kids, 'Your dad was a thief.'"

Arie fought to get the best prices he could get for his employer, all the while telling the seller that he would not take a dime from them. Interestingly enough, Arie had been told by his boss at El Al not to take bribes, but two years after that admonition, this same man was jailed for taking them. Israel is a small country, and people know what you are up to.

Because Arie had connections with wholesalers and knew the business of buying, he became acquainted with Maybo, a company that imported household items. They hired Arie to be the general manager at a salary two times higher than his El Al salary. This job took him away from the family—lots of travel was involved as he worked in sales and distribution to wholesalers and department stores across Israel.

After his work at Maybo ended, Arie took a job with a teachers' association, an organization with 70,000 members. The person who hired him wanted to sell discounted items to teachers, but the company was not well run and it ended up closing in bankruptcy.

Although Rivka was busy with her own career, she still helped Arie open a business named Arkli to import mostly pots and pans made of enamel from a South African manufacturer of household goods. Arie imported containers of goods and sold them to department stores, unions, and companies. It was a tradition for companies to give their employees a gift twice a year, during Rosh Hashanah—the Jewish New Year—and Passover. Rivka helped by loading the car with samples and receiving the orders for the goods during the year. Rivka was also responsible for doing all the paperwork required to keep the goods flowing into Israel, and for dealing with the customs brokers to facilitate the release of the containers with the goods from customs. They did this for about a year and a half.

Chapter 25
The Blessings of Children
(In Rivka's Own Words)

Not long after Steven was born, my parents moved closer to our family in Ramat Gan. This was about the same time that Arie and I bought a used, two-cylinder, two-seater BMW from a coworker at El Al. We rode in the car on Saturdays—our day off—to take Steven to the beach or to drive with friends for a picnic in the country. My father was still the same dictator he had been throughout my childhood, and he tried to prevent us from driving the car on the Shabbat for religious reasons.

Arie said to my father, "This is our life. And we make our own decisions. I am not going to force my wife to do something she does not want to. If she wants to drive, she will drive. I will not lie to you about it."

And I said to my father, "Since I have my own family and life, I am capable of making my own decisions."

It took my father some time to get tired of playing the game of being upset and nervous that his daughter was no longer following his rules, but having no other choice, he got over it and had to agree to my rules despite his reservations.

In 1964, when Steven was two, my aunt Mitzi came to visit from France. Her boat landed in Haifa, so Arie and I took Steven and we went to meet her there, then brought her to visit my parents. She loved meeting Steven for the first time and had such fun trying to teach him French. She asked him to keep repeating her words, like a parrot.

When we went to take Mitzi back to Haifa on a Friday, we found we had locked the keys inside our car. Everything was closed, and our spare keys were at our home in Ramat Gan. It was a nightmare. It was Shabbat, so no buses were running, and we had to take a taxi to go home, get the keys, and go back and open the car. Steven lost his pacifier somewhere along the route and was crying and mad. I tried to find a pharmacy to buy him a new one but was unsuccessful. It was one of those moments when everything went wrong.

Being a working mom was a handful in those days, and having a baby who was needy meant that that I was always tired and had no time to breathe. But Arie and I were children of war, and the way to ensure the continuation of our lives as fulfilled people was to continue to expand the family.

And that's exactly what we did.

Our daughter Liat came into the world on June 10, 1965. She was named after my husband's grandmother, Lea, whom he loved very dearly since she had played quite a role in raising him after he lost both of his parents. Liat's name was originally Lea, but when she became older, she changed her name to Liat, which in Hebrew means, "you are mine." Throughout this book, she will be known as Liat.

On the day Liat was born, I had contractions in the morning and I told Steven's nanny to take him home with her because I had to go to the hospital. Once I got there, the contractions slowed and I had to walk around the yard to get them to come back. Eventually, at around 1:30 in the afternoon, she was born. Liat was a very beautiful girl, with a head of dark hair. She loved to eat, which made me very happy after my experience with Steven.

We celebrated Liat's birth during the weeks after she was born. But the celebrations kept going on and kept me very busy. For boys you have a bris, but for girls nothing, so I baked cakes constantly and had drinks to serve to all the people who came to meet Liat for the first time. It was the custom after the birth of a girl for people to just stop in and visit.

Steven didn't have a problem with having a baby sister. They got along quite well, and as she got a little older they played well together. Liat was very social and loved to play outside in the yard—she taught her brother how to play with the other kids. There were more arguments as they grew up. One day when she was around four years old, she cut the phone cord with scissors during a fight with Steven. And once they were fighting over who would open the door for me when I got home from work, and Liat fell over a drawer on the bottom of a bed. She was bleeding and needed stitches so I had to take her to the hospital. Her hair had to be shaved for the stitches. This was my welcome home after a long day at work.

When Steven was in kindergarten, I got a call from his teacher that he was injured on the playground. While the other children were going down the slide feet first, he went down the slide head first—only to be met with a rock. His forehead was cut. He had been taken to a doctor for stitches and I when I got home from work that day he said, "I was a hero. I didn't cry." To this day he has a scar on his forehead from where those stitches were.

Life went on with both Arie and me working long hours to make a living. Most of the workload was on my shoulders—not just overtime in the office, but also managing our household, which included shopping, cooking, checking the kids' homework, and doing laundry without a washer or dryer.

Steven was 8 and Liat was 5 when the youngest member joined our family—Anat, born on April 29, 1970.

I remember it was around the Passover holiday, and I was already extremely tired. I wanted to get the pregnancy over with and deliver the baby as soon as possible. That night I started to get contractions. I figured, this is the third child, so I stayed up late and fixed clothing and sandwiches for Steven and Liat for school the next day. I finally washed my hands at about 2:30 in the morning, and at 5:00 A.M. I said to Arie, "Let's go!" I called my mother and asked her to come be with the kids so I could go to the hospital, but she said "Wait!" I told her, "I *can't* wait!" So when we got to the hospital, a nurse told Arie to go back home to be with his children—there would be plenty of time before his next child would be born. The nurse got me to a bed, and as soon as I got on it I said, "I am having this baby now!"

I was yelling at the nurse who was now in a panic—she couldn't get the package of sterilized tools open. Anat was born at 5:50 A.M., but Arie was at home with the kids. He took them to school, then came back to the hospital to see his second daughter, who was also born with a lot of hair. Like Liat, she was also very beautiful and looked like a princess. Liat was very happy to have a sister.

By the time Anat came along, we were surrounded with many friends, some of them from our work. All three of our

children were born while I was employed with El Al Airlines. This time we decided to rent a hall and do the party in a more organized fashion. To rent a hall for the birth of a girl at that time was very unusual. So the owner of the banquet hall had to write in the papers that it was going to be a bris. It was funny, but much more comfortable for us than having to entertain people at our house—especially now that we had three kids.

Families always benefit when a sense of humor is shared. Arie was happy and loved to tell jokes and make the kids laugh. We loved standup comedy, and we really enjoyed it when the children did things that were funny. One time, Steven played in the muddy yard in his slippers and he was worried about what I would say when I got home from work. So he washed them and put them in the freezer to dry. I saw them when I went to cook dinner. He said that he put them in the freezer because he wanted them to dry faster! Steven used to catch cockroaches and put them in jars in the freezer. He told me that he needed them for biology class. And then Anat—I used to give her small gummy pills that had fish oil. She threw them behind her bed and the cleaning lady found them.

When Steven was 5 years old, he received a toolbox as a present. One day we came home from work and found that he'd made holes in the walls of the veranda with his tools. He said, "I got this as a present—I had to use it!" Steven's childhood was full of activities and hobbies—he would not stand still, running to everywhere he went. He also loved riding his racing bicycle and would travel as far as 20 miles to school. He enjoyed martial arts, playing the piano, painting, swimming, basketball, European handball, soccer, tennis, Ping-Pong, hiking, and camping.

Steven, Liat, and Anat Ringelstein, 1972

Liat was always looking for attention. We called her "the sandwich kid" because she was the middle child. So in class after the bell rang, she was always the last one to come to class. Her teacher called to tell me that she would come in last just to draw attention. She didn't care how she got attention.

Arie decided to take Anat to ride the train. It was very special since they always traveled by car. During the trip, Anat kept asking Arie if she could have chewing gum. Arie did not like to see people chewing gum and he wouldn't give her any. But she kept nagging so much that passengers nearby wanted to buy her some gum just to keep her quiet.

When we started our family, we didn't have goals—we were busy trying to make a living. It was on us to make sure that we had a good job, and that we earned enough to provide our children with the things *we* didn't have. Arie was insistent that his children not go to daycare. We hired a nanny to be at home with our children. We were going to make sure that our kids would not go through the war experiences and deficiencies we had been forced to experience growing up.

Children always change the rhythm of a marriage. After the

third baby and my three months of maternity leave, life for me was difficult. My job was never nine-to-five because it was an action-filled office—there was never a dull moment in El Al's Operation Division. Arie came home from work even later than I did. During those years, he was hardly involved in raising the kids. I went alone to teacher conferences, and it was not easy.

When Anat was 5, her and her brother and sister all decided they didn't like the nanny any more. Steven and Liat said that they would take turns taking Anat to kindergarten in the morning and picking her up in the afternoon, and they would manage on their own. Liat took charge of feeding Anat lunch and giving her a bath after returning from the kindergarten. We had a family meeting and decided to let them try it.

It only lasted one week.

Everything was fine when Liat picked up Anat from school and helped her with her homework—she helped her little sister a lot. But the problem was in the morning. Steven and Liat would fight over whose turn it was to take Anat to school. The end result was that I had to take her to school and I missed my bus. I had to fire the nanny, who lived in the same building as we did. Fortunately, it wasn't a problem because there were lots of other families who wanted to hire her. Again the burden fell on my shoulders, and I had to learn to cope with every change and situation that was created.

Looking back at the years since the birth of our children, I can see that most of my time was spent working in the office, working at home, and trying to give the kids some quality time as well. I had no time left for myself or for my hobbies or going out for a coffee with girlfriends or doing anything for my own benefit. Other than the hairdresser, I never went to have manicure or pedicure or a massage—this was totally out of my league.

I was constantly in service for somebody else, but this never crossed my mind at the time. I knew I had to make everything possible to run the family just like a business and to make sure everything ran like a Swiss clock. And I did.

Chapter 26
A Glass Half Full

Tension between a husband and wife is common during the time they are raising children, and this was the case with Arie and Rivka. The couple would argue about issues with the children, but they always stayed unanimous. When the children tried to play Arie and Rivka against each other, Rivka would not override Arie's decisions nor would he override hers.

But there was more to Arie's nature to describe his personality in contrast to Rivka's. He was a person of peace, and he was willing to pay any price for that peace. He didn't like to confront people and he never liked to say what he really thought. Rivka was the opposite. She would never let people walk all over her. While Arie would rarely scream, Rivka did not hesitate to scream. If Arie was screaming, you knew that it was the end of the world. He was a peacemaker with the motto of forgive and forget, but he was not able to really do that inside himself. He held his anger inside.

Still, Arie loved to be cheerful and happy and to tell jokes. He had a way of inspiring people to laugh. He would make Rivka laugh even when she was nervous. He always saw the glass as half full.

The Yom Kippur War caught Israel by surprise. Yom Kippur is the holiest holiday for the Jewish people. It's an atonement holiday where everyone prays to God to forgive his or her sins. In Israel, there were no cars on the streets—all was quiet. That is, until the phone rang in the Ringelstein home, and the caller told Rivka that Arie had to report immediately to his regiment. The army sent soldiers to all the synagogues to find anyone they could and tell them to report to their regiments so they could be immediately sent to the front. Word of mouth quickly passed on the street about the war that had broken out. Arie came home and Rivka told him that he was supposed to report to his unit, which he did immediately.

At that time, Golda Meir was the Prime Minister of Israel, and she acted immediately by calling Simcha Dinitz, the Israeli ambassador to the US. She asked him to call US Secretary of State Henry Kissinger and tell him to send arms to Israel immediately. It was three in the morning and Dinitz said it was too early to call Kissinger. Meir told him to wake up Kissinger, anyway—there was no time to waste.

Dinitz called Kissinger, but he was in no hurry to help. So Meir called Kissinger directly and told him that Israel needed ammunition and tanks *now*, not later—Israel's soldiers were being killed on the front line. She told Kissinger that if arms weren't sent immediately, she would order the use of Israel's nuclear weapons. Kissinger replied that first he was the Secretary of State, then he was an American, and then he was a Jew. Meir replied that this was fine, because in Hebrew, people read from right to left. This was her way of saying that first you are a Jew, then you are an American, and then you are the Secretary of State.

Rivka loved and admired Golda Meir—so much so that she highly recommends the theater play, *Golda's Balcony*, which is about her life and her role as Israeli Prime Minister during the Yom Kippur War of 1973. Rivka remembers the era well.

Rivka was working at El Al operations department at the time and witnessed from her office window in the operations department the airplanes coming into the airport one after another, offloading tanks, underwear, and supplies from the Americans. The workers at El Al called it an "air train" in Hebrew, because it was like a train coming into the station with each car full of every supply imaginable. Rivka was witnessing firsthand the historic Operation Nickel Grass, when the United States Air Force sent over 22,000 tons of supplies and war machinery in Lockheed C-141 Starlifter and C-5 Galaxy transport aircraft during October and November 1973.

All the operational and strategic meetings regarding El Al's service during the Yom Kippur War took place in the office where Rivka worked, which was the Operation Division of El Al. her boss, Ben Davidai, the vice president of operations, was conducting and coordinating the strategy meetings with the different authorities within the government and El Al who were involved in this operation. During the war, Rivka worked from 8:00 A.M. to midnight every day, and she drove home by herself with the lights of her car painted blue so they would not be noticed by foreign aircraft planning to bomb the airport. At midnight, Rivka's friend Etty Goldberg arrived at El Al to work from midnight until 8:00 A.M. This went on for six months.

At this time, Arie was on the front in Bir Gafgafa in the Sinai Desert. There was no long-distance telephone service at the time, even though the soldiers had some type of radio communication equipment. Rivka called Arie from El Al's office, and he (and his fellow soldiers) would always be surprised when he received a call from his wife while he was on the front! Rivka also used her connections with the El Al captains who were serving as reserve officers, flying military airplanes as pilots. They helped Rivka arrange to fly Arie home when he had some time off, giving him the opportunity to be with his family for a few hours before he had to return to the front.

CHAPTER 27
MY WORKING LIFE
(IN RIVKA'S OWN WORDS)

I started my career at El Al as a typist at about the same time as I married Arie. The president of the company was a brigadier general from the army and I worked in his office. In 1964 I moved to another office—that of the vice president of operations, Ben Davidai. I was a secretary for two other men besides Davidai: Eddie Lippa, who was the deputy vice president in charge of maintenance, and Captain Jones (from England) who was in charge of flight operations, pilots, and other crewmembers. It was a challenge to work for the three of them.

From 1964 to 1976, I saw El Al grow as my job and duties also expanded. My boss Ben Davidai was nominated to be the first vice president and vice president of operations. He had six or seven divisions under his supervision. My title did not change, but I kept taking on added responsibilities and an increased workload which I initiated, improved, and made more efficient. Eventually, I became the executive office manager. I had an assistant named Ety Goldberg.

When I worked at El Al after the office was re-organized, I would also take the minutes, which was protocol during the weekly meeting of the Head of Divisions, and follow up with them on the action items for which they were responsible. My boss was a person with vision—a fast thinker who spoke very fast as well. He liked things done as fast as yesterday, not today. People were normally unable to cope with his pace. Some would not dare to ask him questions—afraid of looking bad by not understanding what they were supposed to accomplish in their action items, considering the fact that their title was "Head of Division." They would rather make mistakes than dare to ask him what exactly he meant or what they needed to accomplish. To avoid that, after the meetings they would come to me asking when the minutes of the meeting would be ready so they could clarify their action items.

It was a challenge for me to work in that kind of environment, but I was strong, very efficient, time oriented, and I always initiated new work ideas to be implemented. When someone would raise their voice to me, I would react immediately, saying, "Excuse me, but I am not ready to accept that tone of voice," no matter what the person's rank was. I just knew how to stand up for myself.

Within the frame of my own work, I handled a lot of cases in my own way—independently. Almost every day I would get different requests for favors from high-ranking people. One high-ranking air force officer asked some favor for his wife, and I told him to consider it done. He then thanked me and came to visit me in the office. He wanted to tell me in person, "My door is open for you if you ever need something."

In one of the fables of Aesop, a mouse wakes a lion who rises with anger to kill the mouse. The mouse asks forgiveness and the lion sets him free. Later the lion is caught in a net and the mouse hears his distress, gnaws through the net and sets the lion free. The fable proves that an underling can accomplish a big task for a person of great power and that mercy is always rewarded. This is what happened a bit later.

Arie's cousin Shmuel Markowitz studied at the university to be a doctor, and due to his studies, his military service was postponed. When he finally joined the army, they wanted to relocate him in the south of the country from the center of the country to serve as a doctor in the military. However, in the meantime, he had also set up a business in his home to offer health services and didn't want to relocate. So I called the high-ranking air force officer and he returned the favor and arranged for the doctor to be stationed close to his home and business.

While working at El Al, the company began to buy new equipment from Boeing, and for that purpose El Al set up an office in Seattle. El Al sent people to supervise the manufacture of the planes to ensure that they would meet El Al's specifications. My work experience and organizational skills enabled me to develop excellent working relations with the top management of the Boeing Company. Whenever one or more of those high-ranking Boeing managers used to visit El Al in Tel Aviv, I was in charge of coordinating their meetings, seminars, hotel accommodations, and all the other arrangements.

The Boeing representative stationed in Rome, Mr. Hal

Young, came frequently to Tel Aviv for meetings in our office. He was also a close friend of my boss and knew me personally. He therefore recommended me to the rest of Boeing's management, telling them, "Whatever you need, Rivka will take care of it. Contact her directly."

In 1976, I left my job at El Al and took a few months off. I thought I would enjoy doing other things like going out for coffee with my friends. It was an interesting experiment because I found out that I did not enjoy the time away! My next job was with a small airline, Kanaf Arkia.

Kanaf had a fleet of small airplanes like the Islander and the Chieftain that flew domestically within Israel and to the Greek islands. My office was located in the back of an airplane hangar in Tel Aviv, and my duties consisted of ordering spare parts for the aircraft, and dealing with the customs broker to release and ship them to the company. In addition, I acted as the assistant to the manager in charge of the group of mechanics—handling their time cards, sick leave, vacations, and so forth, to report to the accounting department for their salary payments, as well as other related duties.

The situation changed when Kanaf bought Arkia to become Arkia Domestic Airlines. I was working with the vice president of marketing and operations, and eventually became the secretary of the board of directors. During that time, I decided to enrich my knowledge of the French language, and took classes at the French embassy in Tel Aviv. The purpose was to be able to communicate with the suppliers in their own language.

At a certain point of time in my life, I got the idea to leave that job and become a sales agent for different kinds of clothing merchandise. My friend Shoshi encouraged me, and we both decided to have fun and not sit in a cubicle from 9 to 5. It was during the month of November, and the sales agents had not booked any orders, so I took the merchandise collection in my car and drove around looking at storefronts to see which stores we should market the clothing to. After I identified some likely targets, I went in and started selling the clothes to these stores. Eventually I branched out into another type of collection that fit into a different type of store.

This job proved that I have sales power. Then a good friend of mine told me "What a waste—*you* selling clothes!" Even when I had the collections, I went to the manufacturers with cash and bought more clothing, cut out the labels, and sold the clothing to more stores. With the money I earned, I bought more clothes to sell! I think I drove my friends and cousins crazy with this business. One of my close friends said to me, "This job is not your caliber. I have a friend with a company who is looking for someone like you."

It was a company named Maxima that dealt with natural gas that had started up a facility to manufacture oxygen, nitrogen, and argon to sell to hospitals and to the military. When I went to the interview, I told the manager what my list of benefits was and how much I felt I was worth. The manager approved it and hired me immediately. I told him I wanted everything in writing. But, I was still very involved in the clothing business and had to tell the two companies that I worked for as a sales agent that I was going to quit.

This caused a problem. They did want to let go of me, and offered me even more money to stay. I stood firm. "You want my husband to divorce me?" I asked them. "He does not like me selling these clothes."

I went to work as the administrative assistant to the general manager of Maxima, and I was also in charge of the import of gases that were not manufactured in Israel. Maxima's plant was built by the Linde Group, a German company. We imported helium because they were not able to manufacture it in Israel. I was in charge of imports from Union Carbide in the US and other companies. I would take care of the calculations involved in those imports to make sure they were at good prices after determining the expenses incurred with customs and shipping, and how much margin could be made after selling to customers. If there were leaks, or if the quantities ordered didn't match what came in, I took care of it. I was in charge of approving the invoices to pay the suppliers. I would get bills and solve disputes. Companies would send containers with less gas (the gas would evaporate) but bill for the full amount.

In addition to working at my job, I took continuing education classes such as management, exporting, importing, and how to deal with the customs authorities. I had to work with the customs people to make sure that the containers we ordered got to the manufacturing facility in Mitzpe Ramon in the south of Israel on time so they could be delivered to customers on time.

Time was of the essence in this business. I had to argue a lot with the customs people to ensure quick and safe delivery of the goods. I reviewed every paragraph to know how they categorized the item so I could know how much customs tax to pay. It got to the point where the customs employees knew they couldn't mess with me. I would call them and say, "You have to get that container on the premises by tonight!" I was so strict with them, but they were familiar with my work ethic and the importance to have the container at the plant as soon as possible. I actually worked with the same customs broker earlier, during my job at Kanaf Arkia, and now I was dealing with them at Maxima as well.

At the same time as I worked for Maxima, I was working a second job with Arkia as the secretary of the board of directors. I worked at Maxima during the day, and the Arkia board of directors meetings—which took place mainly in the evening—I would take minutes and then do follow up with the people who needed to take action. I was a dedicated Maxima employee, working long hours and not going home before I made sure everything was in place and the urgent issues had been taken care of.

Maxima's chairman of the board was Maurice Kahn, an investor from France. The plant, which was in the south of the country at Mitzpe Ramon, created jobs for the locals, and that is how the company received benefits from the Israeli Government in the form of loans and favorable tax treatment. However, Mr. Kahn was not in the office most of the time due to his travel schedule. He knew who I was, but he didn't know exactly what I was doing. I got to the office by 8:30 or 9:00 in the morning, so people would see me when I came in, but I would stay until 8:00 or 9:00 at night just to make sure that everything was in place. I felt so responsible—as if it was my father's company!

Another employee was jealous of me. She told Mr. Kahn that I was never on time to work in the morning. At one point, Mr. Kahn called me to his office and started to complain about the fact that I was late arriving at the office in the morning. I was very upset and confronted him. I said Mr. Kahn, "I feel sorry for you that you have no clue what I am doing for this company, how much money I save the company. Nobody sees me when I go home so if it makes such a difference for you and it is so important to you that I come to the office on time in the morning and everything else has no value for you, then here is my resignation. I don't want to work one more day for you!"

When the managing director of the company heard this, he went ballistic. He said to me, "No! You are not leaving!"

But the damage had been done. A week later Mr. Kahn apologized to me, but I was determined to leave anyway and I soon resigned my position.

My next job was working as an office manager and sales and marketing for kibbutzim. Each kibbutz had a manufacturing facility for products such as tiles, shipping containers, or tape. A man named Ronnie Zimmerman had the contract to do their marketing. He was never in his office—he would do the travelling and delivery of the goods, and I was supposed to keep the business going. It was here that I experienced some office innovations.

It was new for me to type on an electric typewriter and then to use a computer. I had to take a class to learn to use the computer. I ran the business.

One time I got a call from a bank manager who wanted to speak to Ronnie. I told him that he wasn't there, but I could help. He was not ready to explain what he needed. He called several times, and my response was the same, "He is not in." One time I went to the bank to conduct some personal business. At that same moment, two of the El Al captains where there in the bank manager's office and they saw me. They said to the banker, "Do you know who this lady is? She worked for El Al and she had the position of the executive secretary of the vice president of operations."

Then, I said to the bank manager, "You call me all the time and want to talk to Ronnie. He's never there and you won't let me help you. If you want me to help you, come to my office and apologize to me, now that you heard about my experience and capabilities." The branch manager of the bank was really surprised and felt ashamed about the way he behaved toward me. He came to my office and apologized first before I helped him.

Working for Ronnie Zimmerman taught me that my integrity was too high to work in that kind of environment. It was in the hallmark year of 1987. I was fortunate that Maxima's managing director called and asked me to come back to the company to work for him. I went back to Maxima in 1988, and found that the company had changed after a shareholder had sold his shares, and a retired army officer had become the chairman of the board.

This time I stayed for only a year because Arie was already in Canada trying to get the papers for our immigration. In the meantime, Arie worked for his cousin, the eye doctor. This was the same cousin who, when he lived in Israel, I helped to get a better position in the army by using my connection with the high-ranking air force officer.

Eventually, one of my friends referred me to a company in the clothing business. They used to import unfinished clothing—meaning no zippers, buttons, and so forth—then complete them in Israel. This type of import created jobs for more people, and the company took advantage by getting special benefits and tax exemptions from the government. After the merchandise was ready, it was exported. Once again, my organizational skills and experience with import/export and customs brokers was used to my advantage.

I never wrote a resume. Every job I got was because somebody knew me and knew my capabilities. Once, while in between jobs, I got a call from a new company that was manufacturing computer technology for airplane cockpits. I was recommended to the president of this company by the vice president of Arkia, with whom I had previously worked. He knew my capabilities and experience with the top management of the Boeing Company, which was of great interest to this new company.

I was interviewed for the job by a man who was younger than me, and I ended up interviewing *him*! He was taken completely by surprise with my questions. The job required working hours from 2:00 P.M. to 8:00 P.M. because of the difference in time zones between Israel and the United States. Even though it seemed like a great opportunity, and a very tempting salary, I decided not to take the job. It would have required sacrificing my family and not being available for them, which was not acceptable to me. I then found another position with an electronics company, but I didn't like it and only stayed for six months.

      The point is that I always worked. I always had something to do. I was never out having coffee with friends or unemployed. This was the part of my life where I tried to make sure that Arie and I were doing our very best to provide for the kids.

Chapter 28
Finding Balance

From being an errand girl at a travel agency, to an entry level secretary at El Al Airlines, Rivka's career history tells the story of how she managed to balance career and family at a time in the history of the English-speaking world when women were at the threshold of a movement known as "women's liberation." It's important to note that what she actually experienced as a woman in Israel matched the ideals put forth by the liberation movement in the United States. While women in the United States were vocalizing about how they could and should simultaneously be on a career track and a mother, Rivka was living the experiment. The women's' libbers proposed equality between the sexes in areas of career and family but they did not address the sacrifices involved in such "equality."

The kind of strength it took Rivka to go through a typical day as a career woman with a full-time job in a high-profile industry—and as a mother of three, and a wife—exists only in the highest realms of human energy. Imagine Rivka during a typical day in the early 1970s:

5:30 A.M. Wake up

5:45 A.M. Cook the family lunch and dinner

6:00 A.M. Wake up children

6:15 A.M. Chores such as preparing lunches for the kids to take to school and cleaning up

6:30 A.M. Prepare the kids for school and dress for work

7:30 A.M. Leave for work

8:30 A.M. Arrive at office

Noon Lunch at office

5:30 P.M. Commute home

6:30 P.M. Stop at grocers for food

7:00 P.M. Arrive home, supervise children's homework, and clean up

8:30 P.M. Chores such as cleaning, doing laundry, preparing for next day

9:00 P.M. Prepare for bedtime, reading bedtime stories to the kids

10:00 P.M. Maybe some time to read or have a talk with Arie to see how his day went

11:00 P.M. Finish chores, laundry, set things up for next day

Midnight Sleep, five and a half hours

Normally, Rivka would get home at 7:00 P.M. from work. The Ringelstein family had purchased a washing machine after Anat was born, which was an improvement from the time Steven and Liat were raised without one, and in an era that did not offer disposable diapers.

Chapter 29
Bar and Bat Mitzvah Traditions
(In Rivka's Own Words)

Several memorable family trips were planned around the bar and bat mitzvahs of Steven, Liat, and Anat. In advance of Steven's bar mitzvah, I took a trip to France to buy a dress for the event. After the bar mitzvah ceremony, and the party at the banquet hall, we planned a trip to California for a tour of Disneyland, Sea World, and Universal Studios. Plans had to be changed, however, when Anat got sick with pneumonia just before the trip. While I stayed home with Liat and Anat, Steven and Arie went on the trip by themselves. They had a lot of fun and met new friends. It was a man's trip—no shopping, no women!

Steven experienced freedom with his father—they could do whatever they wanted. Nothing slowed them down. They were very efficient and they saw and did a lot.

As it turned out, there was to be a lot of travel in Steven's future. I arranged for some of this travel through my job and connections with Kanaf the airline. When Steven turned 15, he went to Greece for the first time on his own. The trip came about as the result of a friend Steven had made when on a previous vacation at a resort. Steven's new friend's dad was stationed in Greece working for Zim, an Israeli transportation company. He invited Steven to come back to Greece for a visit. Steven flew to the island Mikonos where he experienced nude beaches for the first time. When he returned home, the girls he met there kept calling him from all over the world. Mikonos became his favorite place through his teen years.

Steven was an independent individual from very young age. When he was 15 years of age, Steven started his first business—cleaning buildings and offices after school. At 16, after working there for a short time, Steven partnered with a catering company to manage the bar at exclusive parties. Soon after that, he started a music company and DJ team—organizing birthday parties, bar mitzvahs, weddings, and other special events. That business brought him a healthy income, and at age 17, he left home to live in a luxury penthouse with two other friends.

In addition to his own businesses, Steven had many summer jobs—working in construction, at a manufacturing factory for leather bags, and as a lifeguard at a local resort. In addition, he worked for the airlines—painting airplanes, working in the engine department for maintenance and repairs, avionics, and supply management. His passion for airplanes and flying started at an early age, and the only dream he had was to become a pilot.

At 16, Steven passed several of the Israeli Air Force tests, and at 18 he joined the IDF and was enrolled in pilot training. The pilot training didn't last very long because, a leader at heart, Steven had hard time following orders. He was reassigned to another school for electronic warfare and continued his service at the headquarters of the Israeli Air Force for a total of four years.

For Liat's bat mitzvah in 1977, we went to Walt Disney World in Florida, then on to Washington, D.C. to see the Smithsonian, the White House, and the Mint, and finally to London. This time, no one was sick and the entire family enjoyed the trip. The kids sat up at night watching TV at the Hilton Hotel in Washington D.C., which was very luxurious. They were tired in the mornings, but it was fun for them.

After Washington, D.C., we stayed in London at a place called the Swiss Cottage that was not at all a luxury—someone had to put money in the meter in the room to turn on the water to take a shower or to turn on the heater. We flew space available—as an airline employee, this was the rule—which meant that there wasn't a plane immediately available that all five of us could all fly on together. So we had to wait for a suitable flight, and we quickly tired of that hotel in London. By the time they found a spot on a plane for the five of us, we were thrilled to be out of London because it was cold and the hotel was awful.

At the time of Anat's bat mitzvah, I was working for Kanaf Arkia airline. I organized a group of family members, including a cousin who was ill, because I knew it would be my cousin's last trip before she would leave this world. I filled up a small Arkia airplane with relatives, including Arie's sister, and we all flew to Koss, a small island in Greece. We had a lot of fun, and since Anat would eat only very small meals, every place we went to eat the owners would say she could eat for free.

When Liat was 15 years old, Arie and I wanted to help her improve her ability to understand and speak English. So we decided to send her to Canada to stay with Arie's cousin Shmuel and his family in Toronto while Liat attended a summer course in English. Shmuel was a doctor who specialized in glaucoma of the eye, and he owned a few eye clinics. This is the same cousin I helped in Israel (using my connection with the high-ranking air force officer) to get assigned close to home while he served in the army. In this way he was able to maintain his clinic.

At the time, El Al Israel Airlines flew to Montreal, but not to Toronto. This meant that Liat would have to fly to Montreal-Mirabel International Airport, then get on a bus to a different airport in Montreal, where she would catch a Canadian Pacific Air Lines (CP Air) flight to Toronto. Although I provided Liat with some written instructions for navigating her journey, she impressed me with her ability to find her way through the maze of airports and bus lines.

While staying with Shmuel's family, Liat helped with their girls—including babysitting—and she rode the subway to school each day. The summer turned out to be an amazing experience for her. The truth is Liat always liked to experience new things, and even if she afraid or nervous she would still try them.

Before Steven joined the army in 1981, he and his dad took another "man's trip" to Germany, France, England, and Austria. Steven took ski lessons in Austria and he remembers that it was very cold, and that his ears froze. It was so cold that he was in pain—the coldest he ever felt. But while Steven was outside freezing his ears off, Arie was inside drinking hot tea. Arie took Steven to nightclubs, and they shopped for gifts for the family. While they were in France, they met my aunt Mitzi and her son George, and while in Germany they toured Munich.

Chapter 30
1987: A Year of Turning Points
(In Rivka's Own Words)

Some years get lodged in the collective memory of a family. The year 1987 was one of those years for the Ringelstein family. That summer, when Steven was living in New York, Arie, Liat, Anat, and I flew to meet him there, and then we all flew to Cancun, Mexico, to stay at Club Med. It was a wonderful week of togetherness, and when the week ended, Steven went home to New York and the girls went back to Israel. Arie and I returned to New York, and then took a flight to San Juan, Puerto Rico, and got on a Carnival cruise for a tour of the Virgin Islands, St. Maarten, Martinique, and Barbados.

One night at dinner, we heard the ship's purser singing "Hava Nagila." We told him, "You sang so well in Hebrew!" and he spoke to us in Hebrew! He asked us to send his love to his mother when we returned back home. I also discovered that Joni Meshulam, who years earlier used to work with me at El Al Israel Airlines in the maintenance department, and as a musician at night, over the years had become the vice president of Carnival Cruise Lines.

While we were on the cruise, my mother was not doing well, and I was anxious to get in touch with her. So I told the ship's officers that I knew Joni, and asked if I could go into the ship's operation room to place a call to my mother in Israel. They let me make the call and speak with her. It was an unusual thing to do, but not impossible. It was reassuring for me to be able to speak with my mother while Arie and I were on that trip.

Rivka and Arie on the Carnival Cruise Lines TSS Festivale, 1987

One day in 1987, Steven came up with the idea to take his 81-year-old grandfather Jacob on a trip to Disneyland. They went to all the parks and my father, ignoring his age, rode all the rides! He never had a childhood, and for him the trip to Disneyland meant a lifetime of fun since he was a workaholic and never knew what pleasures life could give a person.

After my dad returned from that trip, my mom had become very sick. The little bit of happiness he had experienced on that trip barely helped him get through the sadness of losing his wife—my mom—after 56 years of marriage. Steven says it was the most alive he had ever seen him. Says Steven, "He'd never known to fear the motion of a roller coaster so he had no idea what the ride was like. After he rode, his face was red and he said he'd had a great time from the adrenalin rush."

During this period in the history of our family, Arie worked in sales at Eitanit, a manufacturing company with a sales office in Tel Aviv. He lasted one year at this job. Unfortunately, Eitanit manufactured asbestos in Naharia in the north of Israel, and the news had just come out that asbestos caused lung cancer, causing the market for the company's products to collapse. This job with Eitanit marked the end of Arie's career history in Israel.

He moved to Canada by himself in 1987 and worked as an accountant for his cousin Shmuel.

CHAPTER 31
FAREWELL TO MY MOM
(IN RIVKA'S OWN WORDS)

Having a career keeps a person busy about eight hours a day. Yet in the hours beyond the office, the other events in life rise up, happen, and get handled. I was the one who took care of my mom through the time of her final illness. My mom had been sick for quite a while with various ailments. At the same time as my mom was terribly ill and in the hospital, Anat was preparing for her final exams in high school and Liat was preparing for her wedding. My mom liked Liat's fiancé Shlomo very much, and she was excited to attend the wedding and planned to do whatever it took to get there—coming directly to the wedding from her hospital bed if that's what it took. But, unfortunately, these plans did not work out. My mom got worse and passed away on December 14, 1987 at the age of 78.

The girls were understandably very busy with the events in their own lives, but I kept telling them "Grandma is really sick and you have to go see her." Sadly, on the day I finally brought both daughters to the hospital, my mother had passed away just a half-hour before we got there. Liat fainted—she loved her grandmother and was very connected to her. Anat was so busy with her studies that she felt guilty and sorry that she had not visited her grandmother earlier. I embraced my mother after she died. I kissed her. It broke my heart that she didn't live to attend Liat's wedding.

At this time, Steven was a student in New York City and he also felt very sorry that he couldn't see his grandmother before she passed. Because Arie was already living in Toronto at this time, he was unable to be with me during the time of my mother's death. He felt very bad about this. He loved her very much and wished he could have been at her bedside in her last minutes, and he was sorry that he was not able to attend her funeral. My mom was buried in Tel Aviv at Kyriat Shaul cemetery. In 2001, my dad was buried next to her in the plot they bought years earlier.

Once again I had to deal with the death of a close member of my family. It was very difficult for me to come to terms with my mom's death, and later on, with my Dad's death as well.

By that time, I had to make a switch in my life, with my husband in Canada waiting to get the immigration papers, and my daughter planning her wedding. It was sorrow mixed with happiness at the same time. I needed a lot of strength to get through all of that, so I pulled myself together and a few months later—at the beginning of 1988—I started to plan Liat's wedding.

CHAPTER 32
OUR CHILDREN
(IN RIVKA'S OWN WORDS)

At age 22, Steven left military service with the IDF to pursue private life. His dream was to move to the U.S. and become an entrepreneur. During the summer of 1985, at 23 years of age, Steven left Israel with $500 in his pocket and moved to New York City. At first, he stayed with friends of friends who offered him a place to stay. But soon he became homeless while working part time, changing jobs while taking intensive English classes to be able to start his university classes. By the end of the summer of 1985, Steven was accepted as a full-time student to the City University of New York and he found a job with the Israeli Ministry of Defense offices in New York City.

By 1990 Steven resigned his job and was almost done with his undergraduate degree when he moved to Scottsdale, Arizona to start a new life. He took another semester at Arizona State University and graduated that year. By that time, Steven had started up several companies, but he wanted to shift his professional life from the aerospace industry to something new. He decided to attend the Thunderbird School of Global Management and graduated with his MBA and MIM degrees at the beginning of 1994.

Steven was married from 1992 through 1997, but his passion for business and career proved to be greater than his marriage. He was sad to end his marriage, and has been single ever since.

From 1994 through 2003, Steven served as CEO for several companies—routinely working 100-hour weeks, with little personal time to enjoy life. In 2003, Steven realized that his happiness was more important than the pursuit of wealth, and so he shifted his life by designing it from scratch—in service of happiness. He also pursued advanced education in the healing arts where he learned more about massage therapy, Reiki, shamanic healing, and channeling.

Steven Ringelstein, 2005

In 2003, Steven founded The Business Gym LLC, a consulting firm that supports CEOs and leadership teams in Fortune 500 companies. Steven's firm helps them become high-performance teams and individuals by sharing his breakthrough ways to bring playfulness, fun, and spirituality to the workplace. He is a pioneer in bringing spirituality into the workplace. Steven does not shy away from sharing his spiritual gifts, intuition, and the ability to communicate with all life into corporate boardrooms and multinational leadership teams.

Steven is currently using a collective intention process to explore the inside of the global collective intelligence for possible new ecosystems to support the emergence of what's next and beyond. These practices led Steven to recently found another company—Intention Bubbles LLC—which promotes the power of the collective intention setting of humanity to co-create a better world. He is in the process of developing a smartphone app and writing a book on the topic.

Steven has committed his life to helping others and creating new ways for businesses to be self-managed, and allowing all players to be fully expressed and working at their full potential. His passion for life continues with traveling around the world, extreme sports, and lots of fun simply enjoying the presence. Steven is passionate about communicating with animals in the wild, and is also known among his friends as "Magic Man" for his ability to manifest what seems impossible.

The first addition of a son-in-law to our family was when Liat married Shlomo Alus. Shlomo lost his mom at the age of 14 and grew up with his sisters and father. He was born in Israel, but his family's roots were in the Jewish community in Iraq. Shlomo wanted to get an education so he could have a profession and to be able to provide for his wife and later on kids. He went to Technion—Israel Institute of Technology—in Haifa, which is one of the most highly regarded universities in Israel, and he graduated as an industrial management engineer.

Arie and I liked him because he had integrity as a person, showed responsibility, always knew how to honor and respect us, and he had good manners. He did not want to marry our daughter Liat before he would be able to provide for her.

A portion of his studies were paid for by scholarships, and a portion by his father's pension. Shlomo and Liat had dated for a period of six years, and Arie and I could see that it would take a long time for them to get married. We were very concerned he might not stick with his plan to marry Liat, because he might meet some other girls. Lea had never dated anyone else and she was devoted to him. So Arie and I decided to send Liat to New York City to stay with Steven to take English classes and see what would happen.

Liat stayed with Steven in his apartment in New York, and Steven was able to arrange a babysitting job for her with some friends. She ended up staying in New York for nine months. She was very independent, and Steven helped teach her to take responsibility for her life, and how to use the money she was earning to pay for food, clothes, and the other necessities of life.

The wedding of Liat Ringelstein and Shlomo Alus, 1988

In the meantime, Shlomo was very anxious for Liat to return to Israel, and he promised that as soon as he graduated, they would marry. Shlomo kept his promise, and on August 9, 1988, he and Liat were married. He quickly became an integral part of our family.

The wedding of Anat Ringelstein and Moti Markizano, 1990

    Anat, the baby of our family, grew up. She served in the military and then got married—following Arie and me to Canada. Anat met Moti Markizano when she was 17 and still in high school. They started to date. Moti was born in Israel. His family was of Greek origin, and he was the oldest of three children—he had a sister and brother. The couple dated for three years. By that time, Arie and I had decided to move to Canada, and Anat was in the documents to immigrate with us since she was still considered to be a minor.

    So Arie and I met with Moti's parents and told them that Moti and Anat had to make a decision about their future. In order for them to stay together, they would have to get married because of the fact that Anat would be getting her immigration papers in Canada. Moti's parents' response was, "He's too young." At the time, Anat was 20 and Moti was 23. Arie and I then told them, "We are not telling you what to do, but a decision has to be made." Moti could not come to Canada unless they got married. We were also anxious for Liat to move to Canada as well, however, her husband Shlomo was not yet ready to leave Israel.

      Anat and Moti were married in Israel on August 7, 1990. Two weeks after the ceremony, the happy couple moved to Toronto to live with us, with Anat sponsoring Moti after they arrived in Canada. Soon after that, Anat enrolled at York University, and Moti enrolled at Seneca College to study and to improve his English. He then continued his studies at York University and got his Bachelor in Economics. Anat took a major in Economics and then Business Administration. After that, she continued her studies and eventually became a CGA/CPA Certified General Accountant. Moti became an integral part of the Ringelstein family—we treated him as a son. It was difficult for him to leave his family in Israel, and it took him some time to adjust to life in Canada.

Chapter 33
Starting a New Life in Canada
(In Rivka's Own Words)

The year 1989 was another year of geographic transition for me as I followed my husband Arie west to Canada. But as I awaited the approval of my immigration papers, I was hired to work for an aerospace company in Cleveland, Ohio on a special contract for a short period of time. Arie continued to work as an accountant for his cousin Shmuel.

Arie and I maintained our long-distance marriage for two years. Every other week, I would fly to Toronto to visit Arie, and Arie would drive five and a half hours to Cleveland to be with me. This went on until 1991, when I was finally permitted to immigrate to Canada.

It takes a lot of energy to be able to absorb so much and to go through so many changes in life. Sometimes you get to a point where you get tired of starting all over again. This is what happened to Arie and me when we moved to Canada. We were already in our fifties, and to start life from scratch—from finding an apartment, to obtaining jobs, to building a new life in a new country—was like being born again. But since this was what we wanted, we had to try and make the best of it, and we did.

When Arie and I moved to Canada, it was difficult to find jobs. I went on a lot of interviews, and was told that I was overqualified, but the truth was that since they were not allowed to use your age to discriminate against you, they would come up with another excuse. The need to make a living brought us to the decision to open a restaurant. I knew how to cook, but I never thought it was going to be such a difficult job. The truth is that, once I went into that business, I very quickly understood just how difficult it could be.

The restaurant, Smart & Lazy, opened in 1991. It got its name from the letters of the first names of the family: Shlomo, Moti, Arie, Rebecca, T for Itay, Liat, Anat, Zvi (Steven), and the Y from the last letter of Itay, our first grandson at that time.

The business required a very full and tight schedule, which

meant getting up at 5:30 A.M., and going to purchase bread and buns at the bakery by 6:00 A.M. in order to get to the restaurant by 6:30 A.M. All the preparations for the menu had to be ready by 8:00 A.M., when the restaurant opened.

It was a small restaurant, and I cooked a variety of items from scratch, including baked muffins, fresh soups, and salads. I gave people samples of the dishes I made to taste—all kinds of dishes from recipes I made up in addition to the regular dishes, including potato latkes, veggie latkes, chicken schnitzel in a pita, and falafel. We served breakfast and lunch and closed at 6:00 P.M. Arie and I started with one location, and then decided to open another location at a food court in the Hillcrest Mall. Arie worked in the mall and I prepared the food for both stores. On Saturdays, the business was slower, so I used the time to prepare some items that took longer to be prepared, and to freeze them so I could use them during the week. I would stand and fry about 150 schnitzels in three separate pans, and then freeze them. Then I would fry 100 veggie and potato latkes and freeze those too. I was very creative and made up my recipes all by myself, using just my instincts and innovation.

The years working at Smart & Lazy were among the most difficult years of our lives. It was open for business every day of the week except for Sunday. The economy in Canada had slowed down and there was a deep recession. Many stores had closed down, and we were forced to close the store in the mall. In 1995, we were happy that we were able to sell the original restaurant and leave this painful experience behind us.

Arie and I then decided to sell our apartment in Israel so we could purchase one in Canada. It had to be renovated before it could be sold, and I stayed in Israel the entire time by myself, supervising the renovation and dealing with the real estate agents until the sale was finalized. That process took six months. When I returned to Toronto, we were able to purchase a condo apartment and move in. Living in a rented apartment was just a waste of money.

At the end of 1995, a friend offered me a job as a sales representative with a program in Canada known as the RESP, which stands for Registered Education Savings Plan. The plan was put into place by the Canadian federal government to encourage parents to save for their children's post-secondary education. In this plan, parents would set aside in savings some money on a monthly or annual basis—at that time, the maximum savings allowed was $2,000 per year and the federal government of Canada would contribute an additional 20 percent of their annual contributions as a grant. (Later on, the maximum savings amount was increased, and the government contribution also increased to between 20 to 40 percent, depending on the family annual income.)

I received my license to be a Registered Education Savings Plan sales representative, and I have held this position full time since 1995. The job includes booking my own appointments with prospective customers, driving to their homes, and performing a presentation of the plan offered. Eventually, if they sign up for the savings plan, I get paid on a one-time commission basis per customer.

Arie did the accounting and drove me to my appointments. He was able to work from home, which he enjoyed because he loved accounting and using the computer.

In the meantime, our son Steven introduced Arie to doing accounting using Quicken on a computer. My job was classified as an independent contractor, so Arie would do all the accounting for the household and then give the information to our CPA to file our taxes. The flexibility of working from home offered advantages in managing our time. Arie could help our daughter Anat with her kids, and over the years he was the one who picked up our grandchildren from school and daycare. I was the one who cooked for the grandchildren when Arie brought them to our home since their parents worked long hours.

Starting a new career was not easy for me, especially with me being in a new country at my age. It was a real challenge. I had no clue how I would fit into that kind of business since I had no connections with parents—my kids were grown up already. But once again I used my instincts, my intuition, and innovation to develop better sales skills and to excel at my job. I understood that it might be difficult, but not impossible, and today I am still capable of doing my job in a very professional way.

I loved my work and it gave me great satisfaction. I felt it was my mission to teach young parents to understand the importance of saving for their children's education and to build for them a better life and future. My greatest satisfaction after working at this job for nineteen years was when I received calls from parents who I met many years before, when their kids were born. These parents would thank me for offering them the savings plan, because when their kids were ready to go to college, they had the money saved to pay for it. The plan we offered allowed parents to decide how much they wanted to save.

In the beginning, any sales job requires developing a lot of connections and referrals, so I decided to join a networking group that is known around the world and operates in Canada as well. This group is known as BNI—Business Network International. It is the largest business networking organization in the world, and my membership in it has been extremely beneficial to my career.

CHAPTER 34
THE GRANDPARENTS' CLUB
(IN RIVKA'S OWN WORDS)

We were blessed to join the Grandparents' Club when Liat's first son, Itay, was born on August 20, 1990. We were very excited to join the exclusive club of grandparents. For the bris, according to Jewish tradition, the father of the wife is the godfather. But Shlomo's father was quite ill and Shlomo asked Arie if his father could be the godfather. Arie agreed.

Liat gave birth to our second grandchild, Dikla, on August 11, 1993, then Karin Pnina was born September 24, 1996, and Ram was born September 18, 1998.

Liat and Shlomo's children (left to right): Dikla, Karin, Ram, and Itay, 2011

Moti and Anat became parents for the first time in 1994 when their son Leeran was born on March 22. Matan-Matthew, their second son, was born May 20, 1999, and their daughter Maytal Rita was born November 7, 2002.

Anat and Moti's children (left to right) Maytal, Leeran, and Matan, 2011

Anat's move to Canada, and the subsequent help she enjoyed being close to Arie and me, caused quite a rift between the sisters. Liat was raising four children in Israel, and because her husband's parents had passed away, she did not have much help or support. This rift lasted quite some time, but the sisters were able to make amends just prior to Arie's passing and to give him a few days of life in which his vision of oneness in the family and unconditional love and acceptance came true.

Arie came up with a nice idea that that for every grandchild reaching the age of bar or bat mitzvah, we would grant them as a special present a trip to Disneyland, Universal Studios, and Sea World, and to turn it into a family tradition. This would be the best possible quality time we could give to our grandchildren to remember for a lifetime.

The grandchildren in Canada (Anat's kids) naturally got more quality time than the ones in Israel due of the geographical situation, however, all were loved equally. Each grandchild has his or her own personality and gifts, but they are all a great gift to us as their grandparents.

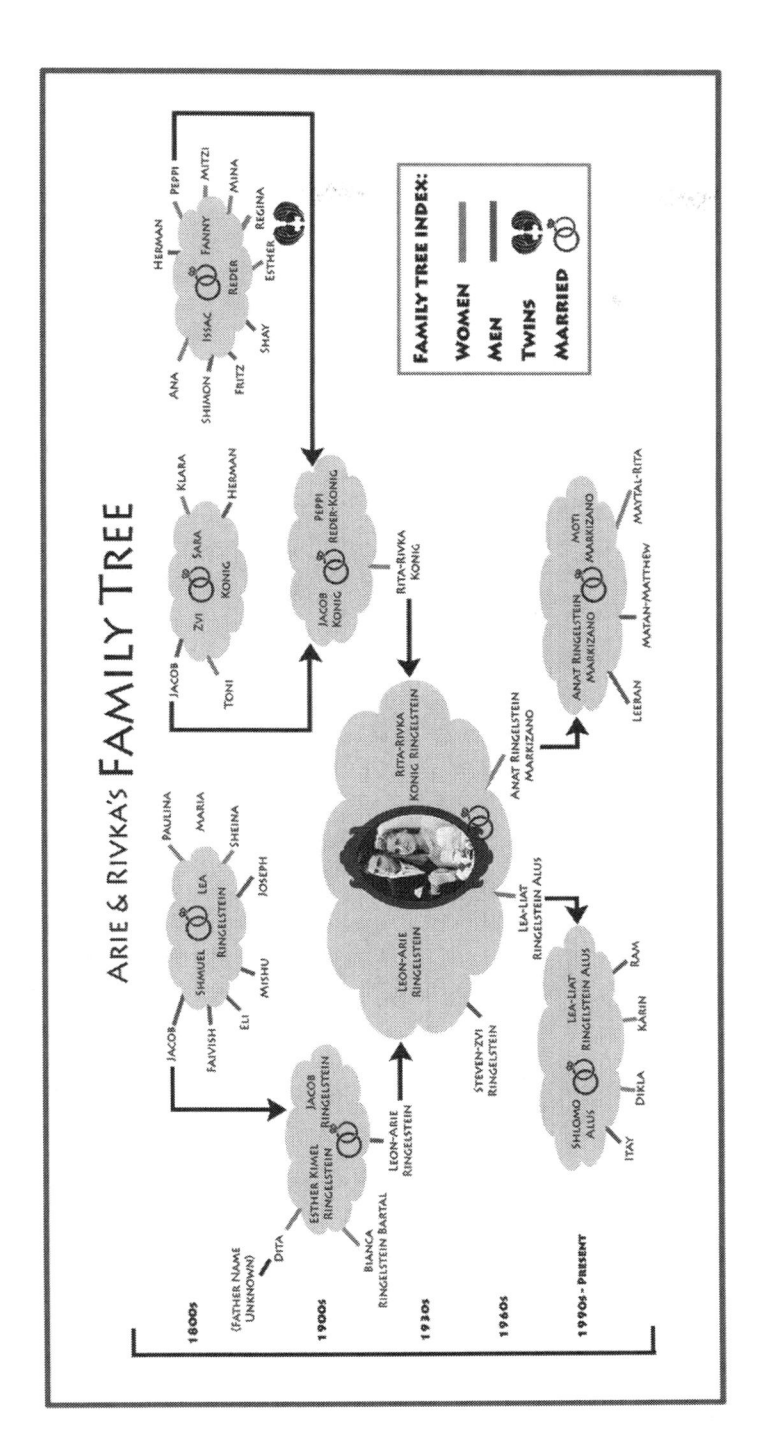

Arie & Rivka's Family Tree

1800s
(Father Name Unknown) — Dita

1900s
Esther Kimel Ringelstein ⚭ Jacob Ringelstein
- Bianca Ringelstein Bartal
- Shmuel Ringelstein ⚭ Lea Ringelstein
  - Faivish
  - Eli
  - Mishu
  - Joseph
  - Sheina
  - Maria
  - Paulina
- Leon-Arie Ringelstein
- Zvi Konig ⚭ Sara Konig
  - Jacob
  - Toni
  - Klara
  - Herman
- Jacob Konig ⚭ Peppi Reder-Konig
  - Rita-Rivka Konig
- Herman, Peppi, Mitzi, Mina, Regina, Esther, Fanny Reder, Issac, Shimon, Ana, Fritz, Shay

1930s
Leon-Arie Ringelstein ⚭ Rita-Rivka Konig Ringelstein

1960s
- Steven-Zvi Ringelstein
- Anat Ringelstein Markizano ⚭ Moti Markizano
  - Leeran
  - Matan-Matthew
  - Maytal-Rita
- Lea-Liat Ringelstein Alus

1990s – Present
Shlomo Alus ⚭ Lea-Liat Ringelstein Alus
- Itay
- Dikla
- Karin
- Ram

FAMILY TREE INDEX:
- WOMEN
- MEN
- TWINS
- MARRIED

Arie and Rivka's Family Tree (1800s to Present).
Please visit www.arierivka.com for detailed color family tree.

Graphic by Jamie Dickerson.

Chapter 35
Honoring My Father
(In Rivka's Own Words)

After my mother passed away, my father was diagnosed with colon cancer in 1989, and he continued to live in Ramat Gan. At that time, I was already working in the US and Arie was in Canada. After the diagnosis, my father was operated on, and the doctors removed his cancer without the need for chemotherapy or radiation. But, he was overweight and the stitches opened, requiring him to have another surgery. This time he got worse and had to be in the ICU since he had been a heavy smoker in his youth and also suffered emphysema. After the second surgery, he was very sick and on a respirator. The doctors gave up on him and even the nurses didn't take good care of him because they thought he was dying. He was almost dead and not one person believed he would make it.

I was extremely upset about this set of circumstances. Arie and I decided to take care of him personally every day, and at night we hired a nurse to watch him. I argued with the doctors and nurses and gave them hell—I could not believe how badly they treated my father. I told the doctors that they should be ashamed of themselves—they must have forgotten what their doctor's oath meant, to save lives and not let people die.

It was really a miracle that my father overcame all of that at the age of 89, and he did pull through, even though he also developed bedsores due to being hospitalized for eight months. He got rehab and started like a newborn baby to learn to walk. He showed so much strength. All the doctors came to witness the miracle—they even brought the professor of the department involved to study his case.

I received a lot of help from my daughter Liat and her husband Shlomo during the time my father was hospitalized, as well as from my daughter Anat and her boyfriend at the time—soon to become her husband—Moti. They all kept coming to visit and buy my father food and stuff he liked since the food in the hospital was quite bad.

After my father was discharged from the hospital, he came to Anat's wedding in 1990 and by then he was doing much better.

He came to live with me and Arie in Canada in 1997. Although he had beaten the colon cancer, by then he'd gotten bladder cancer. He passed away in January 2001, at the age of 94 years.

What I went through with my father during this illness was yet another test of my strength. I remembered this struggle with my father during the time of my own husband's illness. My father had been so strong to pull through the first round of cancer. I saw him beat it, and later, when Arie became ill, I used to tell myself that if my father could survive, then Arie could be strong and do the same.

That, of course, remained to be seen.

Chapter 36
Emergency!
(In Rivka's Own Words)

Arie suffered from back pain throughout his life, and problems due to an enlarged prostate starting at the age of 50. The Canadian doctors wanted him to have surgery, but I wouldn't let him. In Israel, people with prostate problems get surgery right away with a laser or some other up-to-date technique. It is done in one day so the patient does not have to endure traditional surgery with a long recovery, as it was done in Canada at the time.

After the death of my father, we flew his coffin to Israel. It was at that time that Arie had a serious medical crisis. Right after sitting shiva for my dad, we were still in Israel. Arie couldn't urinate, and he didn't tell me until it became a serious medical emergency. I drove him to the emergency room, which luckily wasn't overcrowded. They were able to take him right away and insert a catheter. Due to the fact that he did not urinate almost the entire day, he had accumulated a huge amount of urine. This in turn caused his blood pressure to go up to 220 by the time we arrived at the hospital. If we had waited a little bit longer, he could have died.

During the time he was in the hospital, the doctors asked him why he wouldn't have surgery for his prostate. We explained that Arie was not ready for surgery because we were scheduled to fly back home to Toronto soon. The 12-hour flight would be challenging with a catheter, but no other choice was available. Before we left Israel, I called Anat in Toronto and asked her to schedule an appointment with Arie's urologist so he could check Arie out and hopefully remove his catheter.

The Air Canada hostess was an Israeli who lived in our building. I confided in her about Arie's situation, and she did her best to make Arie comfortable. The 12-hour flight was very difficult, and as soon as we landed we went straight to the hospital to meet my husband's urologist who immediately removed the catheter. Arie continued to take his medication and went for check-ups regularly to maintain his prostate health. The urologist felt that if he could be treated with medication, no surgery would be needed.

Living with someone who experiences frequent pain is not easy to witness. Arie lived for 18 years with an enlarged prostate. He also suffered terrible back pain due to the fact that his spine was deteriorating and he had arthritis in his bones. He went to chiropractors and used special equipment, but nothing worked and his pain continued to worsen over time. Regardless, Arie never focused on his health problems. He had a remarkable ability to accept life as it was, and to tolerate pain and still smile.

Chapter 37
Arie's 70th Birthday
(In Rivka's Own Words)

In September 2004, we went to Israel for Rosh Hashanah to be with our daughter Liat and her family. Before that trip, I booked a banquet hall to host a surprise party for Arie's seventieth birthday. I invited all our friends, plus Arie's cousin Shmuel, his sister Bianca, and her husband Simon.

I invited about 40 people, plus at that time Moti's grandparents were visiting from Israel and they decided to extend their stay until after the party. I made arrangements with Steven to come to Toronto and for Moti to pick him up from the airport one day earlier. He would sleep overnight at Anat's house and I made sure the grandkids didn't give out the secret.

The following Friday evening was set—it was earlier than Arie's official birthday, so that he would not be suspicious. I ordered a special cake from a bakery that my friend Etty picked up for me and brought to the banquet hall. I made sure everything was being taken care of carefully to make it as a total surprise. I told Arie that he did not have to pick up the grandchildren from daycare and school that Friday, since Anat was going to get them.

I suggested to Arie that, since Moti's grandparents were in Toronto, we should go out and meet with them at an Israeli restaurant named Hava Nagila, which was also a banquet hall and served Middle Eastern and Israeli food. Arie agreed. He asked me how to dress, and I said, "Well you better be in a nice suit." When Arie asked me what Steven's plans were that same weekend, I told him that he went with friends to the lake to go camping.

I constantly kept in touch with Anat to make sure that everyone had arrived at the banquet hall. As it turned out, the party venue was shared with another Jewish couple who were celebrating their engagement. Arie's party occupied four tables of 10 people each, and I hired an Israeli singer, a friend whom I knew very well, to sing and entertain, along with a live orchestra.

As soon as we arrived and stepped into the banquet hall, the orchestra started to play the "Happy Birthday" song for Arie, and he was so confused he had no clue what is really going on. Then he saw his family members and friends, and the biggest surprise was when Steven came out to hug him. He was so excited that he had tears of joy in his eyes—he never dreamed of having such a wonderful surprise. I wrote a rhyming poem in Hebrew to honor Arie, which made him both emotional and excited. Liat called him on the phone from Israel.

The party was a huge success. My friend, Polly, gave Arie a present in the form of a belly dancing show. The music and the Israeli songs and dances helped to make everyone so happy, and it turned out to be an unforgettable evening for years to come. Our friend Itzik Cohen videotaped the birthday party, and we sent a copy to Israel for our daughter and the family there to watch.

Chapter 38
Arie's Health Takes a Surprising Turn for the Worse
(In Rivka's Own Words)

During the course of a routine exam, Arie's doctor discovered that he had an iron deficiency. He was given medication, but the doctor also recommended a colonoscopy—Arie had never had one. We were visiting Arizona and our world at that time was so perfect! We always had good times with our son Steven during our once-a-year visits with him in Arizona. We worked out in the gym and danced twice a week. We spent a good amount of time with Steven and we were so appreciative that we had each other. We experienced the heaven here on earth.

When we returned to Toronto, I called a private lab to make the colonoscopy appointment. The receptionist gave me lots of dates to choose from—I don't know why or how, but for every date she gave me, I said no. First there was Passover, then the Passover Seder, and then Anat was visiting Steven. I had the intuition that I did not want Arie to go in for the colonoscopy until after Anat returned home. Then the receptionist offered the date April 21, and I said yes.

When we arrived for the colonoscopy, the doctor asked us why Arie was there, and Arie told him about his iron deficiency. The doctor said that he would do the colonoscopy, and if nothing was found, he would perform a gastroscopy to check his stomach. Arie was wheeled in for the procedure. The wait was long and difficult and when the doctor showed up he said, "I don't have good news."

My heart started to pound as the doctor showed us a photo of an open and bleeding wound in Arie's stomach. The doctor said right away, "It's cancer, Mrs. Ringelstein, you are not going home now—you are going to take him straight to the hospital and Dr. Klein is waiting for you there." I pulled myself together and drove like a robot to the hospital with only my instinct getting me there. I was hallucinating, thinking, "This is not happening, this is not happening." I called the children to let them know the bad news. Steven's reaction was very strange—it was as if he already knew.

Anat visited him in Arizona, Steven had told her that he didn't know how he knew it, but that he just knew Arie didn't have much longer to live. He did not tell me that back then.

There was more waiting at the hospital, then finally Dr. Klein told me, "We are going to do a blood test and a CT scan." It turned out that Arie needed surgery and Dr. Klein would be the surgeon. He was one of very few surgeons in Toronto who did non-invasive stomach surgeries. He explained to Arie and me how he was going to do the procedure, telling us, "I am going to do it the Japanese way. The Japanese have the highest rate of stomach cancer in the world due to the food they eat and the spices they use." The procedure he was going to use would take a greater circle around the margins of the site of the cancer to make sure it would not spread to other organs, and Dr. Klein said he was consulting with another oncologist from Ireland.

The surgery was to take place at Humber River Regional Hospital in Toronto. However, the first step was for Arie to start nine weeks of chemotherapy to shrink the tumor. Then Dr. Klein would be able to perform the surgery.

Some friends of Steven introduced the family to Marcia K. Horn, president and CEO of ICAN, the International Cancer Advocacy Network. Steven made a donation and found assistance and support for Arie and me. Ms. Horn lost her husband to cancer while raising a young child so she dedicated her life to helping people who were battling cancer.

Marcia was another wife who got the message out of the blue that her husband had cancer. It's hard to understand what's happening and you feel so lost during something like this. She actually sent me a whole list of questions to take into our meeting with the oncologist and had also researched Arie's oncologist to make sure he was good. Once the doctors went over the diagnosis, I was very connected to Marcia. She coached me on what to say to Arie's doctors—things like, "Bear with me and explain this to me like I am a little child. Don't give me big medical words because I won't know what they mean." The doctor would answer all my questions and was very nice and then I would email all the information back to Marcia.

After talking with Dr. Klein, and based on results of the CT scan, they decided that Arie had to start chemotherapy to shrink the tumor because the surgery could not be performed until the tumor had shrunk. The surgery normally would take a few hours, with five days to recover, but there could be complications.

Dr. Klein explained what the surgical procedure included, and how it was going to be performed. They would first remove the stomach, and then connect the esophagus to the small intestine. The doctor explained that there was a 35 percent chance of a leak—in other words, complications. At this point, we weren't thinking—and the doctors didn't warn us—about what Arie's body would be like after nine weeks of chemotherapy. We didn't think to ask what the surgery would be like for him after the chemotherapy treatment to shrink the tumor. The only thing I was thinking was, "How can my husband's life be saved?"

Some people turn their illness into a positive. Arie seemed to use his diagnosis as a catalyst to step into his spirituality. As soon as Arie was diagnosed, he started to meditate and understand things like never before. He was talking to the spirits of his parents and his aunts, and writing about his deeper understanding of life through meditation. I kept asking him, "Are you sure you want to do the surgery? It is so complicated." Being the dominant person in our marriage, I was so skeptical and wanted to convince Arie not to get the surgery considering the risks involved.

Because of my experience taking care of my mother and father, I wanted a second opinion. After I met with Dr. Klein the first time, I told him, "I don't want to offend you, but I always like to have a second opinion." And I told him the story about my mom, when she had a wound on her foot that wouldn't heal and went to one of the largest hospitals, and the manager of the department—who was a surgeon—told her that her foot would have to be amputated. I heard that and said, "We need a second opinion from a doctor who is an expert in blood vessels." I found a blood-vessel specialist and he ended up doing bypass surgery on her foot and everything turned out fine—no amputation needed. It was the same with my dad—he had cancer and I got a second opinion.

Dr. Klein gave me permission to get a second opinion, so I said to Arie, "Meditate and ask yourself if you are sure you want Dr. Klein to perform the surgery." He did as I asked, and said he was sure about Dr. Klein. So against my rules and reservations, we didn't go for a second opinion because Arie told me, "Through meditation I have come to understand that Dr. Klein is going to be my angel and he is going to take good care of me."

During all of Arie's meditations, he kept telling me that he was talking to the spirits of his parents and grandparents, and they told him that at the time they died there were no medications, and that he was lucky that today medicine is so developed and that it could save his life. Arie's grandfather died of an infection of the prostate because he did not have the proper medication. In one meditation, his grandfather—who had been distant from Arie during his childhood, completely the opposite of Arie's grandmother who took care of him—came to apologize to Arie for passing on the prostate problem to him. In another meditation, Arie asked what would happen if he did or did not have treatment. Arie's decisions were based on his meditations, so I lost control. I am a very controlling and dominating person, and I made a lot of the decisions in our marriage. But this time I let him make the decisions. Steven kept telling me, "Leave him alone and let him follow his own guidance." I couldn't fight it.

The oncologist decided that nine weeks of chemotherapy were required to shrink the tumor to a sufficient degree to conduct the surgery. Every three weeks, we spent a day in the hospital for chemotherapy, and at home Arie had to swallow additional chemotherapy medication daily. In Canada, medications are free for seniors, but I had to pay for Arie's oral medication.

During this whole process, I was reporting back to Marcia Horn by email what was happening because I was looking for help for Arie in every way possible. Marcia helped me understand the doctors' recommendations, and she supported the chemotherapy. But I was still uncertain.

I had heard about a rabbi in Israel who was known for helping people with cancer, and his advice was found to be 98 percent accurate. So I faxed everything to my son-in-law, Shlomo in Israel and asked him to contact the rabbi. The rabbi was very busy and hard to contact, so I asked Shlomo to help. I had to do everything possible in good conscience. Shlomo sent Arie's information to the rabbi and talked to him and asked, "Is this the right thing to do for Arie?" The rabbi replied to Shlomo, "This is a very aggressive treatment, but it is okay and Arie should start the treatment."

Finally, during the course of his meditations, Arie communicated with his parents, and they also agreed that chemotherapy was the right course of action.

Arie's chemotherapy started on May 20, 2009, on our grandson Matan's Birthday. The chemo went well, and Arie didn't suffer many side effects other than weakness. He received medication to control nausea and he didn't lose much of his hair. Every day I cooked and made Arie dishes that were nutritious and had lots of vitamins. I watched him like I would watch a little child to make sure that he was eating and sleeping. It was a very challenging time. I hired two different ladies who were doing work with energy because Steven had suggested I look into that. They were moving energy within Arie body during his chemotherapy so the medication would be absorbed easier and help Arie heal faster.

One lady told me that twice a day, when he took his medication, I should touch certain points on his body for 10 to 15 minutes in order to move the energy. She told me that when the energy was working, I would be able to hear noises in his stomach. When the chi energy of the body is moving, you can feel it in the practitioner's body too.

I watched Arie closely and wouldn't allow him to go into public places for fear he would catch a cold since his immune system was in a weakened state. I had to take him to the lab every week to have his blood work done to test his hemoglobin and other levels. I would ask for the test results—I always demanded all the information I could get. The medical personnel got to know me, and I made sure they brought me the test results each time. I was just like a project manager taking care of everything. I faxed everything to Marcia, and she told me what looked okay or not, and she answered my questions.

Chapter 39
A 50ᵗʰ Wedding Anniversary
(In Rivka's Own Words)

During Arie's chemotherapy, he decided he needed to speak with the grandchildren. He told them about his illness and said, "I may not be able to hug you because I am not allowed. My immune system is getting weak." He started chemo on May 20, and he continued with this course of medication for nine weeks, until the end of July. He was supposed to finish earlier, but one time his blood chemistry was not at the right level, so he had to continue. This overlapped with our fiftieth anniversary plans.

On July 8, 2009, we were supposed to have our fiftieth wedding anniversary party. Every Friday we would go to our daughter Anat's home for Shabbat dinner with Anat, Moti, and the kids. In order for me not to get suspicious, Anat got all the email addresses from our computer—along with our photos—and she and Moti called and organized an early surprise party for our fiftieth anniversary. Arie had prepared a greeting card with a story about this anniversary that he wrote for me for that purpose. He did not know, however, that there would be a surprise party, and it was a total surprise for me as well. It is not so easy to surprise me, since I always use my premonitions.

Here is the greeting letter Arie wrote to me:

> *To Rita, my loving and wonderful wife,*
>
> *Congratulations on our 50ᵗʰ anniversary today! Indeed this is a long way that we have succeeded to pass together, through all the obstacles of life, and to stay united around the ball of love which helped us on our path of life.*
>
> *Many people throughout different generations have tried to define, "What is love?"*
>
> *Some of them said, "It's a sexual attraction, which in time fades and then love ends."*
>
> *Some said, "This is a mutual interest in communal*

subjects."

Some said, "This is actually because of the opposites of character."

Some said, "It is kind of a compromise."

Some said, "It's a different level of education."

Others claim, "There are a lot of theories, as many as the number of people living in the world."

I see our love as an energy ball that came out of a supernatural power of divine energy as a mission on Earth. Inside the body of a human being, the spirit and soul are the energy that are supposed to guard the body, to navigate me in order to experience the test of life and physical conditions of the human body.

This ball is built like any other star in the universe, with one pole plus and the other pole a minus. On the one hand, the opposites between the sides, the minus and the plus, keep the equilibrium and balance of the ball together on the path of life.

I arrived to Earth five years before you. But both of us have felt the special experience, to enter into a physical body without any knowledge, without knowing in the beginning how to use our wonderful bodies and how to benefit and enjoy all the things on the path of life.

It's true that we received a very sophisticated body with genes from our parents, with full support until we reached a status where we are able to navigate our own way. In time, getting older, conditions have been created where it doesn't matter the distance of the different families. We still were able to find each other and to unite again to that ball of love that went on its way supported by the Divine who is the original creator of love.

From the moment we met and knew each other, until we got married on July 8, 1959, we understood that we belonged one to the other. Without even knowing how, we became united to that ball of energy which is the ball of love.

On the one hand, the two poles of the plus and the minus, with excitement, emotions, and sex life, dissolve and feel like one body. On the other hand, on a daily basis we come across obstacles, difficulties and opposites. This creates distance and we are separated from the love of the Divine, like the side of the globe that recedes from the sun and the cold that is in that area.

Now comes the miracle. Our first angel, our son Steven, was born to us and brought new happiness into our lives, new energy to remind us where we come from. Only with mutual assistance, we are able to overcome obstacles and to stay alive on the globe of love, which continues to lead us easily on the path of life.

I remember picking up Steven, he was so little and scrawny and he looked just like the other babies. So I picked up another baby, and only after you started to scream at me, "This is not our son!" did I pick up Steven. By then I was already confused.

After him came the second angel, our daughter Liat, with a head so full of black hair that she could already be going to the hairdresser. You couldn't miss it, her smile was so warm and it filled our heart with love. Again we got closer to the energy of the love of the Divine.

Our third angel was in the form of our daughter Anat, with a sweet smile that again brought us a lot of love and new energy.

The kids grew up, matured, and started to find their way in life. We started to feel again the imbalance, wasting energy on unimportant things with our arguments. This is probably the way of most people's lives.

Now, again, here arrive four new angels, grandchildren from Liat, and three angels, grandchildren from Anat. They are the new re-charging of our love energy. We are excited and our hearts are filled with love.

Our son Steven didn't bring us angels in the form of

grandchildren, but look at the miracle where he himself reached the level of being able to communicate with the supernatural and to fill himself with love and to send us that energy of love to re-charge ourselves. We are getting older but we still have patience to wait for another angel from Steven and more angels of great grandchildren.

I will end with the story that I keep telling…that as long as our ball of love will exist, we will continue passionately, with the passion within us to be sexy Grandma and Grandpa, so that the great grandchildren will continue to come.

Love you now and now is not a time but an eternity of kisses,

Arie

Anat didn't say anything about the surprise. It turns out that it was Moti's idea to have the party at their home—and I didn't think anyone was coming for the Shabbat dinner. Our grandson Leeran came to our house and kept us busy until Anat and Moti completed the arrangements for the party. Neither Arie nor I had any clue that something was going on. Then Leeran said, "Can you take me home, since we are all going anyway for the Shabbat dinner? I said, "Okay," and because I didn't know a thing, I was dressed very simply. Arie loved going to Shabbat dinner with the grandchildren—he would go to the backyard and enjoy the green grass and sitting on the swing, and talking to the grandchildren or meditating a little until food was served.

This time it was different.

As soon as we arrived at Anat and Moti's home, Arie was quickly on his way out to the backyard. But this time Anat made sure that none of their friends' cars were parked nearby—she knew I would remember the license plates of their cars. Anat made sure everything was perfect for the surprise.

Arie and Rivka's 50th Anniversary, 2009

Anat was in touch with Steven by cell phone. When we walked into the house, we couldn't believe it when we saw that all of our friends were already there and waiting for us to celebrate our fiftieth anniversary. It was a great surprise!

It was the first time in my life that I could remember being surprised in this way. I told Anat, "You could have said that at least some other people would be at your house. I would have dressed better!" Arie was so surprised and so happy—it was a very emotional experience for everyone who was there to share this very special occasion with us.

CHAPTER 40
LETTERS OF LOVE

Once it became clear that Arie was going to go forward with the surgery, each member of his family wrote love letters to him that would be read aloud in his presence. The idea was to set an intention for Arie to gain the inner strength required for him to be well again. It also reflected a refusal to believe that Arie was too sick to be helped, or that he might pass away.

These love letters reflected the power of togetherness that united the entire family to focus on one thing: Arie's healing. Arie had a hard time accepting love from others, and hearing the content of these letters read to him was the first time he opened himself up to receiving love. He realized that people actually loved and cared for him deeply.

My Dream Husband (by Rivka)

I met my dream husband when I was 18 years old and he was 23 years old. We started dating and we knew just a short while later that we were soul mates and that our hearts had been connected with a special bond. We knew we would get married and have a wonderful family.

We got married one and a half years later in 1959, surrounded with love and affection. As of that moment, harmony started to take charge in our life.

Our children were born. First Steven. This was a very exciting moment for us, to become a first time mom and a first-time dad. Three years later Liat was born, again joy came into our life. Five years later Anat was born, another bundle of joy for our family.

My dream husband always makes sure that we were happy, no matter in what direction life took us. Of course, the main concern was lifestyle and the cost of living and to be able to give our children the best. It was very important for us that our kids would not have to encounter in their life any of the difficulties that we had been through.

My dream husband always makes sure that we look forward with the utmost positive attitude towards anything in life.

My dream husband is my best friend. We share our love to each other and a lifetime of experience, solving problems, keeping the family together, loving our children, sons-in-law and all the grandchildren that God blessed us with. Every child and grandchild, and of course our two sons-in-law, is an integral part of our wonderful family.

I dream of celebrating our 50th anniversary and our milestone birthdays.

I dream of spending the rest of our lives together; doing things together, going places, enjoying nature with our children, sons-in-law and grandchildren.

My dream husband always knows how to cheer me up, especially on a cloudy or rainy day. He always says, "Remember the sun always shines beyond the clouds."

Also I feel even when the rain is falling like it is today, that we are showered with blessings and love from a supernatural power above. Every drop of rain has love in it, and the more the drops fall down the more love they bring to us. It seems unstoppable.

It is just like an ocean of love, that every wave brings more and more blessings and love into our hearts. Every wave is a new wave that was not here before, and so is every drop of rain. Once the drop gets to the ground it gets absorbed into the earth, but then some new raindrops are following and they are newcomers. They also are anxious to participate in that party of love showered over our whole family.

I know that my dream husband is strong and confident that he will be able to beat anything and to be with us for many more years of pleasure and joy.

My dream husband has a history of survival, since he was a child. Unfortunately he did not have a childhood period in his life, losing his parents while being so young, having to spend his life in an orphanage, going through the Holocaust. Then joining the army in Israel and fighting on the front in four wars. Now you understand how strong he is, and how every test that life presented to him made him stronger.

The test that life presented to him now is his health condition. I am more than confident and so is he that he can pass that test as well, as he did before, because he knows he has still so many projects to complete. He has to finish his book that he started to write about his life. Also, he will enjoy the bar mitzvah of our grandchildren Ram and Matan and bat mitzvah of Maytal: the trips to Disneyland with all of them and much more. I can see ourselves becoming great grandparents as well.

All of these projects will be achieved and completed only with love, confidence, appreciation, affection and by living a conscious life all of us together.

Your loving wife, Rivka

May 9, 2009

My Dream Dad (by Steven)

I would like to be able to say for the rest of my life that my dad was able to transform his life from being unconscious to living consciously. I would like to say that he is the father of my conscious family, a family that will continue to impact many souls on this planet with their awakening to divine life.

I would like to say that my dad is a hero, not for being a warrior all his life but for the courage to allow love to conquer all obstacles in the way of living life.

My dream dad is living connected, conscious, in constant communication with all life. He is always finding a way to allow love over fear, to choose consciously his way of expressing his soul through his actions. My dream dad will allow me to simply witness him from far and from within, from by his side to being an integral part of who he is with no separation any more.

My dream dad is not a dream, but a reality of how one spirit is more powerful than millions of unconscious lives. How one spirit with the freedom of choice can create miracles on Earth? How one spirit teaching can impact millions of others in sharing and expressing his journey with the world?

My dream dad will write a life-changing book that will help transform millions of lives from ignorance to living consciously, creating families that are living in integrity with themselves, and living for the greatness of humanity rather for the self, living for the passion of experiencing and living love.

My dream dad knows the difference between right and wrong, not in the human level but in the spirit one. My dream dad lives life as an explorer and a teacher rather than limited by old beliefs.

My dream dad is living from guidance from his inner soul rather than from outside forces. Making every breath count, every step matter, and every word means something. My dream dad does not say much but what he says is what's important.

My dream dad is a living example for how love, self-love, and allowing universal love to reverse his body condition to a healthy one. He is a living example to the power of individual conscious choice. He is a role model to his children and grandchildren and great grandchildren to come for mastering one's life in becoming ones leader who is responsible, choosing consciously, and living as a pure expression of love.

My dream dad is able to connect in the spiritual realm to prepare for the passing to the transition when he is ready so that it is smooth, loving and pleasant. My dad is having this connection with the rest of us, so we can be loving witnesses for him and for each other in our journeys.

My dream is to take my dad and rest of family to Romania this summer to connect to the roots of our family, connect to our grandparents, his parents and other family members who have passed and share with them our gratitude for the sacrifices they have made in their life for us. To acknowledge their greatness, and help them get complete with their lives so they can also continue their journey to the light.

I dream of taking my dad and rest of family to Hawaii to witness the volcanoes as they erupt and witness the creation of earth from fire under water and experience that kind of evolution within our family. I dream of celebrating 50 years of life together for dad and mom and the birth of a new life that is available to them today - conscious life.

I dream that my dad will experience the infinite nature of love and will be able to create and chose many more moments of such love while living here with us, as they will forever remain with his soul and will help him continue on his eternal life with so much love that it will be able to move planets and create new worlds. That is the power of my dad.

I dream of simple but special moments of connection when I sit with my dad on the beach looking at the ocean together with no words. Just moments of love, connection, and appreciation when tears are filling our hearts; tears of joy and gratitude for us coming together this far.

I dream of dad experiencing this loving connection with mom, Anat, Liat, and their families. I dream of dad experiencing this love from friends and strangers, from known and unknown spirits, from all life including the trees, the flowers and the water.

When I dream of my dad, I do not see time as a factor. I see the quality of time as what matters. One can live 100 years unconsciously and that is as not living at all, while one moment of conscious life can mean a lot more than a 100.

May your life, dad, from this point and on be filled with as many conscious moments as you can possibly create. May we, your family, be your loving witness.

We are with you. We love you. We cherish you. We admire you. We salute to you. We are grateful to you. We are the manifestation of your love in this world and for that no words can describe the experience for us.

Love

Steven

A Love Letter to a Dear Father (by Liat)

A love letter to you, my dear father!

First we would like to tell you that we are very happy to get this moving and tearful mail. Of course you are a dad, a grandfather, and the most-loved person in the whole wide world.

Always surrounded by friends and family, all of them around you are feeling just the light and happiness. You will always continue to be the entertainer with all your jokes. You always know to pick up what is the best in everything.

We all hope that you will be able to get through this difficult time and we will continue to be together and celebrate all the upcoming events. Maybe even you and I will go together for spinning. That would be my dream come true. The most perfect thing I might have.

Dad, you are very strong person. You always think positive and that's just so wonderful to be like that. That's why you will be able to go through everything and smile to the world and the world will continue to smile to you. The sun will always shine on your face with lots of light, love and happiness.

Here in Israel we sit and think so much about you, that only God in heaven will send you full recovery. It's Friday night and Shlomo and I are now doing the Shabbat candles, praying to God and hoping that he is listening to me, and that he will make my dream come true that my dad will be strong and healthy.

Love you from the bottom of my heart,

Liat

My Dream Daddy (by Anat)

I dream of jogging on the sand close to the sea with my daddy. This time I'm not sprinting ahead and leaving him behind, but just jogging next to him side by side. We can feel the warm sand under our feet and the little waves hugging us. The wind is blowing and helping us advance forward while the sun is patting our backs. The smell of salted water fills the air.

After we get tired we stop and continue to walk, looking over the horizon, admiring the endless ocean, the birds in the sky and the trees. Such a spectacular view from every side.

Maytal comes along. She also wants to share the love and the beautiful connection. We are all collecting seashells and we use them to decorate the sand castle that we build. Matan also joins and builds a moat around the castle; he brings water to fill it up. Leeran also joins the team, offering a unique design idea.

We look up and see parasailing in the horizon. "Daddy, let's go flying," I say. We are on top of the world, like two birds flying side by side. So light, so free.

I dream of going hiking, all of us: Moti, me, the kids, mom and dad, Steven, and Liat, Shlomo and the kids. The way up is tough but we feel so powerful that together we can challenge every obstacle. We reach to the top and just sit there admiring the striking sights. The sky is so colorful and so are the mountains.

I dream of celebrating Matan's bar mitzvah, feeling the love just filling the air. There is music and laughter everywhere. Daddy is dancing with mom, showing off the great new steps that they just picked up.

I dream of Maytal's bat mitzvah. She is so beautiful and grown up. Daddy is reading his speech next to mom. He has tears of joy in his eyes, proud to be able to take part in this event and celebrate her life. She saves him a dance. All eyes are on them. Everyone can feel the special connection they have.

I dream of enjoying juicy steaks in our backyard with all of the family together, listening to the birds chirping, watching the sunset and catching up on the events of the week.

Daddy, I dream of you continuing to be in our lives for many more years, where we join your new world of consciousness with no limits, just pure abundance.

Love

Anat

A Letter to Arie from the Alus Family

Dear Dad,

You and we have gone through not an easy time. We your children that not long ago didn't know what a worry in the world meant. We didn't understand the meaning of the word health.

We understand that life cannot be taken so easily for granted. It was very hard for us and we felt fear and deep horror.

Here you are on your right path to celebrate your birthday and many other events—bar mitzvahs, weddings, grandchildren, etc., because you shouldn't be in a hurry. God in heaven decided that you have to be here.

We cannot give you up. So we will wish for you from our hearts that the smile on your face will always be there, that you'll be able to go back to your sports and that your body will get stronger and go back to your daily routine. Because we believe that you are on the path to full recovery.

Loving you very much,

Liat, Shlomo, Itay, Dikla, Karin and Ram

To My Dear and Loving Grandpa (by Itay)

To my dear Grandpa,

I am Itay, your firstborn grandson. I wish you lots of health, happiness, and that you will always be the funny grandpa, the swimmer, and the sports guy.

I remember you taking me to my bar mitzvah trip. We had such a special quality time. We were talking, eating together, going to all the rides. We had such a wonderful time and it is a pity that time is flying so fast and it has been 6.5 years since.

Now I'm about to join the army. I was dreaming and hoping to see you before joining the army. But I guess my dream will not come true this year. In any case I wish you to get healthy and that you will win the war of that disease and not that the disease will win you.

You have this year a lot to look forward to and to celebrate: your 50th anniversary, my dearest grandma's 70th birthday, your 75th birthday. You have to go through all the treatments with great success and with all your power that God will send you, amen, so that you will have all the time in the world to celebrate all the events.

You should not even think that you are weak or that it's too difficult for you. You have a long path that you have to finish and I wish you to get healthy soon, lots of health and love, even though we are here in Israel and far from you, you are in our hearts all the time. In our dreams at night and during the day, we keep thinking of you. How our grandpa will be healthy and whole.

Endless kisses, hugs, love you from the bottom of my heart,

Itay Alus

To Grandpa (by Dikla)

I would like to express my love to you and my feelings to you as a granddaughter, to my dear grandpa. You are the best grandpa in the world. I will never forget our trip to Disneyland. We had so much fun and we went totally wild as if you were 18 years old, but in your spirit you really didn't behave like a grandpa. You behaved like a friend for life and that is such a great, the best feeling in the world. My heart is pounding when I'm thinking about all of that.

I'm so emotional and thinking maybe there will come a day and it will happen again. You are healthy. Who said that you are sick? You have to remove all your bad thoughts from your body. Think positive and then for sure everything will be fine. God in heaven will listen to every prayer and will help you to get well and to continue to dance with grandma and with the rest of the family in every family event.

And of course how is it possible to forget dear grandma who is always taking care of you, not to forget to take your medications. She's treating you like a son and not like a husband. She's always at your side, helping you, supporting you, worrying, not sleeping at night, and during the day her head is full of thoughts that everything will be fine and that the whole family will celebrate only happy events.

So to summarize I would like to wish you, grandpa and grandma, who are the most dearest in the whole world to me, that I love you both and would like to get only good messages because you are very dear to me.

With all my love,

Dikla Alus

I Dream (by Leeran)

I dream that I will finally beat Saba at Chess. Saba isn't just my grandfather. He is my adviser, my lawyer and my escape from the world. Saba is a person with so much experience of life and advice, and he's just a phone call away. Also when I talk to him he doesn't treat me like a child but treats me like an old friend or an adult. In the end I know I have to face my challenges but for a short period of time I can think and feel without being judged or annoyed. I can tell Saba anything and everything and sometimes I do before I even tell my parents. We have discussions about my hopes and dreams that I would have to work for to succeed, and his hopes and dreams that he already achieved.

Saba in my life is just that more enjoyable.

He takes me to the movies and plays backgammon, which we started just recently to play. By the way, we are in a tie in that game. The series is 2-2. Also in a harsh winter where it's really cold and icy, I call him to come pick me up and in a snap he, without even thinking, just jumps into the car and picks me up. Just think of it: I could have frozen to death if Saba wouldn't have come.

I have a loving grandfather that will always play with me from when I was little, all the way to a teenager and I hope until I'm 40. I support him and love him and pray to God that he gets well (which he will).

Now Saba, let's talk a little about you. A smart, loving grandfather that words cannot even express how much love and respect I have for you. I have read your meditations and I am both proud and surprised that you have accomplished so much. I one day want to be like you—strong, healthy, with a loving family and wife. You have inspired me to go after my goals and advised me what to do in certain situations.

I dream that one day we can play soccer again like we used to in Newmarket. All that running and playing…It was always fun to play with you even though you would let me win. I know you are strong, so I know you will get through this bump on the road of life, because we have so much to do still. You are going to be that someone that helps me out when I will climb the Grand Canyon, or when we have a race in swimming just to have fun and to practice. Let's face it Saba, I see you there in a nice tuxedo standing by my side, and then looking at my wife and congratulating me. You also will be there when our hearts are trying to grasp love from you. Your love is so strong that everyone feels it and feels a little warmer inside.

> I dream that my Saba is right there beside me when I turn around to him.
>
> I love you so much Saba that I almost cried when I was writing this (which you know is a big thing for me).
>
> To show the love I have for you, I took some of Safta's talent and wrote you a poem:
>
> A person I can look to
>
> When my world is turned around and I'm in a zoo
>
> A quiet island that can play a game
>
> The game of life that got your name
>
> Movies, sports and popcorn too
>
> Having fun with you is not new
>
> When I came from school and was singing the blues
>
> You patched me up just like a bruise
>
> I can go on and on with so much to write
>
> You're as strong as a medieval white knight
>
> I end this poem with a high note
>
> Maybe we can go fishing on a big white boat.
>
> I love you so much Saba. Please, please, please get better.
>
> Leeran Markizano, A loving grandson

To Dear Grandpa (by Karin)

To the dearest grandpa and most loved in the world,

I'd like to tell you that I love you very, very much. You have done for me things that I have to thank you, like going on trips with all of your grandchildren while visiting in Israel, and trips to Disneyland, Sea World and Universal Studios. I had a wonderful time all my life with you and love you forever.

I am crying every day and miss you. But at least we had the chance to go on the trip that I just mentioned with you and Grandma and Steven. This was the perfect trip that I will never forget, your idea to take every grandchild to a trip to Disney when they are bar mitzvah or bat mitzvah. You had so many friends that love you, even in California every morning you would walk with Steven on the beach and the birds would follow.

You are a very special person and good hearted and I hope that you reading this letter will understand how much I love you. We the family and friends will make your dream come true by being a connected family. I wanted so much to see you for the last time. You will always stay in my heart and I will never leave you. I will never forget you.

Love you, hug you, miss you,

Your granddaughter Karin and the rest of the Alus family (Liat, Shlomo, Itay, Dikla, Ram and me)

Wish for Grandpa (by Ram)

I wish you health, happiness and lots of love, dreaming that you will be going through all the treatments and God will send you a full recovery. Now is your time to be happy. To look forward and to believe that there is a ray of light in the darkness, to understand that there are lots of people that love you here, and that are at your side every moment.

Remember we are always there for you. We will always be there for you. So take your time to get stronger and to recover, so that we will be able to see you showering us with a sea of smiles because you have a lot of goals in your life.

You have to celebrate your 70th birthday. You have to

celebrate your 50th anniversary with grandma. May God send her lots of health, amen. You have to take me to my bar mitzvah trip to Disney, to enjoy with me the rides, the restaurants and to get wild like an 18 year old and not really like a grandpa. Like a friend for life. You still have to take Matan for his bar mitzvah trip and you have to take the beautiful and wonderful cousin of mine Maytal to her bat mitzvah trip.

You still have a long way and you have to know that you will get your treatments and you will be getting strong for all your kids and grandkids who love you.

Love you from the heart and the soul, from the bottom of my heart,

Ram Alus, your grandson

My Saba (Grandfather) (by Matan)

I dream of Saba and me in Disneyland trying out all the rides. I can hear him telling me new stories and lots of jokes. I feel him holding my hand when we watch a movie with everyone on Friday night. I see him eating grapefruit after he wakes up. When I see Saba my heart pumps so fast because it's happy to meet his grandpa's heart and I'm happy too to see my Saba.

Thank you Saba for all the stuff that you did for me, like taking me to the movies and letting me have lots of treats. I know that the cancer will go away, just keep believing in yourself.

I dream of my Saba getting all the help and treatments and the doctors kicking the cancer out of Saba. Saba will not be weak because I will give him all my love.

Love

Matan

CHAPTER 41
THE SURGERY
(IN RIVKA'S OWN WORDS)

The surgery was originally scheduled for September, but the date was moved up to August 21, one month after the chemotherapy ended. Dr. Klein called me and told me that the oncologist said that two months was too long to wait, and that the tumor had shrunk. Every day I asked Arie, "Are you sure you want surgery?" Arie loved to eat, so to have his stomach removed was unthinkable. He loved steak and fish—to him a meal without meat wasn't a meal.

Arie wrote a letter to the kids saying he would fight and he would do his best. He also wrote a letter to our grandchildren. He told them, "You know me, I was a fighter in the army and I will fight. I'm sure I'm going to get through this, but if I don't make it, you should know that Grandma will continue the tradition of trips for bar mitzvahs and bat mitzvahs and go to Disneyland. She will continue to be there for you even if I'm not here any longer." He told them to always uphold what is important in life and to keep their priorities straight.

Liat arrived from Israel on August 17 to spend a few days with us before her dad went in for surgery. Steven was supposed to arrive in Toronto from Arizona the night before the surgery. The evening of August 20 we planned to go out to a restaurant to have a steak the way Arie liked it, and to be together with all the kids. Unfortunately, Steven's plane was diverted to Buffalo due to poor weather conditions, and he didn't get into Toronto until 10:00 P.M., so we couldn't go to the restaurant. There was a Middle Eastern restaurant nearby—we ordered dinner and took it to Anat's house and enjoyed being together. After dinner, we had a photo taken of our entire family.

The next day we went to the hospital for Arie's surgery. Arie got dressed in the hospital clothes and prepped for surgery. Dr. Klein met with Steven, Liat, Anat, Moti, and me. He was very nice—he kept joking, and smiling, and he said, "Don't worry, everything will be fine."

Dr. Klein said the surgery would take four hours, so we sat in the cafeteria at the hospital. Steven went outside onto the grass to lie down and meditate. When Steven came back it was three hours into the surgery. He said, "You know what? He went out of his body. He was floating and he didn't want to come back. I took his hand and I tugged him back and I said, 'No way—you have to go back to your body.'"

When Dr. Klein came out he said, "The surgery is over and he's okay. He's now in recovery and you'll be able to see him a little bit later." Once Arie was taken from recovery to his room, all four of us sat there, by his side. He was very thirsty and the nurse gave him water. We decided to take shifts and decided who would stay with him and when. Of course, I took the first shift and stayed the whole night. Arie didn't want to sleep that night. I kept telling him he needed to sleep and get some rest, but he kept opening his eyes to see if I was still there.

According to author Joan Borysenko, the stomach is the place where you digest your life—when there are things in your life that are hard for you to digest, you suppress them and then the cells go wild and create a tumor. Arie was unable to digest all the situations encountered during his life—from being an orphan, to later being a soldier on the front line of five wars, and other life challenges.

He felt so powerless when his friends were killed in the wars. Family disunity further bothered him and this affected his stomach.

Steven explained to me that because of the disease, Arie developed a higher consciousness. When people face fear for their life, they become more conscious. They try to understand how to go inside the body and learn more about themselves. When Arie began to meditate, he kept a journal of his experiences. One morning, when Arie documented his daily meditation, he wrote that his stomach had been healed by the chemotherapy. So I begged him not to go for the scheduled surgery. I kept asking him, "Why would you go for surgery if your stomach has healed?" But Arie insisted that medicine had advanced considerably, and he had to do it.

The idea of not allowing Arie to have the surgery that might save his life was a very heavy responsibility for me to bear. If something went wrong, then everyone would blame me. So I had to go along with Arie's wish to have the surgery and his stomach was removed. The tissue was sent off to pathology, and the result was that Arie's stomach had indeed been healed. Unfortunately, the damage had already been done. I was so upset—I couldn't forgive myself for allowing Arie to have the surgery.

The day after the operation to remove his stomach, every time Arie wanted to talk, he couldn't catch his breath. He wasn't allowed to eat, and whenever he was thirsty they gave him water. I asked the nurse, "Are you sure he's allowed to drink?" The nurse said, "We do what the patient wants." I said, "Don't you have instructions from the doctor?" Because I was worried about Arie, I called the doctor's office and said to the receptionist, "You have to find Dr. Klein for me." She paged him at the hospital and he came to Arie's room.

By the time the doctor arrived, Arie's lungs were flooded with water. He had to go into surgery again at 1:30 A.M. to remove the water from his lungs. They put some tubes into both sides of his lung, and then admitted him to the ICU. From that moment, for two and a half weeks, I had to see him with a breathing tube in his mouth. It was heartbreaking. He could not talk and he was in and out of consciousness from the huge quantities of morphine they gave him for his pain.

Most of the time Arie was asleep, and he didn't know what was going on. We would sit at his bedside, but he never knew we were there. Then we found out that one of his nurses was an Israeli because she heard us speak in Hebrew. She was so helpful. It was the only place in the hospital where the nurse really cared about the patient. My daughter Liat had to go back home after two weeks—she had to go back to work or she'd lose her job. Steven had to go back to Arizona to prepare for a presentation he was scheduled to make at a conference. I said to them, "Go. You do what you have to do."

I was there day and night. After two and a half weeks, the nurse told me that Arie would not recall anything. Steven told me that he knew Arie didn't want to go back to his body—his body was so injured that he didn't want to come back. When Arie finally awoke, he didn't remember anything. I told him he couldn't remember because he had been given so many drugs for the pain.

Finally, Arie was taken out of the ICU. They had to keep doing lung X-rays, and feed and give him oxygen through tubes. The nurses gave him liquid protein through his feeding tube so that he would gain some strength. This was difficult for me to watch because his tube would get blocked every time, and he would not get the food. I got so angry with those incompetent nurses—they never knew how to handle the tube or how to be compassionate to a patient.

I went to the chief nurse and told her, "Listen, my husband is a very sick person, and the girls keep changing shifts. By the time they know the patient, they leave." I was there every day until 9:00 at night, and then went home for only an hour. I gave hell to the nurses because they were behaving terribly. Only one or two of the nurses were compassionate. They would only do their job and go home and didn't seem to care about the patient. One time they did an X-ray, and said everything looked fine and that he could have some solid food without the tube. They brought him yogurt, but I knew that he was not allowed to even have any liquid!

Arie continued to suffer, and I continued to monitor his condition. Leakage from the stomach, which was a surgical side effect predicted by Dr. Klein, did occur. The leak was through the stitches between the esophagus and the small intestine. The area became infected and just did not heal the way it was supposed to. They assigned a therapist to come and help Arie go for a walk with a walker each day.

Many of Arie's friends followed his situation through me. I kept telling Arie how many people called and asked about him—all the kids' friends kept calling and asking about how he was. Every time I went to the hospital, I would tell him, "Jews, non-Jews, everyone is praying for you." He said, "I never knew that so many people liked me." One of our closest friends, Izzy Finkelstein, kept coming to visit him, to massage his feet, to shave him, and to talk with Arie for hours. I will never forget the love that he provided to Arie during those difficult days of his life.

We got to September and Rosh Hashanah, and I kept praying to God for Arie's recovery. One of his lungs had water in it again and he had to begin receiving shots to help control his blood sugar. I asked the chief nurse for a list of the medications he was receiving, and I called Dr. Klein and asked him what the purpose was for each of them. For example, Arie had a hernia and took Prevacid, which is prescribed for persistent heartburn caused by excess stomach acid. They continued to give him Prevacid even after his stomach was removed!

I was so upset and asked, "How is this possible?!" Dr. Klein said that he told the staff not to give Arie the Prevacid, but I knew that there were no written instructions. This was undoubtedly the most difficult situation I had ever managed. I was at the hospital day and night to monitor and care for Arie. I discovered that the health system was so poor and careless. I felt like contacting the local newspaper to have a reporter write about the horrible state of patient care.

Friends came to visit, and even with so many tubes in his body, Arie still kept his morale high and would tell our friends to smile. He also told them, "If it wasn't for my wife, I would be dead." Every day I was there to make sure he received the best treatment. Moti would come and shave him, give him a massage on his feet, and talk to him for hours. The grandchildren came too and Leeran would tell Arie about his projects at school and how successful he was. Arie would be so pleased to see the progress they were making in school.

Arie's sister Bianca and her husband Simon came to visit him too. I kept encouraging him and telling him that everything would be fine when we got him back home. We would hire a helper from the Philippines, because we had a friend who was bringing nannies to Canada from there. Arie kept assuring me that he would come home, but he never did. They kept transferring him to different floors and different rooms. Then they found something wrong with his heart.

I continued to follow up on every small detail and ask the nurses many questions—I wanted to know everything they were doing to Arie and what was happening. One night a nurse even came with the wrong injection—thankfully I caught it!

Once, during Arie's first visit to the ICU right after surgery, Steven and I took a walk around the neighborhood before going to visit Arie. While on the walk, Steven noticed a falling sign by his feet that read, "Funeral." He pointed it out to me and I said, "Don't tell me that you see a funeral!" Then he retracted a bit because he didn't want to admit it to himself.

I tried so hard to save my husband, but unfortunately this was not in my hands. My hardest moment was watching him disappear in front of my eyes. He had lost so much weight. One day, when he was going for physical therapy, I saw his legs and they were so thin he looked like he had just walked out of a concentration camp. I said to the therapist, "He fought in wars and stayed alive and now this disease is killing him." I cried every time I left the hospital, but I didn't want Arie to see me cry. I had to keep up the façade and play the game to show him my strength in the hopes that it would encourage him to get better.

When the nurses failed to follow feeding tube instructions, the food got stuck, so he had to get a new tube in order to eat. Then Dr. Klein brought a lung specialist in to see Arie and another procedure had to be done because his right lung was blocked by the feeding tube leakage. That ended up being another two-and-a-half-hour surgery. The doctor came out and said, "Your husband is a very strong man." But Arie ended up in the ICU again after this surgery.

I would think, "He's going to get better and then he will come home." I said to him, "You've been all over the hospital, and now it is time to come home." And Arie kept repeating, "I'm coming home." He could only whisper as he had lost his ability to speak because the tubes irritated his throat. I gave him my cell phone to talk with Steven and the grandchildren from Israel as well as Liat and Shlomo—the others would come visit him at the hospital.

And then I said, "You have to be home by your birthday on October 15. Steven said he would come to Toronto to celebrate both of our birthdays—my seventieth and your seventy-fifth birthday." Arie kept asking, "When is Steven coming?" He was so anxious to see Steven and to talk to him.

Leeran came often to visit his grandpa, with whom he liked having discussions so much. Arie used to always watch Leeran play ice hockey and Leeran was doing his part to support his grandfather during this difficult time. Liat, Shlomo, and their children were monitoring Arie's progress every day, as was Anat's family. Many of Steven's friends, some of them spiritual leaders, were all praying for Arie and monitoring his progress. At this time, there was a lot of attention being given to Arie in the hope that he would recover.

We treated our daughter's husbands like our own sons the moment they joined the family, and at the time of Arie's illness, these two men treated Arie like they would have treated their own fathers. Arie and Moti shared a strong bond. Moti left his family behind in Israel at the age of 23 when he married Anat. This separation from his family is what made his bond with Arie so strong. When Arie was in the ICU the first time, Moti came to visit him and would talk to Arie even though Arie was unconscious. Moti kept talking to him and telling him, "You are my second dad."

Shlomo, who married my daughter Liat, loved Arie so much. They also shared a strong bond. The two men often went out for coffee to talk during our yearly visits to Israel. Shlomo was the youngest in a family of 10 siblings—eight girls and two boys. Arie would joke, "Your dad wanted boys and he wouldn't give up!" Shlomo loved Arie very much and he felt so sorry that he couldn't be beside him at this most difficult time of his life leading up to his death and funeral. He was very upset that he couldn't be with him. He knew this kind of sorrow from having lost his own dad. He really loved Arie from the bottom of his heart.

CHAPTER 42
THE FINAL TWO DAYS
(IN RIVKA'S OWN WORDS)

On Thursday, October 8, Dr. Klein ordered yet another procedure in the CT room to drain the leakage. For every procedure Arie had, it was difficult to transfer him from a stretcher to a new bed. It was such a hassle and so hard for him. I used to bring pizzas, bagels, and other food every day for the staff and other employees in every department that Arie was in, including the ICU. I treated them like human beings and everyone came to thank me. They told me, "No one treats us like this—they only complain about us." A nurse said, "You treat us so well Mrs. Ringelstein." I did this because I wanted Arie to get the best treatment he could possibly get.

I got to the hospital at 8:00 A.M. and learned that they could not do the procedure because they didn't have blood test results. Dr. Jacobs, who was supposed to do the procedure, told me that he had other patients so the procedure would have to wait until lunchtime. As Dr. Jacobs went to lunch I said to him, "I hope that when you come back from lunch you will still be on your best to perform the procedure because when your belly is full, you get tired. You have a big responsibility."

When Dr. Jacobs came back I asked him "Did you have a good lunch?" and he said, "Yes." I told him, "Take good care of my husband. I hope you're not too tired from the food you ate." He went in to do the procedure at 1:30 P.M., and thirty or forty minutes later, I heard all the loudspeakers in the hospital blare "DR KLEIN! ANY DOCTOR IN THE BUILDING, COME TO THE CT ROOM!"

I started to scream, "What happened to my husband, tell me!" and they wouldn't tell me. Dr. Klein was not in the building, so I asked another doctor who was working with him, and was headed to the CT room. When they opened the door, I saw Arie on his belly on the CT table bleeding. Blood was coming out of his mouth and I kept screaming. I called my daughter Anat and said, "You have to come right away." She said, "Mom take it easy. Everything is okay." I said, "No, come here right away. I'm telling you."

Anat came to the hospital, and we waited together to hear something about Arie. Then Dr. Jacobs came to us and said, "I'm so sorry, I'm so sorry." I said, "What is wrong?" Dr. Jacobs explained that when he put a tube into Arie body, he hit a blood vessel which caused the bleeding. He said that he got it to stop, but that Arie needed three units of blood. The doctors transferred Arie to the ICU to be watched for 24 hours because another CT scan had to be done to make sure the bleeding stopped. It took a long time to get Arie into the ICU. Once he was there, I went home to rest and came back on Friday morning. The next day, Dr. Jacobs was on rounds, so I said to another doctor, "My husband needs another CT scan—Dr. Jacob ordered it." The doctor on duty said, "No he doesn't." I didn't know what to do. I couldn't argue with the ICU doctor so I sat with Arie and waited.

I kept praying, "Please God!" for my husband to get well. On that Friday, around noon, Dr. Klein came to check on Arie with an entourage of doctors. After checking Arie, Dr. Klein said, "He looks good and his hemoglobin levels look good." So at 7:15 P.M. on Friday night, the nurse told me to go home. She said I could come back at 8:30 P.M. that evening, when the shift changed. I was exhausted and I couldn't sleep more than two hours at a time. I would call and talk to the nurse every night, and then first thing every morning I was back at the hospital.

I hugged Arie and kissed him and said, "I wish you a quiet night. I am going to Anat's house for Shabbat dinner." He was looking into my eyes—it was such a deep gaze. He didn't say anything, but just looked straight into my eyes. I didn't dare ask what that look meant, but in my heart—my intuition—I said to myself, "I hope to God that you aren't telling me goodbye." When I arrived at Anat's home, I told her what I felt. She said, "Why do you think so?" I said, "I don't know." I went home after Shabbat dinner and was very tired. I was so exhausted and I said to myself, "Okay, I will get some sleep now and then wake in the night and call the ICU."

I was just about to call the hospital at 2:00 A.M. when the phone started ringing. The nurse from the ICU said, "Mrs. Ringelstein, your husband is not doing well." I asked, "What happened?" and she told me that his blood pressure was dropping, he vomited food from his feeding tube, and was choking so they had to intubate him. She asked me, "Do you want to come?" and I said, "I am coming right away."

I called Anat and asked, "Do you want to come?" and she said, "Yes." I was so confused and scared and not in my right mind for driving a car—I missed the entrance to Highway 407, and had to put the car in reverse to continue driving to the hospital. My daughter called and asked, "I thought you were coming to pick me up?" and I said, "No you need to come in your car. Please come. He is intubated and he can't talk."

When I got to the hospital, I saw that he had a catheter and that there was blood in the catheter. I asked, "Why does he have so much blood in his urine?" There was a very experienced nurse there that night that I used to see all the time in the ICU. She was Romanian and Arie would speak to her in Romanian. He once told me, "God sent me this Romanian nurse to help me." The Romanian nurse said that Arie's condition was not good. Anat and I were there all night.

The next morning, I called Dr. Klein and said, "Something is wrong." Dr. Klein said that he was on the first day of his vacation and he had his son's birthday. I said, "I don't care, you are his doctor and his surgeon. He is your patient. I demand that you come to the hospital right away." The strange thing is that on Friday after the procedure, Dr. Klein had come to check on Arie and had said he was doing well. I told Dr. Klein that Dr. Jacobs said he needed another CT scan, but that the other doctor had said not to move him. But at the same time, Dr. Klein was saying that Arie was doing well.

I called Steven and said, "Something is wrong, very wrong." Steven called on all of Arie's spirits and asked them to call all the angels and see if they could help. That Saturday morning, I begged Dr. Klein to come because I felt I was losing Arie. Steven called and said that he learned by connecting with Arie's spirit that he was bleeding inside and yelling for help. In the middle of the night, Steven woke up feeling very sick to his stomach, and he sat down to write what he was feeling. He was channeling his father—who was telling Steven that he was bleeding and that he needed help. I said to Steven, "If I tell the doctors that Arie is bleeding inside because you know this by ESP or channeling, they will think

I am crazy."

I made Steven tell the doctor what he knew and the medical staff continued working on Arie. Moti arrived and saw the situation was getting far worse—at this point, Arie could not express himself any longer. It was the seventh day of Sukkoth, and eventually Arie's blood pressure got a bit better. Steven told Anat and me to go home and take a break, and we followed his advice. Moti stayed at the hospital to watch over Arie.

Five minutes after I got home, Moti called and said, "Come back" and then the Romanian nurse said, "Please come back, it's his blood pressure." Moti saw what was happening and went home in order to bring the kids back to the hospital—he knew it was over. My 10-year-old grandson Matan said to Moti, "I know you came to pick me up because Grandpa is leaving us. I spoke to his spirit and he told me that his body is so badly injured that he cannot stay with us anymore."

Moti brought the kids, and our granddaughter Maytal brought a birthday card for him that said, "You are the best grandpa in the whole wide world." I kept shaking Arie's head and saying, "Please come back to us. If you are going out of your body, you cannot come back to us." Arie continued to bleed internally, and the inconsiderate doctor kept saying, "He's not going to make it." I gave him a piece of my mind and I screamed at him, "How can you say that?!?"

A few hours later, the other doctor asked me if I wanted Arie to be resuscitated. I told him to speak with Steven on the phone and Steven told Dr. Klein not to do it. Through that entire time, Steven was on the phone with me calling from San Francisco, and had another dear friend of his who could also channel Dr. Linne on the line to negotiate with Arie's spirit to stay. Steven said that Arie's spirit is leaving the body, and not coming back. Steven pulled his arm back to his body, and being next to Arie we noticed that his life signs were returning. Then Steven told me over the cell phone, "He's waiting for your permission to leave. Please let him go—give him your permission. This is his last wish."

I hugged Arie and kissed him. I told him, "I love you so much. I know you are suffering, and with all the pain in my heart, I understand I have to let you go. I know this is your wish and that we have to let you go." The minute I said, "I am going to fulfill your wish and let you go" he left and I saw a straight line on the monitor. Steven later shared with me that he held his hand while passing to the other side to be welcomed by his parents. Steven then came back from the other side and felt a big punch in his stomach. He burst out crying after facing the death of his dad.

It was a very emotional transition. The nurses asked me if I wanted to see Arie after they cleaned him up and took out all the tubes. I said, "Yes." The family members went in to see Arie. I kissed him again. He looked so peaceful, as if he was sleeping. I couldn't believe he was not alive anymore. This was Saturday night, October 10—five days short of his seventy-fifth birthday.

Steven was in California when Arie passed, yet he was with Arie in spirit. I was comforted to know that he'd taken Arie's hand and walked him over to the other side. When he passed, Arie was not suffering any longer, and he was happy and free of the pain of his injured body.

Steven arrived in Toronto on Sunday, October 11, as did Liat. Liat was in Israel when I informed her on the phone that her dad had just passed on. She screamed and Moti had to continue the call. Even though it was difficult for me to talk to anybody, we had to make arrangements for the funeral on Sunday night as it would take place on Monday. Steven, Anat, and Leeran prepared a eulogy. Leeran happened to be wearing Arie's shoes—the shoes that Arie had worn to Leeran's bar mitzvah. Leeran said, "I am wearing his shoes, but I'm not sure I'll be able to walk in his shoes." Then he added, "If I have a son, I will name him Arie." Maytal was still six years old, and she wanted to put the birthday card she'd made for Arie into the coffin with her grandfather. I convinced her to let her keep it with his papers and treasures.

Steven wanted to see the body, so he went to the hospital with Moti to see Arie's body. They let Steven put his hand on Arie's forehead to connect to his spirit. Steven invited Arie's spirit to continue to live through his body and enjoy the beauty of life here. Indeed, Arie continues to travel with Steven on his journey to this date.

I went to the airport to pick up Liat on Monday, and I said,

"Daddy didn't come to pick you up from the Airport. Dad will never come again to pick you up from the airport." She started to scream. "My daddy is not dead!" and as soon as she entered our apartment she looked at all the pictures and then collapsed. Steven worked to relax her. After that, we went to the funeral home, and before everyone else was allowed in, they showed him to us. They told me to bring his tallis and they enveloped him with it. His face looked so beautiful, but he was ice cold. Even though it was hard, Liat knew she had to touch and kiss him to say goodbye.

Chapter 43
Arie's Voice from the Other Side

As I lay on the hospital gurney, with doctors and nurses and my loved ones buzzing all around me, blood draining from my mouth, I knew that my physical life was about to end. But what was to follow? Isn't that the eternal question for which we all want to know the answer?

The doctors had done all they could to try to save my body—to extend my physical life—putting me on weeks of chemotherapy, removing my stomach, sending me off to X-ray machines and CT scanners, and probing and prodding me in every conceivable place—but there is only so much that mortal beings can do to affect the course of events that has been laid out for each one of us by the Creator. We all have a role to play in the great story of the world, and then it is our time to move offstage, as each of us eventually transitions from the physical world to something better.

In an instant, I was in two places at once—still residing in my physical body, but also pure energy, a spirit, floating above the bleeding, cancer-ridden body I saw below me. From this vantage point, I could see my beloved Rivka, daughter Anat, her husband Moti, and my grandchildren Leeran, Matan, and Maytal. Rivka held my hand as I began to explore the other side—tethering me in place. There I met my parents, who I had lost so early in my life, and thousands of angels who were ready to help me begin my journey.

In the end, the power of togetherness bound me so tightly to Rivka that I could not make the transition to the other side. While I did not want to leave the love of my life, my reason for being, I knew that it was time—the angels were calling me, and my parents were waiting there for me to join them. I also knew that I would always be with Rivka, that every day of her life I would walk by her side, and that one day we would be reunited for all eternity.

I heard Steven calling to me through the ether—imploring me not to leave my family behind. I communicated to him that I was ready to cross over, and that I had made my peace with my death and that it was time to continue my journey. But before I could transition to the other side, I needed Rivka to let me go.

Steven called Rivka on the phone and told her that she needed to give me permission to leave. "I love you so much," Rivka said to me. "I know you are suffering, and with all the pain in my heart, I understand I have to let you go. I know this is your wish and that we have to let you go. I am going to fulfill your wish and let you go."

With those words, I joined with my parents and the thousands of angels who were waiting for me. Together, we walked into the light.

As the white light increased in intensity, it filled the room—blinding me, consuming me, and scattering my very being into a trillion subatomic particles that swirled like a powerful cyclone into the hospital room, through the loved ones gathered around my bed, and swiftly into the heavens.

I am one.

CHAPTER 44
EULOGIES

The Rabbi Tuvia Gabriel's Eulogy

Today we bid farewell to Arie Ringelstein...Arie Ben Jacob...a man who exemplified the true meaning of human life—a man who placed the lives of others in place of his own; a survivor, who squarely faced life's adversities and challenges with courage and dignity...and at the same time a man who conciliated and brought about peace; a man who saw a cloud as the overture to a bright sun; a man who imparted to his family and all those who knew him with the noblest of moral values; a man for whom the word "negative" was virtually non-existent...a man whose biggest source of pride and everlasting treasure was his beloved family...and a man who lived to the fullest—always with an indelible smile on his face!

Our Arie passed away on a Shabbat which was also a festival—tradition has it that righteous persons have that Zchut, that honor...and the last chapter of his life on Earth coincided with the reading this weekend of the last chapter of our Torah and the passing of the foremost leader and prophet of our nation: Moshe Rabeynu.

This reading begins with the last blessings bestowed upon the Israelites by Moses and in this context, the Torah refers to Moshe as "Ish Ha-Elokim" the Man of God—an accolade never before conferred to Moshe in the Torah. The Midrash tells us that from midway down, Moshe was an Ish—a man, and from midway up—"Ish Ha-Elokim" to mean that he was both an Ish and Elokim—an angelic being.

In what way? Our Biblical commentators explain that Moshe achieved the spiritual stature of an angel but without the accompanying pitfalls of an angel.

Our tradition has it that angels performed the divine will with robotic perfection and consistency—they would not tolerate imperfection in any way, shape or form. When God consulted them regarding his intent to give the Torah to B'Nai Israel, they vehemently—and with disdain—objected and insisted that the pure, sacred Torah belonged to the pristine realm of the heavens, and should not be allowed to descend into the human world of greed, jealousy and lust. Overriding the objection of the angels, God nonetheless gave the Torah to the Israelites—planted its values, teachings and commandments precisely into a world of imperfection.

Moses's absolute devotion to God was unequalled and thus rose to the level of an angel. However, unlike the dry, strict, unforgiving, and insensitive nature attributed to angels, Moshe's stature did not lead him to feel disdain towards the less perfect members of the nation, towards those who were still human. He was always there for his people, in good and in trying times!

Imperfection enriches our lives, because it brings out the values, the ideals of generosity, compassion, respect and honesty of purpose in a person. Without the flexibility inherent in imperfection, we could not learn and grow—we would effectively stagnate under the stiff, unchallenged umbrella of perfection and we could never reach our maximum potential! Indeed, if we come to think of it, we worship a God of imperfection!

Our Arie exemplified the ideal of living as an angel amongst human beings, of perfecting oneself by giving to others, and identifying with the needs of others. He leaves a rich legacy to his family, to his friends, and to all those who had the privilege to know him. Yehi Zichro Baruch! May his memory be a blessing to all of us!

To relatives, we express our sincere condolences! May his legacy be a living one, a true example to all of us, amen!

And remember: Death may end a physical presence...but death will never end a relationship!

Tehi Nishmato Tzrura Bitzror Hachayim—may his soul be bound up in the bond of eternal life.

El Maleh Rachamim—God full of mercy.

Steven's Eulogy

Imagine it is March, 20° C, and you are enjoying a vacation at your son's for a month in sunny Arizona. You are training in the gym three times a week, swimming three times a week, taking dancing lessons twice a week, walking an hour a day, and feel the best you have ever felt. Then one day you go to get checked for an iron deficiency and the doctor performs a colonoscopy. Your colon is fine, so the doctor inserts the camera into your stomach and discovers a bleeding cancer tumor. You came for a checkup, and you leave the doctor's office with a diagnosis of stage IV stomach cancer. The doctor's recommendation is to undergo nine weeks of chemotherapy, followed by surgery to remove your stomach, and then nine more weeks of chemotherapy. What would you do?

My dad chose nine weeks of chemotherapy and was determined to be cancer free without surgery.

So what happened?

What Happened

After a successful nine weeks of chemotherapy, the doctor was ready to perform the surgery. After successful surgery, they opened the stomach and found all cancer cells dead from the chemo. Arie was cancer-free. Following the surgery, however, there were complications. After seven weeks in and out of intensive care, fighting for his life, Arie consciously chose to pass over on the seventh day of the week, departing from bed number seven at 7:45 P.M. If you add 7 and 4 and 5, it is 16, where 1 and 6 add up to 7 again.

In the morning of his last day, tears were pouring from his eyes. He knew he was about to depart from the life as he knew it. He passed on Saturday, October 10, 2009, five days short of his seventy-fifth birthday.

His Last Few Hours

My mom, sister Anat, and her husband Moti, and the grandkids Leeran, Matan, and Maytal were with him as he transitioned at the hospital bed. I was in my San Francisco home connecting to his spirit, begging him to stay, but when I felt the peace he connected to, I knew he wanted to continue his journey. My fear of losing him and refusal to accept his departure disappeared and I felt his peace. I stepped outside to the yard, overlooking a motionless ocean with no waves, no wind, as life stood still. A few drops of rain touched my head and a hawk landed by me, Archangel Michael. The hawk looked at me right in my eyes and I knew it was time. My dad's transitioning journey was now safe. The hawk then flew away.

The whole time, I was on the phone with my dear friend and angel Dr. Linne, who helped me guide his spirit back to the body in the last hours of his life. I was also on another phone with my mom and sister at the hospital, text-messaging instructions for them to repeat for his return to the body. My dad started to wander around on the other side, not wanting to come back. He wanted to join his parents who were with him at the transition. He asked us to respect his will and to accept his conscious choice and let him go. Surrounded with thousands of angels that had gathered his family members on the other side, I told my mom on the phone to let him go, to tell him that we honor his choice and let him go. "We honor your choice," she yelled repeatedly to him.

He was lying there with icy glazed eyes. The doctor got on the phone letting me know that his life signs were dissipating and requested permission to not revive him once his heart stopped. I told the doctor that it was okay to let him go. He was ready and it was his wish and choice.

The Transition

I stood tall over the ocean witnessing my dad passing over and his spirit leaving his body. He was floating over his body, looking down at the blood coming out of his mouth. I suddenly and violently puked my guts as he transitioned smoothly to the other side. I promised my dad that I would be with him when he was ready to transition and I was—not by his bed, but by his soul. I had the honor of walking with him in this life for 47 years and to walk with him all the way to the other side, holding his hand in safety and peace, just like he held mine when I came to this world. No son can ask for a greater honor.

I then came back to my body, feeling the enormous emotional pain of losing my dad. My heart is bleeding with the pain of love as I miss my dad, no words can describe my love or my pain. Thank God love is eternal and thank God we have your love, friends, and family, to support us.

About My Dad

Born in Romania, a Holocaust survivor who lost his dad at age one and his mom at age seven, and survived a collapsed house in an earthquake at age six, he grew up as an orphan with no family of his own during World War II. In 1948, with the establishment of the state of Israel, he found his way to become a young soldier serving in five wars on the front line, witnessing most of his young troops losing their lives while protecting their country.

He was the officer in charge, not only on the battlefield, but also the one who went in person to the grieving families to notify them of their loss. Compassion was one of his greatest gifts. Shifting to civilian life, my dad dedicated his life to create a loving family that is connected and strong. I was the firstborn, followed by two beautiful sisters. My dad didn't have much in the way of parenthood role models to learn from or any formal education, but he was able to fill our hearts with the most important ingredient to a strong family, and that is unconditional love.

He was always adventurous at heart, taking in life always with a smile, very adaptive to any new conditions. He demonstrated that in a bold move of the family from Israel to Toronto, Canada. My dad and I have shared many memorable trips in the wild from hiking the Grand Canyon, to Alaska, whitewater rafting, to traveling around the world with no plans other than being in the moment.

In the past six months I had a distinct honor to journey to guide and accompany my dad in the process of his consciousness awareness awakening. I witnessed him connecting to his body and his spirit and he was even able to clean his body from cancer completely.

His true victory in his life was the level of consciousness he was able to achieve. For the first time, he was able to communicate with his parents that he lost as a child and other lost family members from the Holocaust. Can you imagine how much it meant to him to speak to his parents? He was also able to connect to the angels that were with him. He was open to receive all the love that was sent his way from all of you, his friends and relatives.

My dad lived and dedicated his life for his family and friends. We were all the meaning of his life. He always put first everyone else but himself. For years I had been begging him to put himself first and allow himself to accept your love, just like he loved you. I begged him to allow us to care for him for a change and to not feel guilty about receiving. But he was a proud man.

In the last few months of his life, my dad finally surrendered to accept love, and opened his heart to receive all of your unconditional love. He was shocked and surprised to learn how many of you loved him. He couldn't believe that you simply loved him for who he was and wanted nothing from him but his company. He couldn't believe all the hospital visits, notes, cards, and wishes you all sent him. You were all the angels in his life and I thank you for giving him the ultimate gift of unconditional love. During chemo he said to me, "A moment of consciousness of love is worth a whole lifetime of ignorance." My Dad got the meaning of his life and I was blessed to witness it.

We will miss his laughter, jokes, and being the life of a party, but I will especially miss our long, into-the-night conversations about the meaning of life and death. My dad was my teacher and also my student. It is my aspiration to be the same to all of you.

I want to thank you all for your prayers, support, and love you have extended to him, to my mom, to my family, and to me. Your unconditional love is so precious and means so much to us.

His Dream

I often asked my dad about his dreams and he had joked about like winning the lottery or riding horses in nature, but the only dream that really mattered to him was oneness in our family, where the three of us children are being loving and connecting with our parents, our children, and with each other. Like every family, we the kids had our share of differences over the years, but recently were able to bridge the gap among us to become Oneness of Love in our family. I want to thank my sisters who joined me in manifesting my dad's dream.

"Do you have oneness in your family?" he would ask if he stood here now. "Because nothing else matters," he would add. And that would probably remind him of a joke and he would have forgotten what he was speaking about.

About My Mom

My pain, although unimaginable, is nothing compared to the pain of my mom Rivka Ringelstein who lost the love of her life. Can you imagine losing 53 years of a friend, lover, and a husband?

The last six months of attending to a helpless partner, witnessing the suffering of a loved one is no walk in the park. I have never seen such commitment and dedication to a loved one. My mom put her life on hold for a while so that my dad could have his. Following the grieving, my mom will begin a new phase in her life, life without a loved one, but will be surrounded with all of us to love her as she loves us, and more. She is a powerful soul, who together with our family, came to teach the world the true meaning of love. At the hospital everybody knows her, loves her, and came to hug her, because she represents unconditional LOVE that we are all yearning for in our lives.

I always felt uncomfortable about consoling others when they lost a loved one, especially if I didn't know the passing or the family that well. What do you say? What do you do? What is the right thing to say? I now know that it is not about the right words, but maybe about sharing your own feelings, and definitely about expressing your love in your life, because after all, we are all connected. Love yourself, love your family and friends, and therefore you love us too.

I also invite you to extend your love to my mom. To support her journey of grieving, longing for dad, and missing him, to allow her with this big shift in her life. Her heart is more vulnerable than ever before, her appreciation for all of you has already touched her soul.

On Saturday, October 24, 2009, we will be celebrating her seventieth birthday and the life of my dad.

Moving Forward

I could never pay back my dad for all that he has given me, but I can pay forward to you and to the world. As a student of life and the divine, and gifted with the love of my parents, I will continue my father's teachings and values of a strong and loving family. I will live my life with the only relationship I now know matters and that is a relationship of unconditional love and unconditional acceptance with oneness in my family, with yours, and with all life.

Closing

Last night I went to the morgue to see my dad's body. He was lying cold on the bed. I put one hand on his heart, the other on the top of his head. I took a few deep breaths and invited his spirit to use my eyes to see you all here, my heart to feel your love so he can experience his dream not only from above but from within.

My dad had a dream: Oneness in the family with unconditional love and unconditional acceptance for all.

That was my dad's dream not only for our family, but for yours. That dream was worth dying for my dad, and it is worth living for all of us.

Anat's Eulogy

His parents called him Leon, his grandma Leonash. We call him Aba, his grandchildren call him Saba. He was a loving father to my sister, my brother, and I, and to his two special sons-in-law who he considered to be his adoptive sons. He is loved and admired by his seven grandchildren (Itay, Dikla, Karin, Ram, Leeran, Matan, and Maytal) and held a special bond with each and every one of them. He was loved and admired by all of you who are here today and those that couldn't make it, but still hold a special place in their hearts for him.

I remember as a little girl back in Israel jogging with Aba on the beach. I used to sprint off wanting to win the race. Although he started slow, he was still able to pass me on the way and to continue for miles further. He taught me a very important lesson that time. I focused on the destination and forgot to enjoy the journey. I didn't even notice the beautiful sunset or the playful waves. He continued to teach this to his grandchildren and always praised them for their achievements.

When I turned 12, my parents filled up a plan with our closest family and friends took me to Greece for my bat mitzvah trip. I remember going out to local Greek restaurants and my dad dancing on the tables—he was always the life of the party, bringing joy and laughter to everyone's faces.

When I was 16, we went parasailing in Mexico together and I remember this as one of the greatest experiences of my life. Me and my Aba, riding the skies together like two birds, so light and free, carrying no luggage.

He did the same for his grandchildren by devoting special time with each of them—jumping in the pool and splashing water at each other, taking them to the movies, playing board games, cheering at their hockey games, and simply swinging in the backyard, listening to them and giving them love.

Moti said he has two dads, one in Israel and one here in Canada who was here by his side for the past 20 years. Moti cherished the time they spent together, going out to restaurants, enjoying the juiciest steaks, as they are both meat lovers. They spent hours in the restaurant, talking and sharing experiences. My mom used to call and ask if they were okay and if they were still there, but for them the time just flew by.

Aba didn't just watch us grow, but participated in every part of our lives. He showed us unconditional love. Every night when I left the hospital he said, "I love you, thank you for coming, and don't forget to kiss and give a big hug to the kids from me."

When I told him that all our friends are asking about him all the time, wanting to know how he is doing, he said, "I'm so honored that so many people care about me. Tell each and every one of them I said thank you and send them my love."

Aba, Moti, and I will miss our talks and our special bond. We will miss his laughter and his love of life, but above all, we will miss HIM.

Love,

Moti, Anat, Leeran, Matan, and Maytal

Leeran's Eulogy

Arie Ringelstein was not only a great grandfather, to me he was also a best friend, a teacher, and my protector. He had suffered so much in his life by losing his parents when he was young, surviving World War II, and fighting for Israel in five of their wars. Yet with so much suffering he still found happiness, love, and always had a smile on his face, no matter what the situation was.

From him I learned a lot about life. I learned to enjoy it with the people you love to the fullest, without regrets. Saba Arie played with me all the time, took me to the movies, and even picked me up from school when we had a 30 cm snowstorm. He was truly a great man and always gave us something to be happy about and to laugh about. He was such a magnificent grandfather that I even wrote a song with my older cousin Itay about his rules. We named it "The Rules of Saba Arie." These rules are the principles that Saba lived by and I grew up with. What I learned is that no matter what rules or principles you have in your life, it is important that you live by those principles.

He gave us all his love without asking anything in return. I loved him very much and will continue to love him and adore him for the rest of my life. That's why I decided that when I grow up and have kids of my own, I will honor his love that he has given to us by naming my son after him—Arie.

Remember him for the love he brought to us and the happy and funny memories he shared with us. Let's honor him as a magnificent and peaceful husband, father, grandfather, and a friend.

Chapter 45
Memorial, Burial, Unveiling
(In Rivka's Own Words)

It took tremendous strength of heart for me to rise and give a tribute to my beloved Arie before those who gathered at the funeral. When it was my turn at the ceremony to speak, I don't even know how I went to the podium and spoke from the heart. I don't know where I got the courage and the strength to stay there and talk. After the ceremony, we went to the cemetery and buried Arie next to a tree the way he would have liked it—he loved greenery. It was the Canadian Thanksgiving weekend which was a day off, so many, many people came to say goodbye to Arie. Being the person of peace that he was, the name of the cemetery was Pardes Shalom.

Here is the speech I gave at the unveiling ceremony:

Dear family and friends,

It has been more than a month since my beloved husband, partner, friend, father, grandfather, and brother has passed on. No words can begin to describe the loss, suffering, and pain we all feel in our hearts on a daily basis.

Since Arie was always positive and saw the half-full cup, I can say that the half-full cup is loaded with endless words to describe the joy, happiness, laughter, and the difference he made in our family's life, as well as how he touched other peoples' lives during his lifetime.

We will always remember his smiling face, his jokes, his quotes, and kind words to encourage us while facing difficult moments and times throughout our lives.

To express his love for people he would always say, "I don't hate anybody…I don't like their behavior or attitude." He did not love only people, but he also loved nature and animals. Speaking of nature, you may notice that his plot in the cemetery is next to a green tree and also, since he was known as a man of peace, the name of the cemetery is PARDES SHALOM.

He is no longer with us physically, but he will always be in our hearts and watch over us from above with his spirit and be our protecting angel.

I would like to thank each and every one of you, on behalf of our family, for taking the time and coming here today to honor Arie who was a very unique and loving person.

Thank you kindly,

Rivka

CHAPTER 46
SITTING SHIVA
(IN RIVKA'S OWN WORDS)

Sitting shiva the week after the death of a close relative is meant to help ease grief. The love of so many people during this time was very apparent to me, but our son-in-law Moti's actions were remarkable. During the shiva, Moti worked hard to keep the house organized and thank the people who brought food and did the cleaning. When you are sitting shiva, you have to be served and taken care of. Moti worked hard and did everything with love in order to make the shiva work. Considering the number of people who came by, his contribution was exemplary and important.

Many friends helped during the shiva, friends like Ella, who brought breakfast each morning, and our friend Etty Cohen, who came every morning to check on us. Emily, Poly, Tova, Lina, Ofra, and many others took turns supplying lunch and dinner. All of our friends were very involved and cared about our family—even our neighbors from the building and Anat's friends came to console us and bring food and dessert. That is the custom while sitting shiva. Everyone told their remembrances about Arie, always with a smile and telling jokes.

A month later, on November 15, we held Arie's unveiling ceremony. Steven was on his way from San Francisco to Arizona, and he listened to the ceremony through his cell phone. Many people came to attend, there were about 40 or 50. I was so grateful to be surrounded with so many friends and people. Once again, I had to face death in the family. This time it was my beloved husband with whom I shared more than 50 years of friendship, love, appreciation, and happiness. He was my best friend, lover, husband, and a father and grandfather. He always knew how to cheer me up and how to say the right words at the right time. He was so positive about life and saw only the good in every person. We always did everything together.

The most difficult part of losing my dear husband was to witness the torture he went through with his disease. To watch him disappear in front in front of my eyes, to witness him losing his former self and becoming disabled. He was so independent throughout his life, but he was forced to become dependent due to the illness. Words can't describe how heartbreaking it was for me, or how much strength I needed in order to hide my tears and pity.

The night Arie passed on, I felt the world come down on me. I could not imagine being able to continue living without him, and something inside me died along with him. I cried my heart out—I felt like a fragile branch that fell down from a tall and strong tree and was completely broken. I could not talk to anybody because I was crying all the time.

Even today, many years after Arie's death, I find myself, from time to time, crying and emotional as if it happened just yesterday. I force myself to get back to reality and continue my life with pride and dignity—hoping that my good health continues and I will be able to do the things I enjoy in life while still on this earth. The Garden of Eden paradise is here on earth as long as you have a spirit in your body. I know I will have to keep my body healthy so that my spirit will be healthy as well.

I always say, "Life is beautiful, and it is important that I enjoy what the universe has to offer me. For that, I am thankful every day I am here."

A year or so after Arie passed on, I had a session with Ann, who channeled the spirit of Arie. I wanted her to ask Arie why he insisted on having the surgery—even after he learned through meditation that his stomach was healed. Arie's response was, "I just didn't trust myself enough to understand the message I received."

Arie was receiving conflicting messages, and he wasn't sure which ones to heed. On one hand, his parents (through his meditations) and his doctors were pushing him to go forward with the surgery. On the other hand, Arie was receiving messages—pure guidance—from his stomach telling him that the cancer was cured. Arie was unable to trust the pure guidance from his own body, and he allowed his thinking guidance to rule his decision-making process.

Perhaps the biggest challenge in the lives of the members of my family was the illness and death of my dear and loving husband. So many lessons are learned during the course of a loved one's illness and passing, but it was me who was on the front line of Arie's diagnosis, and the story that follows is heart wrenching. It is difficult to watch loved ones suffer, but it is even more difficult to go through this challenge with grace. I believe I summoned an extraordinary amount of grace to live through this episode of my life and to be able to tell the story.

CHAPTER 47
ARIE'S 75TH BIRTHDAY

Arie passed into his new life just five days before his birthday. But that fact did not stop a proper birthday tribute. He would have turned 75 years old on October 15, 2009, and Steven wrote the following:

Happy 75th Birthday Dad from Steven
October 15, 2009

We celebrate 75 years of life with us today
We also celebrate your new life away
You have given us all that a family can hope for
Teaching us that love can open any door

You have shown us the beautiful world outside and from within
You have taught us that everything starts and ends with our being
You gave us the support that allows us to be who we truly are
And that the only thing in our way is our fear of being a star

You have taught us how to fish by asking the right questions
Only when been asked, giving others suggestions
To respect all life by appreciating its beauty
To be willing to make a fool of yourself appearing fruity

To find the humor in the way you are and laugh with passion
But laughing at others with compassion
To always take a deep breath and count to 10 before reacting
To allow the time to take your power back and thinking before acting

How to find joy in connecting and helping
Without expecting, projecting, and correcting
How to be protecting and respecting

To enhance how much we are really affecting

How important it is to speak our truth
And rejoice in our inner youth
To always remember to play
Like actors on stage—a performance on display

To know that we learn our whole life and die stupid, you would say
To not delay what you can do today
To not wear a long face when life shows you dismay
But use a smile to start and end every day

Your life wisdom and lessons are endless to list
Not to mention the ones we still resist
But please be comforted that all you have given exist
With us forever to assist

We also celebrate your new life on the other side
That was only possible when the old you died
We have asked you so many times to put yourself first and you did
To fly high is what you wanted since you were a kid

You have accomplished the biggest victory of any lifetime warrior
You learned to find the eternal peace corridor
Although this is difficult for us to comprehend
The following wishes for you we would like to extend:

May you continue to be the pure love you are?
May you continue to be the student of the world afar?
May you continue to be our leader and teacher?
May you be our guide, angel, and secret special feature?

May you be open to receive our eternal love as we know it?
Giving us time to further grow into even better ways of expressing it
May you be patient with our ignorance and limited view?
Knowing it's true; we want to be feeling like you, free and new

Love is a feeling that is not bound by physicality
No human body is needed to experience its reality
Love is an energy flowing from the soul
Experiencing it may be our only important human goal

Not only did we not lose your love in the transition
It ignited, magnified, and deepened our conscious recognition
Eternal love has been a human tradition
It will continue to be the fire that fuels our way and intuition

May we continue to grow in our loving communication?
With ourselves, the creator, you, and our own creations
May we continue to enhance our relations?
Saying NO to temptation and YES to our vocation to only follow our vibrations

We shall look up to you in admiration
Not expecting any compensation
United family we stand as your congregation
With determination, imagination, and corporation

You have left us with unanswered questions
Accepting it for now is your suggestion
We therefore have accepted your transformation
With one word left to say: Congratulations!

I was so excited to share with you what I wrote
For a moment I forgot, to the other room I went and you weren't there, I choked
I now read to all the people you love, this note
Knowing you can hear us from remote

Love

Steven

Chapter 48
Rivka's 70th Birthday
(In Rivka's Own Words)

Arie and I shared October as our birthday month. When October 24, 2009 arrived, however, I didn't feel at all like celebrating, but my children, sons-in-law, and grandchildren made sure that my birthday was marked by their love for me during this time of grief.

Anat held a small birthday celebration for me at her house and invited her close friends. It was a very nice party. When I returned home after the party, Anat arranged to send me roses as if Arie had sent them, and to keep with his tradition of sending me flowers on my birthday. Anat also wrote a note to go with the roses and Steven wrote a birthday poem to me:

Happy 70th Birthday Mom from Steven!
October 24, 2009

How can I find the right words?
I grab one and it flies away like a bird
I write one and delete it right away
Is it the right thing to say?

Love got redefined for me two weeks ago and knowing
With dad passing it's deeper, expended, and growing
I am not sure how to express this love to you even more
But I am excited to be on this journey and explore

Our hearts are more open than ever before
A childhood past of war feeling ignored, NO MORE
Putting blame, shame, and guilt all behind
Please forgive, forget, and let love be blind

We are oneness in the family and above all
We are in conscious communication standing tall
Love is a flow that requires constant movement
Our core was shaken but created an improvement

I watch the sunrise and remember the gift of being here

My love to you today comes with a tear
I feel a sense of urgency to celebrate life with passion
And to continue to touch each other with compassion

Compassion is another word that got redefined for me
It is a deep awareness of others' suffering I now see
Compassion is truly a divine gift that you possess
Not only in an awareness, but with action to express

I have learned that we really don't know who we are
We discover a scar next to a gift or star
I invite you to start from knowing nothing
So we can together learn everything

I will do all that I can to fill the empty space
Putting flowers in your vase
The gift that you are I will embrace
Who you are I will forever cherish with grace

You will never be alone
Not on earth and not in spirit zone
I will teach you how to spirit listen and talk
How to fly powerfully like a hawk

I am looking forward to our new beginning
Believing, seeing, experiencing, and loving
May you continue to be my teacher?
Allowing love and compassion be your guiding feature

Love

Steven

.

CHAPTER 49
A GREETING FROM ARIE CHANNELED THROUGH STEVEN
(IN RIVKA'S OWN WORDS)

Because my seventieth birthday came quickly after Arie's funeral, Steven used his special ability to channel this message to me from Arie:

Happy 70th birthday Rita from Arie!
October 24, 2009

It has been two weeks since I passed
As you can see time goes by fast
You must know that I am with you all the time
You must know that I am shadowing you like a rhyme

To you I am invisible and not around
Unless I knock a bottle or vase, I am without a sound
You think of a dead body lying underground in the rain
Feeling an empty heart to be only filled with more pain

Why did I leave your mind is eager to explain
What else could you have done drives you insane
How can you accept your life without me?
How can you continue to be?

Today is your 70th birthday, but your heart is sad
You tell yourself that while mourning, celebrating is bad
You feel guilty been left behind
Without communicating with me, you are in the blind

I used to always say that you and I are one
We are ONE, we are not yet done
We are forever entwined
Two spirits in one body are now combined
May you celebrate today as if I was physically around?
Don't let the illusion of physicality bring you down
Imagine me standing next to you gazing into your eyes
A hug, tears of joy, and a kiss from the skies

I am celebrating you Rita for 53 years and more to come

*It is thanks to you that I was and who I will still become
You are the source of my inspiration, strength, and love
A lifelong teacher on earth and now from above*

*I walk by your side enjoying the red and orange trees
Change of season, colors mixing into the breeze
Breathing the fresh air, clearing the mind
Letting the burdens of life wash with the rain to unwind*

*My life was about love, smiles, and joking around
Now it is your turn, your round
May you celebrate life once and all for yourself?
A lifetime lesson for me to remember oneself*

*I learned the greatest lesson of love in putting myself first
How to drink your own cup of love with burning thirst
To allow our children and grandkids to hold your hand
Not as a sign of weakness, but an opportunity to expand*

*May my love be the nucleus of your inspirations?
To live life fully for yourself with no expectations
The first day in 70 years that you can let go of being
A wife, a mom, a career woman, and first time seeing
That nothing else is needed to simply being
No need to prove that you are a love being*

*Starting now may every day be a celebration of Rita
Enjoying a great meal, a glass of wine, or a margarita
Smiling at all that life has to offer and say YES
Appreciating all that there is, God bless*

*Let's start a new life of discovery
No time for us to waste on recovery
Let's together make every day count
Let's continue to make deposits to our oneness account*

*My heart desires to continue our communication
We can do this at first through meditation
I will always be your invisible friend
You will hear my jokes to tell others at parties you attend*

When it is hard for the mind to comprehend

I will help your consciousness transcend
Let's not be sad anymore
Let's allow our love and passion to roar

I love you Rita now and forever
Welcoming our new endeavor
May I be your angel and guide?
I will always be your protector by your side

Love

Arie

Chapter 50
My New Life
(In Rivka's Own Words)

There is a popular song from early in the last century—1929, to be exact—written by Jack Yellin, which goes:

Happy days are here again,
The skies above are clear again,
Let us sing a song of cheer again,
Happy days are here again!

It's a lively song of cheer, but hidden within the words are implied times of unhappiness. The opposite states of happy and unhappy occur in each life, but for me, the list of happy moments is long. When Arie and I got married, we were happy and we were happy to have our own home. When the children were born, one by one, we were very happy. They were something different and they filled our lives with a lot of happiness.

When the girls got married we were very happy. Every parent wants to see his or her child get married. The grandchildren made us happy. To live to see grandchildren—every one of them is so different—we were happy to have reached the point where we had grandchildren to enjoy. While we can list the numerous events in our lives that brought happiness, our true happiness was living our daily life, loving ourselves, each other and loving our life. It was when we got present to appreciate our joy our joy was present.

Arie once said, 'The children are the investment and the grandchildren are the interest!" Indeed, spending time with the grandchildren is a true blessing.

Strength and Confidence

So much of my wisdom came from my experience in the workplace. My strength and confidence in the way I stood up for myself was remarkable. Around 1975, when I was working at El Al, a friend of mine who worked for a manager of an investment company called in distress. Her name was Doris and she said to me, "The travel agency forgot to send my boss's and his wife's passport and visa. Their papers are stuck at the Canadian embassy in Tel Aviv, and I am afraid to tell him! They are supposed to leave Sunday, and as you are aware, the embassy is closed Saturday and Sunday."

I picked up the phone and called the Canadian ambassador at home. His wife said that he was asleep and to call back in an hour. I called back and spoke to the Canadian ambassador and told him I was calling from El Al operations and that we had a problem. I told him that there were two passports in his embassy for some very important people who were supposed to travel to Canada on a business meeting on Sunday. I told him that if they were not released from the embassy in time, this could cause a diplomatic issue. The ambassador promised me personally to take care of the issue immediately.

He got on the phone with embassy security and told me that someone would be able to come on Saturday afternoon and pick up the passports. I called my friend Doris and told her to go the embassy and pick up the passports. She could not believe what she was hearing. I told her "Don't ask me how I did it." I just asked her to make sure that her boss didn't know that I took part in this operation since he knew me personally.

When my parents raised me, I was afraid of my own shadow. I didn't have self-confidence and was shy. Growing up like I did, it is amazing that I was so confident when doing so many different and unusual things. After I got that passport problem resolved, I said to myself, "If I can open the Canadian embassy on a Saturday, then I can do anything that I choose to do in my life." That insight changed my life.

My father was very strict and he thought I wasn't good enough. That is what motivated me to do so many things. He never said in so many words that I wasn't good enough, but I understood that I wasn't good enough by the look of his eyes. I wanted to prove to myself that I could do anything and be good enough. I felt I had to prove this to him and to myself. By doing this, I started to please everyone but myself. I had to learn to differentiate between proving to myself and pleasing others.

I was motivated to satisfy the needs of my family, my bosses, and my friends. I had to do outstanding things so I could prove to myself and everybody else that I had my own worth and value, and this is how I got the drive to continue doing things my way. Every time I was successful at doing something different, it was like a reward to me and it gave me more strength to do more things. I cannot imagine what my life would have been like if I would not have been able to grow in that way. I would probably would have been depressed and frustrated, with an inferiority complex, and would have had no motivation or goals for my life. People told me that I could move mountains and, in a way, it was true. By putting myself last, I felt as if I did not exist.

    I was asked the hypothetical question, "If you could go back and change anything in your life, what that would be?" My answer was "I would practice self-care and loving myself first before attending to anyone else. Once I gave up the need to prove to myself and others that I am worthy, I no longer needed to be a pleaser. I have gained freedom that I have never experienced before.

    I wasn't feeling worthy and deserving of that special dress I saw in March 2007 at Nordstrom in Scottsdale, Arizona. I wanted to buy a dress to wear to my grandson Leeran's bar mitzvah. They showed me a three-piece gorgeous and sexy outfit and I tried it on. It was a perfect fit. I said, "I can't buy it. It's too expensive." Steven was with me shopping and he asked me, "Do you think you aren't worth it?" And my answer was "No," so Steven said, "You are going to buy the dress!" I ended up buying the dress and I wore it beautifully to the bar mitzvah. I felt powerful and free.

    I still find it very difficult to talk about Arie's illness. Steven, Anat, Liat, and the grandkids keep inviting me to change the movie I have running in my head of Arie's suffering, and to also see the other happy and beautiful times and events we had together. They invited me to be thankful for having Arie in my life for more than 50 years. I must admit that although I am grateful for those years we shared together, it is not that easy. At times the most dramatic moments and pictures of Arie in the hospital are playing tricks on me and become present out of nowhere. Questions that I keep asking myself like "What if...?" "What if Arie would not have gone for the surgery or if the doctor hadn't done the procedure that caused the bleeding?" "Why did this have to happen to me?"

CHAPTER 51
MY SURPRISE 75TH BIRTHDAY PARTY
(IN RIVKA'S OWN WORDS)

It was October 2014, that time of the year when the family celebrates my birthday, and when we used to celebrate Arie's birthday. Both are in October. Instead of celebrating Arie's birthday each year, however, we now have a memorial for my dear Arie—husband, father, and grandfather. Steven comes every year to attend the memorial, and so he also came in 2014, five years after Arie passed on.

Steven had made earlier arrangements for us to have some quality time together after the memorial at the Oakwood Resort in Grand Bend, Ontario, Canada. The resort, which is located in a small town, is very beautiful. For several days we enjoyed the sunrises, the sunsets, and the wonderful views with green grass and trees everywhere. It was so tranquil. We also enjoyed the cozy restaurants, which served a variety of wonderful dishes. We had a really good time together, and we relished the opportunity to discuss every possible topic in the world.

After we returned to my home in Toronto, there was not much time left before Steven had to return to his own home in Colorado.

As the date for my birthday approached, I was told that we would celebrate the occasion by going to a restaurant a few days earlier than my actual birthdate. I didn't give it too much thought—it was just another year, another birthday—even though it was a milestone, seventy-fifth birthday. I was not aware, nor suspicious, that something big was cooking behind the scenes and that Anat, Moti, and Steven, were the cooks.

Steven spent the weekend at Anat's house, and my grandson Matan spent his time with friends. Steven had just returned from a very special and meaningful trip for him to South Africa where he learned how to communicate with animals. He brought me a beautiful tunic from South Africa and I decided to wear it to the restaurant for my birthday.

As soon as we arrived to Anat's house and walked in, I was completely taken by surprise. There inside the house were all my friends waiting for me to celebrate my birthday. I had no words to express myself. The surprise gave me a strong sense of déjà vu from five years earlier when Anat and Moti surprised Arie and me with our fiftieth anniversary party. It was very emotional for me.

It took me a few minutes to comprehend what was actually happening. Anat, Moti, and Steven all worked very hard the entire day in the kitchen to be able to present me with the special dishes prepared by each of them. They demonstrated their culinary creativity and skills just like the world's most famous chefs.

Another surprise was the video Anat prepared which showed in pictures my entire life since birth. There were photos of my parents, then me as a young girl, getting married to Arie, our honeymoon, the trips we made with Steven over the years, the trips we made with the grandkids to Disneyland, Sea World, and more. Steven posted it on YouTube for family and friends to watch, and every one of them was deeply touched. I became very emotional. I was watching a movie, but this time I was a star in it, together with Arie and the rest of my family.

All of my friends were amazed by the quantities and selection of dishes that were served, along with the drinks. After we finished our feast, a birthday cake with candles was brought out. This part was, again, very emotional for me. In my heart I knew that Arie was at my side—not in his physical body, but in spirit—and we were together every moment of the event. This had a tremendously powerful effect on me, and tears rolled down my face almost the entire time.

On one hand, I was so honored to have my family and friends celebrating my birthday with me. They showered me with love, which they also expressed in their beautiful birthday cards. But on the other hand, I deeply missed Arie—my love my partner and my friend for more than fifty years. I yearned for him to stand hand in hand with me, as we always used to do.

It was an evening to remember for many years to come. How lucky I am to have so many people in my life who love me so dearly and unconditionally, just for who I am.

My son Steven and daughter Anat wrote and presented me with the following wishes on my seventy-fifth birthday:

Happy 75th Birthday Mom From Steven

It's fall and the change of seasons is once again upon us
Celebrating a full cycle of life, no attachments, no fuss
Celebrating your powerful intention and manifestation
For a life full of miracles since your human formation
75 years of a gift that you are to us all
The world is grateful and so am I to a gift that is never too small

Reading the book of your unfolding life story
I am humbled to have a glimpse into the person who lives with no glory
To you your life might seem ordinary
To me your life is beyond extraordinary
Such a life cannot be considered random, coincidence or left to chance
Skillfully balancing the challenges, circumstances with the magic and beauty into a dance

From very young age taking responsibility for all that you do
Taking on your shoulders more than anyone can possibly chew
Yet always came ahead, found a way, pulled through
Always showed up fully while constantly upgrading your world view
A student of life committed to always grow and letting the knowing go
Shedding the excess attachments and stories like the melting snow

I am celebrating our eternal friendship and bond
Remembering our life before, this one and beyond
We are connecting to source, dad's spirit, and the divine
In simple moments of life when we talk, walk or dine with a glass of wine
Remembering to smile and see the beauty in all
Living a life of passion and standing tall

I am looking forward to continue learning by your side
Unconditional love and acceptance always smiling wide
Tapping into our infinite power, patience and creation
Trusting fully without hesitation
Wishing you many more healthy and joyful years to come

To enjoy your presence and witness how you continue to become

Love

Steven

Happy 75th Birthday Mom From Anat

You have always been our rock,
You gave us a solid foundation and taught us independence.
You wrapped us with your wings and moved mountains to protect us.
Together with Dad you injected love into our lives and your grandchildren,
And filled our homes with the aroma of your delicious dishes.
Thank you for being in our lives.

Love you always,

Anat

Chapter 52
Retirement
(In Rivka's Own Words)

Not long after my surprise seventy-fifth birthday party, in December 2014, I got up one morning and made a decision that changed my life forever. On that morning, I decided to retire from my job as a Registered Education Savings Plan sales representative with Knowledge First Financial. I had worked for the company for nineteen years.

I made the decision to retire with mixed feelings. My job was a source of great satisfaction. I shared with the parents I met ideas for how to save money for their kids' education, which would enable the children to build a better future for themselves. But it was not just the act of sharing my knowledge or selling the savings plans—I deeply cared about the people I worked with. Over the years I watched as their children matured and went off to university and college. When I met many of those children, they had just been born or were just a few years old, and here they were now successful young adults. I felt as though I was abandoning them by deciding to retire and leave them with a new sales representative.

That same night, Arie came to me in a dream—hugging me and kissing me. When I finally woke up I was so disappointed that it was just a dream, it was all so real. But I understood the reason he came to me in my dream was to let me know he supported my decision to retire and to say enough is enough.

I submitted my retirement letter to the company and I felt in my heart I was doing the right thing. My kids and grandkids were very happy with my decision, so we can have more quality time together.

It's amazing to me that when I add up all the time I spent in my different careers over the years, the total is fifty-eight years. Now I am living my life with great appreciation for everything I have accomplished, and I continue to enjoy life with my family and friends. Getting up in the morning and not having the burden of going to work is an unbelievably good feeling. It's as if a huge weight has been removed from my shoulders, and I can make plans to do whatever comes to my mind, and enjoy whatever the universe sends my way every day.

This is a great gift—first to be present and to enjoy the beauty and wonder of the world around me, and second to be healthy, alive, and able to enjoy life with my family and friends.

After I retired, and my clients were transferred to a new sales representative, I kept getting email messages and phone calls from them. They wanted to express their thanks and gratitude for my help, and for the wonderful customer service they experienced from me over the years. They all wished me good luck in my new direction in life.

CHAPTER 53
RIVKA'S LIFE TODAY

Rivka had to adjust her life to be fully independent without her partner Arie. It became an entirely new way of life. Her strong desire to not have to depend on anyone else has pushed her to learn to do all that Arie used to handle, including such things as finance, car maintenance, home maintenance, and repairing what is broken.

Rivka continues to live her life in a state of grace and appreciation. She feels blessed and grateful for her wonderful and loving children, sons-in-law, and grandchildren. She thanks God every day for them.

Rivka lives in Toronto, Canada. She retired in December 2014 from Knowledge First Financial after nineteen years as a sales representative for the Canadian Registered Education Savings Plan. She continues to enjoy meeting new people, and she recently completed a three-year Spanish language course—happily putting it to practice wherever she can. She has always closely followed world events, and would gladly discuss with you her views.

Reading

Rivka loves to read books, and has been reading them since she was a child. She particularly enjoys reading spiritual and philosophical books. One of her favorite philosophers is Osho, and Rivka has read many of his works. She also like romance novels, especially those written by Danielle Steel. To Rivka, books contain important life lessons, which she likes to implement and practice in her own life.

Cooking

Rivka's passion for cooking and creating dishes from around the world remains her hobby. She doesn't like to follow recipes, but brings her own innovation to the kitchen. She is known to make extraordinarily decadent dishes that are infused with her special sauce, love.

Walking Outdoors

Rivka takes time each day to walk outdoors when the weather permits. She enjoys taking a deep breath of fresh air, experiencing nature's scenery, and just relaxing.

Listening to Music

Rivka's passion for music has been a lifelong source of delight. She has enjoyed listening to music since she was a young child. She likes different kinds of music—classic and easy rock songs from the '50s, '60s, and '70s. It makes her feel good and gives her a sense of cheerfulness.

Family Life

One of Rivka's top priorities is to connect with her children and grandchildren by having quality time and meaningful conversations. She enjoys learning from her children and grandchildren and taking on new perspectives that are different from her own. While she will always be a mother, this does not stop her from being a student of the young ones.

Rivka also likes to keep up with latest technologies—from iPhones to tablets to computer software—and she is always open to learning new things. She finds it necessary to keep up in order to stay connected to the young ones.

Meditation Practice

Rivka is practicing meditation more than ever before in her life. She finds the practice an eye opener about herself, and it helps Rivka connect more deeply into her true essence. It is still challenging for her to sit in silence without the mind chatter, but it does not prevent her from meditating.

Writing poems

Rivka began writing rhyming poems many years ago. She would write greeting cards to family and friends for their birthday. This gift of writing poems remains a joyful hobby for her.

Intuition

Rivka has known for many years that she is intuitive, and

she has noticed that intuition plays a much greater role in her life now. She is especially interested in learning more about the invisible powers of the universe. She loves enhancing her psychic abilities and intuition through practice. She notices and celebrates the magic and supernatural synchronicities occurring in her life more than ever.

Chapter 54
Together Forever
(In Rivka's Own Words)

While the power of togetherness pulled Arie and me tightly together from the moment we first met, competing forces constantly threatened to tear us apart afterward, just as they do for any other couple in love. We were challenged in many different ways during the course of our long relationship, and it sometimes took everything within us to prevent these challenges from overwhelming us.

For Arie, the meaning of family was very important, as he lost his parents at a very young age and spent most of his childhood being brought up by members of his extended family or orphanages.

For me, the meaning of family was also very important, as I grew up an only child with no brothers or sisters.

Arie liked his job in the army very much, and it gave him a lot of satisfaction. He had a large number of soldiers and junior officers under his command, and much responsibility. Eventually, Arie was selected for promotion to the rank of major, but this would have required our family to relocate to Beersheba in the south of Israel.

I was working for El Al Israel Airlines at the Ben Gurion airport, and we already had our first son, Steven, who was about 1 year old. I knew that when you are in the army, they rule your life and you have to abide by their laws. In other words, whenever the army decides it's time for a soldier and his family to relocate, you are required to do it.

This way of living did not fit into my vision of the family I wanted to raise. I didn't want to be always on the move with our kids—transferring daycare and schools—and for me to have to keep changing jobs from place to place.

This was the first major challenge in our life together.

We had to make a decision together, and it was very

difficult. Arie was the one who decided to give up the job that he liked so much in favor of keeping our family TOGETHER.

The second major challenge was when Arie was called to serve as a reserve major, both during both the Six Day War, and then especially during the Yom Kippur War. Arie spent six months in the Sinai Desert while I was working for El Al Israel Airlines from 8:00 A.M. to midnight every day. We were both under tremendous stress and apart from each other. I didn't know if Arie would return from the war alive.

I missed Arie so much and could not imagine my life without him. The war ended, and luckily Arie returned home safely and we could continue to maintain our unity and TOGETHERNESS as a family.

The third major challenge during our marriage was when Arie was let go from his job due to the closing of the company he worked for. It was very difficult for him to find a decent job that fit his skills. Change knocked on our door once again, and Arie's cousin who lived in Canada offered him a job in one of his companies.

Arie was excited to make the move to Canada—he saw it as an opportunity to live a quiet life with less stress than in Israel. After living in Israel for about 40 years, and serving in the military during five wars, from his point of view it seemed a perfect change.

I, on the other hand, had a great job—excellent salary, perfect benefit package—and I was independent as an assistant to the general manager of the company. Here again we had a conflict of careers between the two of us. And, again, the decision was mutual, but this time I was the one to give up my job and career for the unity of our family and to maintain our TOGETHERNESS. I agreed, and we relocated to Canada.

To keep a family TOGETHER you learn to make concessions that support the greatest priority which is family. We had to develop and introduce into our life new habits, such as learning to accept and love each other unconditionally. We also had to develop a deep connection, communication, and trust, to be united not only in our bodies—but also in our souls—to respect each other, to devote ourselves to each other, and to deal with all the challenges that life presents to every couple.

But just as we had challenges in our lives together, Arie and I also shared joyful moments and events which not only shaped our lives, but also pulled us even more closely together. These included:

Our first trip to Europe as a married couple, while I was working at El Al Israel Airlines. In London we had to deposit coins in a timer in our hotel room to take a shower, and in Paris we went to a show at the Lido Cabaret, where it was obligatory to buy a bottle of Champagne. We drank the entire bottle and laughed the rest of the night away.

Our trip to Vienna where we visited a friend there who was a trauma doctor. He was our tour guide as we visited beautiful landmarks, saw a show at the beautiful and famous opera house, and visited the palace in Salzburg. We went to a special restaurant in the middle of the forest where the chef took the fish right out of the river and then prepared it in front of us. It was quite a culinary show!

Our trips to Arizona, where we visited our son Steven who always made sure we enjoyed our stay. We felt so happy every moment and we thanked God for being healthy and able to enjoy life every day.

The birth of our kids—our firstborn son and then our two daughters—brought us lots of excitement and pleasure as we became parents. For me as a Mom to experience pregnancy and to deliver healthy, beautiful babies was something very special. And for Arie to become a father was so inspiring—he longed for those moments. Our kids are unique and special and we felt so blessed to have them.

The weddings of our daughters expanded our family with two wonderful and special sons-in-law. This is every parent's wish to live to celebrate their children's wedding. Each of the weddings was special and unique in its own way, and a great celebration for Arie and me, and for the rest of the family.

The births of our seven grandchildren brought us much excitement as we joined the Club of Grandparents. First was our grandson Itay, then Dikla, Leeran, Karin, Ram, Matan-Matthew, and the youngest one Maytal. Arie and I were so delighted and enjoyed spending quality time with each and every one of them.

Bar and bat mitzvah trips with each grandson and granddaughter was a tradition that Arie started, taking them to Disneyland, Sea World, Universal Studios, Mexico, and Hawaii. We made those trips with each of the grandkids with Steven's help. Unfortunately, Arie was able to have these trips with only four of our seven grandchildren before he passed away. I, with Steven's help, have continued the tradition, and we have only Maytal left to take on her bat mitzvah trip.

Real life as we learned over the years was like a rollercoaster—the way was not smoothly paved. It had its bumps and challenges, and we had to make a concerted effort to maintain our relationship as a happy, loving couple. There were times when we felt like we were at the very top, and there were times when we hit bottom. There is no such thing as a perfect couple. However, in order to overcome any obstacle that might try to divide us, we needed to have something very strong to keep us together no matter what happened.

The one thing that played the most important role in keeping us together as a happy couple was love and care. We felt we could deal with anything, and that nothing would tear us apart. In our marriage vows, we say "For better or for worse, in sickness and in health, until death do us part." That phrase is not just a collection of words—it has a very deep meaning. Arie was my partner, my best friend, my lover, and my soul mate.

As time went on, we became stronger and better able to deal with anything life presented to us. We were able to deal with challenges and climb any mountain, no matter how high it was. We discovered courage and energy that, before we met, we didn't realize we had inside of us.

I believe our TOGETHERNESS goes on even though Arie is no longer here with me physically. He is definitely with me and our family spiritually, and is watching over all of us every day— me, the kids, the grandkids, and the sons-in-law.

My love for Arie continues and is like an ocean—deep and immeasurable. It's just there every day, always and forever.

Arie and I succeeded in keeping our unity and TOGETHERNESS as a couple for 50 years with love and care. Despite our challenges, we also had many happy and loving moments, and we created a loving family.

And we will always be TOGETHER FOREVER.

The End

APPENDIX I
ARIE'S MEDITATION TRANSCRIPTS

During Arie's final six months, he used meditation to help with his healing, and to connect to the divine and his spirit. He wrote the meditations in Hebrew. These are the translated copies of his meditation. These meditations appear on the Internet by way of the ICAN web site in service of helping and supporting other cancer patients who are dealing with similar situations at: http://www.askican.org/namedprograms/aringelstein.html

2009-04-28 MEDITATION—SURROUNDED BY LOVE AND FAMILY

I got up late this morning, after a difficult evening last night. Having eaten dinner late, I became bloated. I ate without being hungry because I know I have to gain my strength.

This morning at 8:05 A.M., I entered the bath with positive energy. With deep breathing, I felt I was in the middle of my stomach, apologizing for my behavior yesterday.

The stomach answered, "You are right. I did not feel good. I would like you to understand that I know exactly how to operate independently."

"So do I," said the liver. "All we are asking you is to listen to us only, and not to any other rules like that…that you have to eat or drink. We will transmit to you when and what to eat and to drink. The rest of the job is on us."

I thank all the parts of my body and go on to the dream with the frequency of the light, to another world where my mom and dad are hugging me strongly. I can feel strong heat. Both of them are young and beautiful, the way I know them from the photos, forever young. All of a sudden, Rivka's mom, Peppi, joins us with a wide smile. I am really excited to hear her say to me, "I loved you from the first minute I saw you. I cared about you and hoped you would have a good life with my daughter, who I felt has taken after her dad Jacob, who did not know how to show love, and he hurt me many times with his behavior."

I am more surprised when Rivka's father approaches and asks me to forgive him for the way he treated me so badly while he was a living person. Only now does he understand how much love I radiated to him. Both of them radiate love towards me.

Also joining is my uncle Mishu from Beersheba, who knew Rivka's parents even before we knew each other and who lived a long life. Then my grandma Liat joins with a wide smile and with her heart full of love, radiating love and calling me the way she used to, "Leonash." My grandpa Shmuel joins us and apologizes for not showing me the love he had in his heart for me, because he was busy fighting an infection of his prostate which caused him to pass away at a young age. He keeps telling me that he felt a big responsibility by passing on to me in the genes his enlarged prostate, but he said he was making sure that I will not have to have any operation.

Then my aunt Nutzi joins, and so does Shimon's mom—both passed away from cancer—and they thank me for being there for them during the difficult moments of their lives. Also joining me is my aunt Maria who used to give me a bath in a small tub (gigit) and then Shmuel's mom, Aunt Shaina, joined me. She was very proud of my dad and she was the one to pass on the love of the family.

In short, I was so excited that I don't remember who else was there. Everyone expressed their love to me and promised to help me on my way to continue to live a healthy life with my loving family.

Here in the march of love, guiding me back to the route of life, is the spirit of my loving wife Rivka, joined by the spirit of my son Steven, who taught me how to enter the wonderful life of the spirit.

Anat, our youngest daughter, joins us with Moti her husband. I can feel their love. Even though in the daily routine Moti does not know how to express love, I feel it without words. I can also feel the support of our daughter Liat and her husband Shlomo, while their love is expressed by way of a quiet prayer.

I am most excited by the support of my grandchildren, with each and every one of them (Itay, Dikla, Karin, and Ram) in their own way sending me the energy of love, along with the grandchildren from here (Leeran, Matan, and Maytal). It is interesting how, without understanding, Maytal and Matan are transferring lots of good energy to me.

Leeran is thinking increasingly in the way we are programmed as we grow up. I feel his love in a different way, which actually takes us away from the original energy. Maytal and Matan are not yet contaminated with the program of life, and they are therefore closer to the original energy without any effect of the conditioning of people. They connect very clean energy to me, which helps me feel stronger.

I am very excited about all the love that is guiding me on the path of life. I give thanks to the closest spirit to me, my wife Rivka, who is driving courage within the whole group. I am awake with a smile from the journey which excited me, and I get up as a new person from the warm bath.

2009-04-29 MEDITATION—LIGHT AND COLOR

Meditate three (3) times a day:

1. Imagine yourself inhaling white light into your stomach, and circle it clockwise for one (1) minute.

2. Imagine a blood red color in your stomach, and circle it clockwise for one (1) minute.

3. Imagine yellow sunlight, and circle it clockwise for one (1) minute.

4. Imagine orange light, and circle it in a counter-clockwise direction.

5. Bring back the white light for one (1) minute and complete the meditation.

2009-04-30 MEDITATION—ASKING SPIRIT AND BODY

In the next few meditations, please ask your spirit and body the following questions. Please ask only one question per meditation and take time with it. Do not rush the answers, they are important.

1. If I stay on the current course without doing a thing, how long do I have to live?

2. Why have I created this condition?

3. If I am able to reverse this condition, what will I live for?

4. Do I need a biopsy to determine how my body will react to chemo, or does my body approve the proposed pills?

5. Should I start the chemo treatment? If yes, when?

6. When did the entity in my stomach form and why?

7. What was the energetic signature behind that?

8. What feelings, sensations, or thoughts are captured in the energetic signature that was the moment of conception for the entity in my stomach?

Allow your body and stomach to lead you to the moment of conception and experience the thoughts, feelings, and sensations at that particular moment. This moment is very important to connect to. Once you connect to the conception moment, stay with it and follow its growth until your reach the TODAY moment.

Thank your body for the journey, come back, and write about your experiences.

2009-05-01 MEDITATION—THE NEED FOR MEDICAL INTERVENTION

9:30 A.M. I am already half an hour into pampering my body and myself in the warm and pleasant bath, while the warm water is patting my body. I am starting my deep breathing and reaching out to my stomach, which is bothering me a little with some pain in the middle.

I start by asking my stomach, "What is bothering you and how can I help?"

I also want to ask, "How do you feel? Do you think that you are able to overcome and manage on your own, without any *outside help? If you will not get any medical help, how long are you able to maintain yourself until the other organs in the body stop functioning in harmony, and cause the body to collapse? And then for me, my soul, I don't have any hold in this world any more..."*

Without getting any response from my body, I am trembling and out of balance. I can see a huge light. Is this God? This is the superficial power that others have successfully used to get close to him.

Yes, I have a direct question. "How long can I go on living without any medical intervention?"

A warm voice envelops me, "Your soul and other souls are part of my own energy. The duty of the soul is to reach a point of understanding and connection with the body. The body is a very sophisticated and miraculous machine, which consists of many cells that work in full harmony, but they still need the connection with the soul without causing any damage to one another.

"The minute that a situation has been created where a part of the body has been hurt, it begins to get out of control and also disturbs the other cells. There is a need for medical intervention by bringing in the good energy of love. I have given the scientific and medical knowledge only to very special scientists and doctors. They are my angels and they, on my behalf, give the correct medications. I have given Dr. Klein the knowledge and the art and the good energy to be able to perform the surgery to save the body, which in turn will continue to serve as a house for your soul.

"Without the help I am giving you, your body would be able to sustain only for 3 months."

Suddenly, I find myself surrounded by my mom and dad and my grandpa Shmuel and my uncle Faivish—my dad's brother and the father of my cousins Aharon and Efraim. None of them received medical assistance in time, and they passed away without being able to complete their missions in their lifetimes.

My dad Jacob was thrown out of a train by anti-Semitics, and his legs were amputated. He did not get medical help in time and he passed away. My mom Ester was sick with tuberculosis. There still was no medication to deal with that disease at the time, and she passed away. My grandpa Shmuel passed away from an infection of his prostate—again, because there were no medications invented yet to help. My uncle Faivish was bitten by a fly that carried the typhus disease, and he passed away within three days without being able to get proper medical attention since there was no invention or cure for that disease.

All of them together are transferring to me love energy and are congratulating me for living in an era where God has increased and transferred the knowledge to his missionaries to help people. In spite of the many dangers and statistics, I am in the right and good way. All the parts of my body join in with the congratulations. All of them are sure we will succeed together in that mission and goal.

I thank all of them, very emotional and excited walking out of the meditation, very encouraged and ready to cooperate with everyone.

2009-05-02 MEDITATION—MY STOMACH RESPONDS

Today I started my meditation with a clear thought to discover the answer to the question my son Steven raised: What caused the cancer tumor in my stomach?

I started by congratulating my stomach and the other parts of my body. Then I went straight to the stomach, asking: "How did it start? Why did it start?"

I consider myself to be a quiet and balanced person, the kind of person who doesn't hurt anyone, and who always looks for the best in everyone—a person of peace. And then my stomach started to respond.

"It's true you don't hurt anybody else but yourself. It's true you are looking for what is best for everyone else, a peacemaker for others while fighting with yourself. As you are aware, every action in the head promotes feelings. Every feeling is releasing a physical acid or hormones. For example, when you used to jog, hormones were released into the body that made you happy and laugh.

In your case, you just shut down all your feelings in order not to hurt others.

Lots of people get heart disease, like the saying, "He took it too much to heart."

In your case, you took everything into your stomach. I will remind you of a few events during your life—you concentrated all of them into the stomach. Every event caused you pain in the stomach. You declared that your intestines are turning over, being so nervous. So in all those cases, you released acids that damaged and injured the stomach inside.

You started at a young age. During the war, when an earthquake occurred, you thought that your mom deserted you. Afterwards, after you lost her, she passed away. During the war, being lonely without parents and love—the period when you stayed in the orphanage. Later on, your experience in the army and the wars that you took part in. On the outside, you portrayed the hero, but for every soldier who was killed or injured, you gathered within yourself bitterness and blame, without even mentioning that you couldn't cry. Later on you had your own family and you wanted to be a role model. Every person has different ideas and feelings, but for you, every different kind of behavior towards you turned into an injury that you took into your stomach and you turned everything into a war against you.

The most important thing for you was the unity of the family; this is sacred. That's why you also honored and behaved nicely with your wife's parents. The death of Peppi, the mother of your wife Rivka, left a huge pain, and you blamed yourself for the fact you have not been at her death bed because you were out of the country. You did not show anything on the outside, and everything went into the stomach. Out of love you offered a proposal to bring Rivka's dad to Canada in order to give him a better life in his lonely and old years. However, here again you were hurt by him. Instead of gratitude, you got bad behavior. The pain got even worse when your wife suffered because of that as well.

Do you want some more examples? I have a lot. For example, when you moved to Canada, the business you had with Shmuel and Ellen. You felt such helplessness being in a situation where you had to depend on someone else.

The most painful part in your stomach was the lack of love and unity between the kids, especially between Liat and Anat. Outside you said you don't care, you gave up; but that kept hurting your stomach. After selling the restaurant, the disappointment that you were not able to support the family and you had to depend on Rivka's work. You started to understand that there is some cooperation, that you are contributing your part, and you started to be more happy.

The worry about money also caused you bad feelings. During a discussion with your son, you told him, "I'd be better off dying and not having to depend on my children."

I was very emotional when Steven insisted that his duty is to take care of his parents, that I have no right to take that privilege from him. He stated that he will always be able to support us.

During our trip to Oregon, we discussed much with Steven, the fact that we have to take care of the quality of our lives and to enjoy every minute since we will not live forever. It is an opportunity to enjoy from a healthy soul and body on this earth. My wife Rivka and I have accepted the declaration in our imagination that we actually have 18 million dollars in the bank and we don't have to worry about our economic situation.

During our recent trip in March to Arizona, I have declared that I am fully surrendering and will not hurt any part of my body, and I will continue to implement all that we have decided and to free ourselves from any worry and bad thoughts.

After our return home from that trip, I received the message that the damage had already been done. I understand that it is not easy, and there is only a short period to help you, my stomach, to get rid of all that energy and poison that has been accumulated over the years, but I will do my utmost to inject only good energy and not to hurt you anymore.

I am very happy that love has burst out among the children. I feel that it was within, but was not discovered. I allow myself to cry being happy about that. That event keeps me from taking so hard the fact that I have that disease.

Suddenly I feel a call from my parents, Mom and Dad, sending me love and reminding me that I have to forgive and forget. They mean my sister Bianca, and to tell her about my disease and to get her love. I thank you from the heart, and after leaving my parents, I am thankful for the open discussion with my stomach. The stomach will do the best it can to get the love of all of them and to try to repair itself even before the medical attention will come.

2009-05-02 MEDITATION—INVITE THE RIGHT TREATMENT AND TEAM

Now, in your next meditation, please ask the following questions:

1. *Is the proposed chemotherapy the correct one for my body?*
2. *Is anything missing? Or too much?*
3. *Is the frequency of the treatment appropriate?*
4. *Is there anything else my body would need?*
5. *Is there anything my body recommends to change from the current treatment proposal?*

In addition, please consider the following:

1. *Add to your healing team a professional massage therapist who will treat you weekly.*
2. *Add to your healing team an energy worker practicing modality; like Reiki, Polarity.*
3. *Use your intuition to find and invite the right team members.*
4. *Create a routine for body movement; like walking, stretching.*
5. *Keep meditating and writing down what you receive.*

2009-05-12 MEDITATION—CYCLE OF LIFE

Childhood—still full of energy; learning; absorbing everything; enjoying to play; to touch trees; to lie on the soft grass or to walk into the mud; everything is so awesome.

But the grownups start to annoy with all the rules: do this don't do that, this is not allowed. So the rules and the "don't" take away from the child the pleasure. And if the child is upset, the child immediately translates it that the parents don't love him. So you learn to lie to cover up, otherwise you are not able to enjoy. So slowly we are getting programmed up to approximately age 13, and that is how this cycle of life comes to an end—the childhood.

Competition and Achievements—they start at approximately age 18. These include achievements in studies and achievements in sports, and you enter more and more into the materialistic world. Everything depends on money, and you become brainwashed that it is important to get ready for your lifestyle.

When you start socializing, the first question is "How much money have you earned?" and the more the better because if you have money you'll live better and that goes on until you go to the university or you choose a profession.

In countries where joining the army is mandatory, you mature faster and turn into an adult and start feeling the responsibility for your life, and that life is actually quite short and you are able to lose it in no time.

The period of time where you grew up passes quite fast, and then you start the cycle of life of an adult who enters into the madness of competition and how to succeed in life.

How is success in life measured? By making money, purchasing stuff like a house or a car and other products which, in a way, you actually don't even need. So you become totally a slave to your work and you also build a family, have kids, and the responsibility grows. You educate your children the same way with the same style as you have been brought up, and that is another cycle of life passing through.

A NEW CYCLE OF LIFE. You start at the age of 60-65, which is when you wake up and watch how life is passing by like an hourglass. Some people wake up with their own consciousness, some start to fight sickness, and that is when the questions start to pop up:

WHEN DID I EVER HAVE SOME TIME FOR MYSELF?

WHAT HAVE I DONE FOR MY SPIRIT?

WHAT DID I CONTRIBUTE TO SOCIETY?

WHAT DID I CONTRIBUTE TO MY FAMILY IN TERMS OF VALUES?

And some more questions like this.

In the best-case scenario, you start running against time.

You start to dedicate some time for yourself. You read, you walk in nature, watch the skies, smell the flowers, and discover the beauty of the universe. It was there all the time, however you never paid attention to any of it.

You start feeling the wonders of the spiritual world. You get connected to the cosmic energy, and suddenly you feel LOVE everywhere. In every wave of the ocean, in every drop of rain, you watch the rabbit in your neighborhood, and especially you try to keep more love towards your family, your children, your grandchildren and those who live to have great-grandchildren—who continue the roots of the family.

In this short cycle, you're anxious only for one thing: to get the additional time in order to guide the next generation with the knowledge that there are more important things in life other than the madness of the job and daily runs.

It is important to teach and to develop, but not for the purpose of competition—only for love to do what your heart desires, to be open to listen, and to get advice to listen to other ideas and not being compulsive only in order to learn from the experience of others.

To learn to differentiate between work and to take care of the body's spirit and to enjoy every minute to give the proper attention to everything surrounding you: nature, smell, and to be present.

The past is gone and the future is unknown, so we have only to enjoy and feel the present, which is actually a present—a gift.

The love of one person for another, the family connection, without any conditions or competition, such as who is smarter or who is better in math, is what matters most.

The real life is when everyone is contributing his or her gifts—and everyone has a gift. This mission is the main purpose of a parent and educator. Society will be better without hatred and wars and everyone will enjoy the most important present, which is the present of life.

2009-05-22 MEDITATION—THE FEAR OF THROWING UP

Good morning, my organs! I would like to thank you and to congratulate you on your cooperation to receive the chemo, and on the other side, to permit me to live a normal life by making every effort to take advantage of the medication, to recover, and for not letting me have the side effects that the doctors are trying to scare me with. I trust that you know better what you have to do.

This morning I would like you to help me find the reason for my fear of throwing up.

The stomach starts and says, "First of all, you have to understand what it means...throwing up. My duty as a stomach is to pay attention that I get only food and drinks that help to nourish all the cells in the body, and to turn them into energy which lets the living body function.

"The minute I feel that some food or drink that came into my body are causing damage, I don't have time to check or to let it go, because the damage can be harsh and immediate and can cause damage to all the organs (the heart can be affected and a heart attack might occur, the blood can be tainted, etc.). So the fastest way, in cooperation with other cells, is to eject the food or drink through the mouth, and that is throwing up in order to save the soul.

"Rotten food that comes to me may not be done on purpose, and may not be my fault, but most of the time, food and drink are being pushed to me without control. For that you are to be blamed."

Let's remember previous times where I threw up and caused the fear.

I remember being a young child during the Second World War when we did not have food. I went to look for some food, and I found some potatoes. I filled my pockets and brought them to my grandma to cook them. After we ate, it appeared they were frozen and were very spicy and rotten. I still ate them since I was hungry, but in no time I started to throw up my soul—an expression in Hebrew. I was scared and thought I might die. I feel myself again as a child who is afraid to die, but I understand the feeling and the action of throwing up, so I am releasing that fear. I let it evaporate, I have no room for that feeling in my body. All you have to do is to learn to pay attention to what you are throwing into the stomach.

The second severe case that I remember is when I was living with my grandma and I used to sip some wine with her from a special bottle called a dabijan. In time the bottle was empty. At that time people would use some lamps for light since we did not have electricity. It turned out the dabijan was filled with gasoline.

One night I was sneaking into the room where I knew the bottle of wine was, not knowing that it now had gasoline. I poured it into a glass and drank it in one sip.

Immediately I felt very bad and again I threw up. I felt as if I was going to die. Again, by not paying attention, I caused damage to my stomach. The stomach had done what she knew she had to do, the right thing to save me from dying. I feel the experience of fear, understand the process, and let this fear evaporate and release it from me.

Another severe case that I remember was when I was serving in the Army as a young commander. We went off on a special mission, a 120 km walk for the completion of the recruiting period for the regiment. I did not pay attention to drink enough water. With the heat in the Negev, I became dehydrated and started to throw up. This time, I felt the responsibility as a commander and I continued to walk and encouraged other soldiers to continue as well. I continued to throw up. I was then removed on a stretcher and treated for the dehydration. Here again I was afraid that I would die. Now as I relive that feeling, I understand that because of my lack of attention, the stomach had done its duty perfectly again. This fear is being released and evaporated from my body.

One more case was while I was on a business trip to Romania, when Romania was under the communist regime with President Nicolae Ceaușescu. I was trying to do business between Romania and Israel. There I met a Christian Arab from Nazaret and we decided to go to a restaurant in the Athénée Palace hotel in Bucharest, Romania, which once belonged to the King of Romania Mihai. While sitting and waiting for the food to come, we drank lots of wine. The food never arrived because they did not have any food. Drinking the wine, my head started spinning and it was the first time I got drunk. The Arab guy helped me to my room and in my room I started to throw up like hell. I was so scared to be all by myself in a room in a communist country. I could die and nobody would even know or find my body.

Now that I relive that scary feeling, I understand again that because I did not pay attention to my deeds, the stomach had done her job and saved my life. I release that feeling as well.

Thank you organs and thank you stomach for the lessons I have learned. I release those fears and make room for new and healthy cells in my body.

2009-05-23 MEDITATION—THE BURDEN OF WORRY

I just finished brushing my teeth. My wife is tired and went to sleep after a long day of cooking and baking a cake for our grandson Matan. She went to his birthday party for his friends. I have sent him my best wishes. He understands that I am a bit weak from the medications and that I am not socializing at this point to avoid getting sick.

I was sitting on the wonderful and magic seat that Steven has sent me, close to the window's fresh air. With a few breaths, I am with you, my organs. First, I would like to thank you today for your cooperation and for the decision that there is no place for side effects from my medications.

I would like to ask you, my small hernia on the right side, why are you making me feel uncomfortable. What is it that bothers you? I am not standing on my feet long hours, not making any efforts, and still it bothers me and is causing a little bit of pain.

"I am glad you are asking me. I have been trying to talk you for some days now, but you did not have time for me. It is very

simple. You have to pay attention every time you are trying to have your stool. It is just impossible, and you are using force and pressure on me in such a way that I am unable to bear the pressure, therefore pushing myself out and that causes us both to be uncomfortable. You have to pay attention that the problem is due to the iron pills and the medication, so you have to take a higher dose of the softener and you will see the results."

Now I would like to ask you, my back. I noticed that recently you are bothering me less. What happened? Are you more considerate?

"No, that is not the reason. I am glad you give me the opportunity to talk to you after so many years.

"First I have to explain to you that every organ in the body is doing a difficult job in order to keep the soul inside us, which gives us life. So we work in harmony and help each other without counting who is working harder. The only one that is causing us difficulties is you, and I will give you some examples.

"As a back, my duty is very difficult. To keep the whole heavy body supported is okay. I can do it with much love. But your burden on me over the years with your different worries is causing me to not function properly. I tried for years to explain to you, but in vain. You kept adding more worry and burden before the previous ones were gone. I tried for years, but you never had time for me.

"The first example was after you were married. Before that you had no idea about money and nothing would bother you. It was something not important to you. As you entered into the responsibility of family, however, even though your wife's parents bought you the apartment, your ego did not let you rest. You put a lot of worry on me. Half of your salary went for the food and the other half to pay back Rivka's parents the debt on the house. Sometimes you would skip payments for the groceries, etc.

"The second example was when you bought a car. Your salary did not get higher, but you increased your debt and your worry. Then you renovated the house, you enlarged the family, you had kids. You tried to give every child the best you could. Steven was talented. You wanted him to get musical education *and purchased a piano. Rivka took a loan from her job, and paid installments for the piano. Then you wanted to give the girls some music education, too. Then you changed your apartment, moving to Herzliya.*

"The point is that everyone in life is trying to improve and to get more, but what you have done is put more pressure on your back and not release the pressure—putting in more worries. If you want to do something, do it with love, but don't accumulate so much worry. Try to have a priority in making decisions, and not to worry.

"The pressure you put on me over the years was harder than the pressure to keep your body healthy. This caused a lot of damage to the spine, and it started to touch the nervous system. You went to doctors, chiropractors, acupuncturists…you tried everything. Only when you became conscious and you learned some good exercises and correct posture could we work together to ease the pain. The chair you got from Steven is helping us— both for the meditation and for the right posture. So you accept and experience the pain and let it go. That way you will learn to let the worries go and disappear. The burden will disappear as well."

Thank you, my back, for the wonderful lesson. I promise to learn from that and to behave accordingly. Good night, organs.

2009-06-03 MEDITATION—THE LEGACY YOU LEAVE & VALUES THAT ARE MORE IMPORTANT THAN MONEY

Hello organs, I wish to thank you for the cooperation and the results that helped me to feel well today. What do you have to tell me about my blood work tomorrow? Will we get good results according to your work?

"Yes, we confirm together and everyone separately. The blood work results will be okay according to what you feel."

Thank you, I am now encouraged for another week.

I would like to get deeper into my soul and concentrate on the question of the money I would like to leave for my children. That is a very complicated question.

"In nature, and in the world of the animals, there are very

clear and simple rules. The mother or parents teach and support the little baby. Born to be independent and to be able to get their food, they learn how to protect themselves not to be killed by other animals, and how to act when danger is coming—as an individual, or as a family.

"At the end of the learning period, and when the child has grown up, responsibility is transferred. The parents are free of worry or responsibility for the kids, other than the collective responsibility for the family or tribe in the jungle that is threatened in every corner, and every minute, in order to protect their well-being.

"With people, in most of cases the parents continue to hold on to the responsibility for their children, even when they are already grown up and even after they have their own family. Maybe that is the case specifically within the Jewish community.

"In that case, if you take away from the kids the possibility to rely on themselves, they may not develop any self-confidence and remain dependent on their parents. On the other hand, the parents become slaves and continue to hold on to the responsibility for the lives of their children, which causes frustration and pain. This leads the parents to not be able to live their own lives. It also causes friction and inconvenience, which eventually leads to disease. Suddenly you wake up and discover that life is over."

I remember the wise saying, "Teach your son to fish, but don't give him the fish." We can find that kind of wisdom in animals as a simple fact of life. People, who are supposed to be smarter, are more complicated. The fight between logic, feelings, and the need to help causes only confusion, hurting the kids and the parents, instead of living in harmony and loving consciously. Conflicts are being created that hurt both sides. And to whom? The people who are so close to you and who you love the most, a piece of your own flesh and blood.

I remember points where I have been confused and debated with myself.

"Why do I want to give to my children more than what they need?"

I also tried to protect myself by saying, "In my heart and soul I want to give to my children the things that I had not been given as a child," due to the situation at the time, being a child without parents and having to face wartime. Here the feeling worked. The need is that the cow wants to give to the veal more than the veal wants to be fed.

I have continued this theory during my life. We have helped with money and gifts, as per the circumstances, to each and every one of our kids and also to the grandchildren, while my wife and I were the last priority.

Only during recent years have we reached the conclusion that we need to take care of ourselves FIRST. In that way, we are also doing a good deed for our children in order not to become a burden on them.

What is more important is to provide the children and the grandchildren with values, life wisdom, and our experience. Lots of love for a full life, being conscious and keeping the family together with mutual respect, to take advantage of every minute in living life in happiness and joy.

While our time will come to leave this world—everything we own in terms of assets or money will be going to the kids with love. That will only help them to ease their daily routines or for the purpose of learning, studying, and to promote their way in life.

2009-06-25 MEDITATION—PRIORITIES IN LIFE (TIME MANAGEMENT)

Today in my meditation I went back to when I was 6 or 7 years old. My mom had passed away and I was wondering, "Will I die as well?"

I started to be afraid. I didn't want to die. This means that already when young, without understanding exactly what life is all about and what death means, you want to preserve life. As you grow older, you start to understand that man appears on the globe, plays his role in life, and then disappears as if he was never here. You know that life is short. You know that you want to be able to do as many things as possible.

It does not matter how many years you will live. Eventually you will die and it is always not enough. Even though everyone is trying to hide this fact and put it under the rug, trying to avoid death, nobody knows whether he will reach or have a long life, or will be killed in an accident, or in a fire or drowning.

On one hand, it is good not to know. Otherwise, man would not be able to enjoy anything, produce anything, or enjoy life. He would always be in scarcity, knowing that he will die. But between scarcity on the one hand, or to avoid enjoying life and to know that there is a lot of work to be done on Earth, just for the sake of breathing, the difference is huge.

Most people start their lives studying the rules of society and also studying a profession. The task is finding a job in order to be able to survive, creating a family, and making a run for the money—not only in order to survive, but to buy more things, to buy more houses, to be able to compete within society. A bigger house, and always wanting stuff—more than we need. So you become a slave to the stuff, and you spend more time at work and out of your home.

You hardly have any time with your family or children, and you don't enjoy anything. You don't find your peace of mind or happiness, only sorrow and complaints, and you start to suffer illnesses. If you are able to reach old age, you wake up and understand that most of your life has passed you by. All the money and assets you have achieved do not bring you any happiness. Your body is neglected. The kids have no connection to you. You are very angry and sad and lonely on this Earth.

It is nice to have a big house, there's nothing wrong with that, and also to enjoy all the good things that you can get for your money. Most people do the same things and are going through the same process.

Now that I understand that facts, I see that my mission is to teach the younger generation, my grandchildren, and whomever I meet in my way, to explain that life is much more than just working like a slave.

It is only a matter of priorities and time management. When you decide how much of your time you will dedicate for work or for your family or to be part of your children's lives, take some time to be with yourself to find out what is your mission in life on Earth, what you would like to learn, and what would you like to leave spiritually to your children and society.

You need time to take care of your body, which is so delicate: to eat right, to exercise, to nurture the cells of your body in the right way and not to damage them with poison, so that the body will be able always to function and to fight any disease.

You also need to dedicate some of your time for the spiritual part, a healthy spirit in a healthy body: to walk in nature, to touch earth, to smell flowers, to watch the flow of the water to the waves of the ocean, to feel a part of nature, to have friends and socialize, to have influence and good energy, to make time for everything that is important other than your job, and especially to live life consciously in the present and enjoy every minute of it.

2009-06-27 MEDITATION—BEING PART OF NATURE

I just completed my meditation in the bath. I was walking through my body and thanking all my cells for the wonderful job they are doing, and for another good day feeling stronger.

I am sitting in my chair, breathing the fresh air coming through the window; looking into the night at the trees, the flowers and the lights in the streets.

My gaze is concentrated on a tall tree. Green and beautiful, standing upright, I can feel I am in that tree, feeling the thrill of the breeze that is moving the leaves. I can feel the bird nests, how the birds sleep in it. I can feel a miracle. I can be anywhere, to change shape as I want to. I am looking from the top of that tree, overlooking everything. I can feel the mission that this tree has—to swallow the CO_2 gas, absorbing the carbon dioxide, and to produce the oxygen (O) that gives life to all creatures.

On top of all, I can feel the pleasure of the life of a tree. Even though he spends all his life in the same place, withstanding any weather—strong, not to be broken by the wind. No complaints, no envy about anybody else, not even for the birds that are flying around. Happy that all the creatures are around him and sitting on him, building their nests on his branches or enjoying the shadow sitting underneath him.

A tree reaches a life longer than any other creature. I am returning to my body and thinking to myself, "God has given us life with supernatural energy that lets us be able to move from place to place as we wish. To enjoy all the miracles of nature he gave us the knowledge to produce everything—cars, airplanes, space shuttles—so that we will be able to be mobile and to go places, to see things, to feel things, and to be part of nature without limit. We are able to produce life, and that is because we should know to preserve everything we have been given as a present. If we will not preserve it well, and instead abuse it, then we will destroy the world.

"Our mission is to be part of nature and to live consciously and to learn from the trees to live full lives without complaint, helping others love life and people, and to live in harmony with nature, which we are an integral part of."

ABOUT THE AUTHORS
By Steven Ringelstein

Arie Ringelstein was born in Romania in 1934. An orphan and survivor of the holocaust he found his way to Israel as a boy. He served in the Israeli Defense Forces for years including commanding the front lines in 5 wars, leading his troops to victories. Being an orphan creating a family mattered to him a lot. He was married to his wife Rivka Ringelstein for 50 years. He moved his family in his later years to Toronto Canada to enjoy the remaining of his life in peace until his passing in 2009 at the age of 75. Arie was known to conquer any obstacle in his way and alchemize it into love, playfulness and contentment. Arie was a hero to his family.

Rivka Ringelstein was born in Romania in 1939 only short 64 miles from the birth place of her future husband. A single child who at a very young age escaped the atrocities of WWII in Europe. Rivka also found her way to Israel to start a new life in the newly formed Jewish state. Her dedication, commitment and hard work persisted over the many obstacles life presented. Her love for Arie and unshakable courage has made her a hero to her family. Rivka has survived Arie and is now in her mid-seventies enjoying life of contentment in Toronto Canada.

ABOUT THE BOOK COVER
BY JAMIE DICKERSON

    Together Forever's book cover design is an abstract representation of Arie and Rivka's passions and timeless story. Undergoing such hardships of war and migration, they were still able to feel the joys of life, many of which are represented in the vibrant colors of the book cover. The tree in the center of the splash of life symbolizes Arie's family, his most important value in life. The yellow compass represents navigating the world and their journey to find one another while the dolphin high in the clouds represents Arie's special connection to dolphins because of their playfulness, which he added into every gesture of his life. The wings in the clouds symbolize Arie, as he is no longer with Rivka and his family on earth, but forever with them, in their mind and heart. Arie's previous name was Leon meaning 'lion', the king of the animals, a symbol of his energy and powerfulness. Arie gave Rivka red roses for each special occasion throughout their lives. The intertwined wedding rings represent their unity and infinity to be together forever. The purple faces are Arie and Rivka, as one, who survived war and grievances, shown by the teardrop, but also the happiness of being together.

REFERENCES

http://www.thetrumpet.com/article/5955.4330.0.0/religion/judaism/the-resurgence-of-1930s-style-anti-semitism

[ii] http://www.thetrumpet.com/article/5955.4330.0.0/religion/judaism/the-resurgence-of-1930s-style-anti-semitism

[iii] http://www.myjewishlearning.com/culture/2/Food/Ashkenazic_Cuisine/Poland_and_Russia/mamaliga.shtml#less

[iv] http://isurvived.org/2Postings/Iasi_death_train.html

[v] http://en.wikipedia.org/wiki/Historical_Jewish_population_comparisons

[vi] http://jafi.org/JewishAgency/English/Jewish+Education/Compelling+Content/Eye+on+Israel/Society/4)+The+Mass+Migration+of+the+1950s.htm

[vii] http://www.jta.org/1948/10/24/archive/israel-acquires-s-s-negda-from-holland-official-sees-admission-of-150000-this-year

Made in the USA
San Bernardino, CA
28 March 2017